FREEDOM'S
SALESMAN

DAVID LEYONHJELM
FREEDOM'S SALESMAN

*Collected articles
and speeches by
Australia's senator
for liberty*

Published by:
Wilkinson Publishing Pty Ltd
ACN 006 042 173
Level 4, 2 Collins Street
Melbourne, Vic 3000
Ph: 03 9654 5446
www.wilkinsonpublishing.com.au

National Library of Australia Cataloguing-in-Publication entry
Creator: Leyonhjelm, David, author.
Title: Freedom's salesman / David Leyonhjelm.
ISBN: 9781925642049 (paperback)
Subjects: Leyonhjelm, David.
             Liberal Democratic Party (Australia)--Platforms
             Liberty.
             Legislators--Australia.
             Politicians--Australia.
             Political oratory--Australia.
             Speeches, addresses, etc., Australian.

CONTENTS

FOREWORD

As the first politician to be elected to an Australian parliament representing a genuinely libertarian party, I bear a major responsibility. While the libertarian concept is relatively well known in the United States, and classical liberalism (which I regard as the same) is somewhat understood in Britain and Europe generally, neither is part of the usual political dialogue in Australia.

Before I was elected, I had to endure journalists occasionally telling me I was confused because I supported both left-wing causes (e.g. same-sex marriage and recreational marijuana) and right-wing causes (e.g. low taxes and gun rights). Only after I was elected was I able to inform them that they were the confused ones.

Three years later things have changed. Most journalists, particularly those involved in politics, now understand libertarian principles to some extent. Some second-guess me when seeking my position on an issue. A few even try to tell me that I'm inconsistent or hypocritical for failing to conform to their understanding of the term.

Most of the general public, on the other hand, are still to understand it. I periodically encounter people who describe themselves as 'somewhat libertarian,' in that they support me on one particular issue but have little interest in liberty generally or an understanding of the underlying principles.

It is for these people that I have written this book.

For a minor party Senator, a career in politics is very uncertain. Although I was easily elected in 2013, I was only narrowly re-elected in 2016. If I and my party are to win again at a normal half-Senate election, I need to convince a lot of people of the merits of libertarian values.

Apart from an initial chapter about me and my political journey, this book is comprised of articles and speeches I have written since my election, with some slightly edited to keep them current. Of course, quite a few were drafted by my talented staff but I personally edited them all, sometimes quite extensively, and a few endured so many rounds of editing that it was difficult to know who had made the greatest contribution.

Publishing the articles in this book is intended to achieve the same purpose as when they were first published as stand-alone articles or delivered as speeches. I am simply seeking to expose people to the principles of liberty in the hope that they will agree that less government and more personal responsibility will lead to a much happier and more prosperous society.

A LIBERTARIAN FROM
FIRST PRINCIPLES

What is a libertarian?

Libertarianism is a political philosophy based on individuals being more important than groups or governments. It seeks to maximise autonomy and freedom of choice, and emphasises the values of political freedom, voluntary association, and the role of individual judgement.

Libertarians are generally sceptical of authority, although they vary in their opposition to existing political and economic systems. Some differ only marginally from anarchists, who believe governments are unnecessary, but most accept that functions such as national defence and criminal justice are best provided by governments.

To those unfamiliar with it, the libertarian philosophy sometimes confuses those who like to apply left and right labels to political ideologies. Free trade is considered to be right-wing while drug legalisation is left-wing. Cutting tax is right-wing but defending civil liberties is left-wing.

However, each of these positions shares the common principle of decreasing the role of government. Libertarians differ from 'left-wing' people who often want the government to control the economy but not our social lives, and from 'right-wing' people who want the government to control our social lives but not the economy.

Libertarianism can also be based on two quite different philosophical starting points. Some libertarians believe that free markets and individual freedom should be preferred because they are more moral political systems. Such people argue that it is immoral to take money from people by force and to tell people how to live their lives.

Utilitarian libertarians believe that a small government will lead to better outcomes than a big government. Such people argue that libertarian solutions will lead to greater wealth, less poverty, more diversity and will generally make people happier.

The first philosophical position is concerned with process, while the second is concerned with outcomes. In reality, most libertarians (and most people) care about both.

Acceptance by libertarians of the rights of individuals to pursue their activities, subject to non-coercion of others, does not indicate endorsement of those activities. Nor does it say anything about personal interactions. Libertarians draw a clear distinction between the voluntary codes of behaviour of civil society and coercion by the state or groups or individuals permitted by the state.

The absence of coercion, except to prevent the coercion of others, is the ultimate goal of libertarians.

First principles

In my experience there are two types of libertarian: those who arrived at the philosophy because of a general distrust of authority, and those for whom the lights came on as a result of reading a book or viewing a video, such as Hayek's *Road to Serfdom* or Friedman's *Free to Choose*.

I am in the former category. For a long time I did not even realise there was a word to describe my views. I was also not aware there were millions of others who shared them.

In social policy terms, I have never been anything but a libertarian. Two issues were particularly influential in implanting my distaste for authority – conscription and abortion.

When I was a 20-year-old, the law required me to register for National Service. If my birthdate was selected, I would then have been obliged to join the army for two years. Conscripts were being sent to Vietnam, where some had been killed in action.

I had reservations about Australia's participation in the Vietnam War, but my main objection was to compulsory military service. I am not a pacifist and was not opposed to voluntary military service.

Like many thousands my age, I refused to register. As it happened I would not have been conscripted, as my birthdate was not selected, and I would also have been eligible for deferral due to my university studies. None of that mattered – it was the compulsory aspect that I rejected.

By failing to register I became liable to serve two years in the army or in jail. Only the election of the Whitlam Labor government in December 1972, which abolished conscription, saved me.

A decade later I enlisted in the Army Reserve as an officer cadet, although I only completed two years due to persistent conflicts with my job. I can't say I enjoyed being constantly ordered around, but I accepted it because I was there by choice. It certainly left me with a deep appreciation of our military.

My exposure to the abortion issue arose from the fact that, at the same time, women and doctors in Victoria were being arrested and prosecuted. My peers and I were sexually active, but contraception was nowhere near as freely available as it is today. Condoms were sold by chemists, in packs of three or six, wrapped in brown paper. Availability of the contraceptive pill was dependent on the attitudes of doctors; some simply refused to prescribe it at all, while others would only prescribe it for married women.

I was particularly affronted by the notion that the government could dictate to a woman what she could do with her own body. In other words, if she became pregnant she was allowed no choice but to act as an incubator irrespective of the circumstances.

Thankfully the law changed and abortion became more freely available, although I later learnt that it is invariably a difficult choice. Nonetheless, I never doubted that it was not the business of the government.

There were other issues on which I found it difficult to accept government authority. For example, I smoked marijuana from time to time, and tried LSD on one occasion. Although I could easily see why it might not be wise to do either too often, particularly since my brain was my only asset, I never understood why it was any business of the government. Nobody else was harmed and I resented the inference that I was doing anything wrong.

Later still, I could never see why I required a certificate from the government to tell me I was married. A certificate would have made no difference to either me or my wife in the 32 years we have been together. I recognise that some place great significance on marriage and consider a public ceremony as important, but these are personal views. I don't believe we should allow a piece of paper from the government to define our relationships.

My support for the right to own firearms is also profoundly libertarian. While I used firearms as a kid, shooting sparrows and rabbits, it wasn't until I took up competitive target shooting that I began to realise how important firearms were in the context of the relationship between individuals and the state. It is simply not possible to view a government as serving the people, or contemplate forcing a government from power if it disregards the ballot box, if all the guns are in the hands of those wearing government uniforms.

Such thinking was important to those who wrote the US Declaration of Independence and the Second Amendment to the US Constitution. As the saying goes, when the government fears the people there is freedom; when the people fear the government there is tyranny.

When it comes to economic freedom, it took me longer to realise the government was not on the side of the angels. The old saying, if you are not a socialist at 20 you have no heart, but if you are still a socialist at 40 you've got no brains, applies to me. I studied Marx, Engels, Lenin, Trotsky and Mao, wrestled with concepts such as dialectical materialism, and contemplated whether I supported democratic or revolutionary socialism. Some of my friends were in the latter camp and I joined their demonstrations against the Vietnam War, conscription and apartheid. At one point during the Vietnam protests we all carried red flags on large poles, which came in handy for repelling police horses.

However, my socialism was always highly idealist. I had never known a period when money was not extremely short, particularly after my parents separated. Socialist redistribution, from each according to his ability to each according to his needs, seemed attractive. Indeed, I thought it was such an obvious solution that I became convinced the socialist state would wither away, leaving Marx's perfect communist state in its place.

Reality began to intrude when I travelled to purportedly socialist countries, including the USSR, Poland and East Germany. Rather than socialist nirvana I found grinding poverty and an authoritarian police state. I travelled the length of Africa, discovering that the people in capitalist countries such as Nigeria and apartheid South Africa, corrupt and obnoxious as they were, enjoyed more freedom and were more prosperous than those living under the 'village socialism' of Tanzania. By the time I returned to Australia, I was no longer a socialist.

But believing in a free enterprise economy raises many questions. If complete government ownership, as found in a socialist economy, is not desirable, how much should governments own? And when the government does not own a business, to what extent should it regulate how it should run?

These remain perennial questions, even for libertarians. Is free trade ever unfair? Which is more important – protection of local jobs or a lower price for consumers and businesses? Is it exploitation to employ people at whatever price they agree, rather than a legally imposed minimum? Should the government prevent foreigners from buying assets, even if it means a local seller has to accept a lower price?

As my views evolved, I found myself returning time and again to the same thought: anything other than a free market requires someone (mostly bureaucrats with the backing of legislation approved by politicians) to make decisions on behalf of thousands of buyers and sellers who would otherwise make their own decisions.

And the question I considered was, do bureaucrats and politicians really know enough to determine the proper price of labour, property, or goods and services? Or do they suffer from what Hayek describes as the fatal conceit?

In due course I came to the same conclusion as I had on social issues – most economic issues are not the business of the government. Its role should be limited to protection from coercion. Or, as John Locke would have put it, the preservation of life, liberty and property.

BECOMING
A POLITICIAN

A reluctant politician

It's fair to say I'm a reluctant politician. I'm not an accidental politician – I've always taken an active interest in politics and I know what it takes to win – but for many years I had no aspiration to be elected and become a politician.

It's quite likely I could have become a politician many years ago.

My first foray into the political system was as a member of Young Labor, motivated largely by opposition to conscription. I decided Labor needed an animal welfare policy (I was in veterinary practice at the time) and prepared some thoughts, which resulted in an invitation to join a policy committee of some kind. Due to my forthcoming trip overseas I declined. If I'd said yes and stayed, who knows what might have occurred?

A decade or so later and with a different economic perspective I was in Tasmania, seeking to promote jobs and growth in my one and only stint as a public servant. While there I joined the Liberal Party, rubbing shoulders with numerous politicians. It was a small pond and not difficult to get noticed. I attended a State Conference and spoke against one of the endless motions calling for additional government funding. Had I stayed in Tasmania, there is little doubt there would have been opportunities to become a politician.

Back in Sydney, with growing pressure on private ownership of firearms, I joined the recently established Shooters Party. In 1995 the party succeeded in having John Tingle elected to the NSW Legislative Council. I was elected Chairman of the party in 1998, holding the position for five years. Had I been interested I could have put myself forward as a candidate, either to replace John Tingle or gain what would then have been its second seat.

When I joined the Liberal Democrats in 2005 I remained convinced my role was to create an environment in which others could win. I reorganised the party, established a proper database and a federal constitution, financial accounts and new website. In the federal election I ran for the seat of Bennelong against John Howard, knowing full well I could not win. In 2010 I ran the campaign but did not nominate at all.

It was not until the NSW state election in 2011 that I ran in a winnable spot, as lead candidate for the Outdoor Recreation Party (the Liberal Democrats were not registered for state elections). I was far from devastated when I was not elected.

My reluctance was real. I enjoyed, and still prefer, the business world. It's much easier to navigate, easier to measure performance and, unlike politics, operates substantially on mutual benefit. Since my election, I freely admit there are times when I've wanted to give the job away. As I told the National Press Club, being a senator is interfering with semi-retirement.

Being on the crossbench has given me enormous public exposure, which is beneficial when election time comes around, but also means I have lost my anonymity. I am constantly recognised in public, regularly asked for selfies and occasionally abused. As a hitherto private person, that's not something I enjoy.

Having said that, it's not all bad. It is an enormous privilege to represent the people of Australia in the Senate, to be able to vote for liberty, and to have a forum from which I can advocate libertarian values.

It is also very satisfying to know that, had I not been there, some things would not have turned out as positively as they did. Reluctant politician or not, we all like to make a difference.

Preference whispering

Glenn Druery – known around the traps as 'the preference whisperer' – has had a somewhat complicated relationship with the Liberal Democrats. He joined the party in 2007 and wanted badly to be a Senate candidate. Our problem was that we didn't know him very well and he wasn't even a libertarian.

In the end we nominated Terje Petersen as our lead NSW candidate, on the understanding Druery would be seriously considered in 2010.

Druery was still in the party when the 2010 election rolled around, I still had a very busy business and wasn't enthusiastic about running, so he became our candidate more or less by default. Some long-standing members were concerned about that but there was nobody else either keen to run or capable of doing a sound job of harvesting preferences.

Glenn's flair wasn't for policy, but for politics – particularly the politics of numbers. The plan, if he were elected, was to ensure he hired the right staff, voted the right way and advocated our policies. To give him credit, he seemed happy with this arrangement – he just really wanted to be a senator.

Of course, the plan was never put into effect because he was not elected. He came close to beating Lee Rhiannon of the Greens though, and put a major effort into our campaign. We also learnt a lot about negotiating preferences.

Inevitably, recriminations flow after close electoral losses and, post 2010, Glenn ruminated on what might have been.

He formed the view that preferences from the Shooters would have tipped him over the line and into the Senate.

My departure from the Shooters Party had been acrimonious. I fell out with John Tingle and his cheer squad on a personal level, but I was also unhappy with their social conservatism and tendency to defend liberty for licensed shooters but not the liberty of others.

This stood out in two areas, which between them caused me considerable annoyance: gay rights and mandatory sentencing.

What they didn't seem to understand was that some of the most persuasive advocates for gun rights in the US are gay. Tom G Palmer is probably the best-known example: his possession of a concealed carry permit once stopped him from being beaten to death by a mob of marauding homophobes. Mandatory sentencing, of course, is just illiberal, and represents the usurpation of judicial power by the executive and legislature.

Glenn decided – in order to have the Shooters on side and get their preferences at the next election, when he assumed he'd be the candidate again and nothing else would have changed – that I needed to be removed from influence. Unfortunately for him, the national executive wasn't having a bar of it and a war of words erupted. A couple of people called Glenn a 'prick' and there was a round of finger-pointing and blaming. Glenn didn't take kindly to this and resigned in high dudgeon.

By the time 2013 rolled into view, he had spent some time shopping around for a party to nominate him. He courted the Katter Australia Party and various others, but ultimately settled on acting as a paid preference negotiator, working for the Shooters Party, Fishing and Lifestyle Party, and Family First in Victoria.

Glenn established what became known as 'the Minor Party Alliance.' In the past he had encouraged meetings between the parties with a view to helping each other, but nothing much came of it in 2007 or 2010. However, the more formal arrangements he proposed – where minor parties were to preference each other within the Alliance before preferencing minor parties outside the Alliance, or preferencing major parties – had the effect of creating minor party 'in-groups' and 'out-groups.'

In the WA state election in May 2013 Glenn handled preference negotiations for the Shooters and Fishers Party (as it had then become), gaining preferences from most of the other small parties – even the Greens – with the result that Rick Mazza won a seat in the Legislative Council.

I didn't like the idea of preferencing parties with which the Liberal Democrats disagreed on pretty much everything, and in any case Glenn had now linked himself to the Shooters and Fishers' electoral fortunes. One of Glenn's clients, Family First's Ashley Fenn, wanted to exchange preferences with us in Victoria but was also involved with the Minor Party Alliance. He was very keen for the Liberal Democrats to join, but the Shooters and Fishers wouldn't hear of it.

I still remember meeting Ashley in a McDonald's in the city, when he called Glenn.

'David should come to the next Minor Party Alliance meeting, you know.'

Glenn freaked – I could hear him expectorating into Ashley's ear. The gist of it was simple: I couldn't come, because if I did, the Shooters and Fishers would walk out.

The upshot was that we were excluded from the Minor Party Alliance, and I had to negotiate preferences independently. While I built good relationships with many people from other small parties, I was pretty sure – between the Minor Party Alliance and the relative strength of the Shooters and Fishers in NSW – I wouldn't have a chance.

Much has been made – in debate over Senate voting reform – of the ease with which minor parties (sometimes acting on Glenn's advice, sometimes not) supposedly 'gamed' group voting tickets. If only it were actually easy. Negotiating preferences, as I did for the 2013 election, is one of the most tedious, difficult and unpleasant jobs I've had.

It becomes fiendishly complicated if more than one person does the negotiating, so I spent months and months talking to registered officers from other minor parties, thinking deals had been struck, and then watching them unravel. You really do need a good head for figures, coupled with the ability to keep lots of balls in the air.

I thought if the Liberal Democrats did get anyone elected, it'd be in Victoria where minor parties had a better history of winning seats. And if it weren't us, I suspected the Sex Party was also in with a decent chance.

Enter, at that point, my company's fax machine.

After all their nominations were in, political parties were provided with blank Group Voting Tickets from the Australian Electoral Commission, with 24 hours to fill them in and lodge their preferences. It's a torrid time; I was responsible for lodging two sets of forms – the Outdoor Recreation Party as well as the Liberal Democratic Party (at the time, I was registered officer for both).

Clinton Mead – by then Liberal Democrat Mayor of Campbelltown but founder of the Smokers' Rights Party – was also making use of my company's fax machine to lodge SRP preferences. Perhaps unwisely, I had also agreed to lodge the Republican Party's GVTs for them, basically as a favour – we are politically different.

I figured all I had to do was fill out GVTs for three parties, while Clinton had to do one. This seemed straightforward.

What I hadn't allowed for is how much time it takes to fill out the GVTs for every state without making mistakes, and then get them faxed through to the AEC. Email was not acceptable, despite having largely replaced faxes in business. My company's fax machine was past its best days and not often used.

We were also still getting phone calls from other parties – up until one in the morning – offering us deals. Now that people were willing to talk to me – and, to a lesser extent, Clinton – we thought it only fair to reciprocate. We were keen to maximise our performance, so we negotiated. Sometimes this led to last-minute changes in the order on the GVT. We worked at it so long and so intensely, the numbers on the paperwork genuinely started to blur. Both Clinton and I realised we couldn't keep it up without a bit of sleep, or the combined preferencing efforts of four minor parties would come to nothing.

We slept for about three hours, then woke up and kept on filling out the GVTs. I realised shortly after waking that we were going to run out of time – six states, four parties, and my creaky fax machine. I got multiple calls from the AEC telling me that our faxes were unreadable – even when they'd been pre-printed. We had to re-submit time and again, this time with hand-written numbers. Then the document feeder started to jam; I had to hold my mouth just right to stop it failing completely and damaging the paper.

This is not good, I thought. We are just running out of time.

I enlisted my wife's help: she took on the role of fax-whisperer while Clinton and I continued to fill out GVTs. We got them in for Queensland and NSW after several attempts. We got Tasmania in. And finally we had Victoria ready. Amanda dialled the number for Victoria and pressed send. No answer. So she did it again.

'They're not answering.'

'The AEC is normally pretty reliable.'

We faffed around a bit, the document feeder ate another set of GVTs, and then I thought to check the number. She'd been putting in the voice number. By that stage, it was three minutes to midday. No time to lodge preferences for all four parties. We were screwed. So no preferences whatsoever were lodged. It was gut-wrenching.

With South Australia half an hour behind, we hastily got them in, and then Western Australia.

I then rang the Sex Party to explain what had happened. And they exploded.

Until that point I'd had a good relationship with the Sex Party. Rather than accept our apologies, they assumed that we'd done it deliberately. At one point they threatened litigation.

I get that the dodgy fax machine story carried a whiff of 'the dog ate my homework' excuse, but it happened to be true. They were also forgetting, in failing to lodge preferences for Victoria, that I cruelled not only the Sex Party's chances but our own chances as well as those of three other parties – including the wholly innocent Republicans, who had simply trusted us to do the job.

We didn't even have a box above the line.

A few days later Antony Green's famous 'Election Calculator' came out. I started running scenarios, out of curiosity as much as anything. In nearly all of them it looked like I was going to be elected. At first I didn't believe it. I talked to a few people on the National Executive, who told me I had 'Candidate's Disease.' No-one in the party would believe me.

The concept of 'Candidate's Disease' is something I suspect exists in all political parties. This refers to the phenomenon where an individual convinces himself that getting elected is a forgone conclusion, when in reality he doesn't have a snowball's chance in Hell. I've known lots of candidates to develop the disease over the years, and their inevitable disappointment after the election is always disheartening.

After a couple of friendly disagreements, I decided to keep my mouth shut and wait for Election Day. But I was now pretty sure I would be elected.

Now you're in for it

On election day, perhaps unwisely, Amanda and I shared a bottle of wine over dinner after returning from working on the polling booth. I don't generally drink more than two glasses of wine at any one time, so I was already at my usual limit when early results after polls closed showed me on about 7% of the primary vote. I knew from Antony Green's calculator that I'd be elected at about 3%, and by around 7pm the phone calls, texts and emails started. Hundreds and hundreds of them, mostly congratulatory, but a few negative. It got pretty chaotic.

'Now you're in for it,' quite a few people told me.

Even more unwisely, we moved onto a bottle of dessert wine to celebrate. This meant the next day – when the media decided I was the most fascinating thing ever – I had a fierce headache. I tried to put them off, but when television cameras started appearing outside the front fence, I figured I had to take the opportunity to explain what I stood for. That day, and the day after, there was a steady stream of television crews, other journalists and press photographers beating a path to my door.

And all they wanted to talk about was guns.

A couple of days before the election – in a big story on page six – the *Daily Telegraph* had done a major write-up on the party. Ostensibly, the piece was meant to warn people not to vote for the Liberal Democrats by mistake, but much of it was a familiar riff on the 'gun-toting-pot-heads' fear-mongering that comes libertarians' way. Guns – with photographs of one candidate taking aim – were prominent.

The *Daily Telegraph* piece and its gun obsession set the tone, with the ABC in particular going into doom and mourning while interviewing me: my election was a catastrophe and the sky was about to fall in.

A couple of weeks later I accepted an invitation to write a fortnightly column for the *Australian Financial Review* – my first was published on 1 October 2013. I'm an old hand at writing columns – I'd had a monthly one in *Rural Business* magazine for 20 years followed by a weekly one in *Business Spectator* and then Fairfax Rural Media – although those had always been on agricultural issues.

I developed the habit of putting out a press release early in the morning the day each *Financial Review* column appeared, which meant I spent pretty much every second Friday giving interviews. My objective was simple: to explain – and to sell – libertarian ideas to the general public, using the fact of my election as a sort of bully pulpit.

The reactions were interesting, at the very least. If I talked about letting people decide for themselves whether to smoke tobacco, I'd be described as a right-wing nutter, 'shilling' for Big Tobacco. But if I said the same about cannabis, I became a left-wing loony – probably because we don't (yet) have such a thing as Big Weed.

I anticipated having to explain my political views to the electorate, even before I took up my place in the Senate. I saw that as part of the deal from the day I was elected. And I expected people – from both left and right – to disagree with me. But I did not expect to be criticised for being consistent.

When I published a column suggesting we let gay and lesbian people marry – followed a fortnight later by a column supporting 4WDers, fishers and hunters having access to national parks – I could almost hear people's heads exploding down the phone line when they called me.

The day after I was elected, I thought I would be 'chief salesman' for the Liberal Democrats but not much more. I doubted my ability to achieve anything concrete or make much of a difference, given I had just one vote.

Then it became apparent that the government would need my vote in order to pass legislation that was opposed by Labor and the Greens. Not only did I have a wonderful new forum from which to promote the libertarian message, but there would be times when my vote could actually make a difference.

And so it has proved.

FREEDOM'S SALESMAN

First speech[1]

Mr President, fellow Senators, and Australians.

Last September, the people of Australia chose 40 men and women to represent them here. Together with the 36 elected three years earlier, just 571 Australians have been granted this high honour.

We come from diverse backgrounds and occupations. Beyond this place, each of us has been tempered by the challenges of life. We have all tasted the bitterness of failure and exhilaration of success. Whatever our political alignments, that experience will have imparted in us a collective accumulation of knowledge, judgement, wisdom and instinct that should serve our country well.

Indeed, we are the most representative swill ever assembled.

I also believe we are about to begin one of the most exciting periods in the life of the Senate.

In the service of this mission, at the outset I declare that I am proudly what some call a libertarian, though I prefer the term classical liberal. My undeviating political philosophy is grounded in the belief, expressed so clearly by John Stuart Mill, that 'the only purpose for which power can be rightfully ever exercised over any member of a civilised community against his will, is to prevent harm to others.'

I pledge to work tirelessly to convince my fellow Australians and their political representatives that our governments should forego their over-governing, over-taxing and over-riding ways.

Governments instead should seek to constrain themselves to what John Locke advised so wisely more than 300 years ago – the protection of life, liberty and private property.

When I was elected nine months ago and my party's policies became better known, there was a wave of rejoicing in certain circles. When I said that I would never vote for an increase in taxes or a reduction in liberty, there were people who said there was finally going to be someone in parliament worth voting for. That was quite a compliment.

What they, and I, believe in is limited government. We differ from 'left-wing' people who want the government to control the economy but not our social lives, and from 'right-wing' people who want the government to control our social lives but not the economy. Classical liberals support *liberty* across the board.

I have long thought that leaving people alone is the most reasonable position to take. I always suspected I didn't know enough to allow me to tell other people how to live their lives.

But that didn't arise in a vacuum, so a bit of background is necessary.

I never liked being told what to do, and I tend to assume others feel the same. The simple rule: do *not* do unto others what you would rather them *not* do to you, has always driven my thinking.

At least since I reached adulthood, I have also accepted responsibility for myself and expected others to do the same. Even when my choices have been poor, as they inevitably were at times, I don't recall being tempted to blame others or consider myself a victim.

During my early years, the issues that raised my blood pressure were those of individual freedom. But for the election of the Whitlam government, I would have either served two years in the army or gone to jail. I refused to register for national service. Being forced to serve in the army, with the potential to be sent to Vietnam, was a powerful education in excessive government power.

The abortion issue was also controversial at that time. There were doctors and women being prosecuted over what were obviously difficult private choices. Backyard abortions were common. I *knew* some women affected and could never see how the jackboot of government improved things. I also noticed that those opposed to abortion or in favour of conscription were not interested in trying to debate their opponents: instead they sought to seize the levers of government power and impose their views on everyone else.

As my family never had much money, I used to think spreading other people's money around was a good way to make life fairer. As the saying goes, if you're not a socialist at 20 you have no heart, but if you're still a socialist at 40 you have no brains. By that standard I hope I have preserved a bit of both.

Not long after I started full-time work as a veterinarian I recall looking at my annual tax return and being horrified at the amount of money I had handed over to the government. When I looked for signs of value for that money, I found little to reassure me.

To this day I'm still looking!

Our liberty is eroded when our money is taken as taxes and used on something we could have done for ourselves at lower cost.

It is eroded when our taxes are used to pay for things that others will provide, whether on a charitable basis or for profit. That includes TV and radio stations, electricity services, railways, bus services, and of course, schools and hospitals.

It is eroded when our money is taken and then returned to us as welfare, with the only real beneficiaries being the public servants who administer its collection and distribution.

It is eroded when our money is used on things that are a complete waste, like pink batts, unwanted school halls, and accommodation subsidies for wealthy foreign students.

It is eroded when the money we have earned is taken and given to those of working age who simply choose never to work.

Reducing taxes, any kind of taxes, will always have my support. And I will always oppose measures that restrict free markets and hobble entrepreneurship.

But the cause of liberty is challenged in other ways as well.

Liberty is eroded when our cherished right to vote is turned into an obligation and becomes a crime when we don't do it.

It is eroded when we are unable to marry the person of our choice, whatever their gender.

It is eroded when, if we choose to end our life, we must do it before we become feeble and need help, because otherwise, anyone who helps us commits a crime.

It is eroded when we cannot speak or write freely out of fear someone will choose to take offence. Free speech is fundamental to liberty, and it is not the government's role to save people from their feelings.

Liberty is eroded when we are prohibited from doing something that causes harm to nobody else, irrespective of whether we personally approve or would do it ourselves.

I don't use marijuana and don't recommend it except for medical reasons, but it is a matter of choice.

I don't smoke and I drink little, but it's unreasonable for smokers and drinkers to be punished for their alleged excesses via so-called 'sin taxes.'

Liberty includes the right to make bad choices.

Quite a few people say they support liberal values but claim there are valid exemptions. The most common one is security or safety, something that's become pervasive during the so-called 'War on Terror.'

But as William Pitt the Younger observed: 'Necessity is the plea for *every* infringement of human freedom. It is the argument of tyrants, and the creed of slaves.'

Mr President, perhaps some are scratching their heads right now. How can someone support marriage equality and assisted suicide and want to legalise pot, but also want to cut taxes – a lot.

If you *are* scratching your head, it's because you've forgotten that classical liberal principles were at the core of the Enlightenment, the period that gifted us humanity's greatest achievements: in science, medicine, commerce; and also brought about the abolition of slavery.

Classical liberals do not accept there are any exemptions from the light of liberty. But we are not anarchists. We accept there is a proper role for government, just that it's considerably less than the role currently performed. Government can be a wonderful servant, but a terrible master, something leading Enlightenment figures, like John Locke, realised.

John Locke's view of the role of the state was starkly different from that of another important philosopher, Thomas Hobbes. Hobbes thought the natural state of man was perpetual war, with life nasty, brutish and short. In his view, the only way to achieve civilisation was to relinquish all liberties to the sovereign, who then allowed us certain rights as he chose.

While Hobbes is also known for arguing the sovereign should rule with due regard for the desires of the people, there was no doubting where he thought ultimate power resided or rights originated.

Locke was much more optimistic. Man is peaceful and industrious, he argued. But to establish a society in which private property can be protected, it is necessary to relinquish certain liberties to the sovereign. However, this is a limited and conditional arrangement. Only sufficient powers as required for the preservation of life, liberty and property ought to be relinquished, and ultimate power remains with the people. If the sovereign gets too controlling, those powers can be reclaimed.

Locke heavily influenced the American declaration of independence. As many here will recognise, it says:

> We hold these truths to be self-evident, that all men are created equal, that they are endowed by their Creator with certain unalienable Rights, that among these are Life, Liberty and the pursuit of Happiness. That to secure these rights, Governments are instituted among Men, deriving their just powers from the consent of the governed, That whenever any Form of Government becomes destructive of these ends, it is the Right of the People to alter or to abolish it, and to institute new Government.

When it says, 'All men are created equal,' it does not mean everyone is the same or that everyone should achieve the same outcome in life, but that no individual or class enjoys moral or legal superiority over other individuals or classes.

When it says, 'We are endowed with inalienable rights,' it means rights that cannot be taken from us. Good governments can help protect our rights by reflecting them in governance, but they don't get to dole them out piecemeal. Bad governments may seek to legislate away our rights, but only by usurping them.

The right to life is obviously the most fundamental right of all and no government should ever seek to deprive us of that. That includes not only arbitrary killing, but also judicial killing.

Likewise, it includes the right to protect your own life, and that of others, for which there must be a practical means: not merely an emergency number to call. Self-defence, both in principle and in practice, is a right, not a privilege.

Liberty is not like a cake with only so many slices to go around. It only makes sense when the freedom of one person does not encroach upon that of others, but instead reinforces it. Thus it is perfectly legitimate for governments to place limits on things done by a person that limit other people's freedom. Those include violence, threats, theft, and fraud.

It is not, however, legitimate for government to involve itself in things that an individual voluntarily does to him or herself, or that people choose to do to each other by mutual consent, when nobody else is harmed.

It is quite irrelevant whether we approve of those things, or would choose to do them ourselves. Tolerance is central to the concept of liberty. It may matter to our parents, friends or loved ones, but it should not matter to the government. Such things belong in the private realm.

This distinction between the public and private realms can be traced all the way back to the ancient Greeks and is well known in Roman or civil law. Some things fall within the legitimate scope of government, some do not.

The Declaration of Independence also says, 'Governments are instituted among Men, deriving their just powers...' That means, when governments act to secure rights they are acting justly. When they move to violate those rights, they are acting unjustly. They derive that legitimacy from the consent of the governed – in places like this.

When the people fear the government, there is tyranny. When the government fears the people, there is liberty.

Australia does not have the equivalent of a Declaration of Independence, a bill of rights or even a history of resistance against authoritarian government. The Eureka Stockade – which was prompted by excessive taxation and oppressive enforcement – is about all we have.

That makes it especially important that those in places like this understand the only thing standing between an authoritarian state and the protection of life, liberty and private property, is a vote in Parliament. We must never forget that we are the people's servants.

This means we must be willing to take a light touch; to de-legislate; to repeal. As much as possible, people need to be able to choose for themselves, and be free to choose, for good or for ill.

For that reason, some may think of these as being peculiarly 'American' words, but the ideas have their origins in the Scottish Enlightenment. Although it sometimes seems Scotland has produced nothing but incomprehensible socialists, it also gave rise to the modern world's most liberty-affirming thinkers.

Among them was David Hume, who argued that the presence or absence of liberty was the standard by which one ought to assess the past. And on the subject of property, he said: 'No one can doubt, that the convention for the distinction of property, and for the stability of possession, is of all circumstances the most necessary to the establishment of human society, and that after the agreement for the fixing and observing of this rule, there remains little or nothing to be done towards settling a perfect harmony and concord.'

I don't think the Americans disagreed with the Scots on the importance of private property when they substituted the pursuit of happiness, but if they did, I would side with the Scots!

Notwithstanding my earlier comments, I am not a student of philosophy. While Locke, Adam Smith and Mill have their place in my thinking, along with Friedrich Hayek and Milton Friedman, I consider the Enlightenment to be part of Australia's political and intellectual heritage: it doesn't belong to the Scots, the Americans, or the French.

While I sit in the federal parliament, I don't approve of the extent of its power. Liberty is more secure when power is shared with state governments, independently funded and competing with each other to be more attractive to Australians as places to live and do business, and of course each doing their bit to protect life, liberty, and property.

On the subject of private property, there is much today with which Locke would find fault. Rather than protecting private property, governments federal and state have been retreating from this core duty.

The property rights of rural landowners have been undermined by bans on clearing native vegetation, imposed at the behest of the Commonwealth in order to meet the terms of a treaty Australia had yet to ratify.

Over and over, the value of property is indirectly eroded through government decisions, and typically without compensation. In enacting plain packaging laws on cigarettes, for example, the previous parliament destroyed valuable intellectual property and attempted to legislate a market out of existence: perhaps we all need a reminder of how well Prohibition doesn't work.

We trade years of our lives to pay for the things that we own, and when governments take them from us or try to tell us what to do with them, we lose part of ourselves.

And yet when it comes to property that we own in common, like national parks and fishing grounds, we are often locked out on the claim that nature is far too important to let scruffy humans enjoy it.

Whilst in this place, I shall do all I can to oppose this trend. Environmental fanatics are not omniscient geniuses: they don't know enough to tell other people how to live their lives any more than I do. Indeed, they are the same people who engage in anti-GMO pseudoscience, pseudoscience that is not just nonsense, but murderous nonsense.

The Liberal Democrats are strong advocates of capitalism. But before capitalism, we are advocates of freedom. When people are free and entrepreneurial, free market capitalism and prosperity are what follow.

However, I *am* pragmatic enough to recognise that sometimes two steps forward requires one step backwards. I am only one vote, and one voice.

I am also aware that some senators in this place share my views, but are constrained from speaking openly. Whatever party you are in, if you believe in making the pie bigger rather than arguing about how it is cut up, we have plenty in common.

To all of you, I would say this: when any specific issue arises – be it legislation or advocacy – that advances the cause of liberty, if I can say or do something to help, you only need to ask. In my party, the only discipline I'm likely to suffer will be due to not pursuing liberty enough!

I have pursued liberty through membership of the Labor Party, the Liberal Party and the Shooters Party, so I can say with confidence the Liberal Democrats *do not* seek power to impose our views on the nation. All our policies are about freedom – the absence of control by others. We seek to have representatives elected in order to restrict the power of the state over individuals, to encourage the government to do less, not more.

I view my election as an opportunity to help Australia rediscover its reliance on individualism, to reignite the flame of entrepreneurship, and to return government to its essential functions.

There is much to be done.

Magna Carta[2]

There was a time when women could be accused of witchcraft. All it took was an accusation. Any women accused had to prove their innocence.

They did this with a ducking stool.

Ducking was seen as a fool-proof way to establish whether a woman was a witch. It comprised a chair, hung from the end of a free-moving arm. The woman was strapped into the chair, which was beside the river. The woman would then be lowered into the water until submerged. The duration of immersion was determined both by the operator and the seriousness of the crime of which she was accused. It could last for just a few seconds, but in some circumstances the process would be repeated continuously over the course of the day.

But ducking stools were expensive and required skilled carpenters to construct. So, during the witch crazes, ducking was often inflicted without the chair. The accused witch's right thumb was bound to her left toe. A rope was attached to her waist and the she was thrown into a river or deep pond.

Whatever method was used, if the accused woman floated it was deemed that she was in league with the devil, rejecting the 'baptismal water.' If she sank, she was innocent.

In medieval and early modern Europe, few people could swim. In proving their innocence, accused women often drowned.

We don't do that now. If someone is accused of a crime, the accused person does not have to prove anything. The accuser must make the case.

This concept, which we now know as the presumption of innocence, arose in only two civilisations, Rome and England.

Despite attempts to prove the English legal system was influenced by the Romans, we now know the concept evolved independently in both societies. If you are French, you have the presumption of innocence thanks to the Romans. If you are Australian or American, you have the presumption of innocence thanks to the English.

And, because England has a remarkably complete and detailed historical record, we can even identify the crucial document in which the concept was spelled out with clarity for the first time.

That document is Magna Carta.

Mr President, this year, Magna Carta has its 800th anniversary. It is appropriate to speak in this place of its central importance to our liberal democratic heritage.

I spend a lot of my time here talking about liberty, and have berated both government and opposition for failure to uphold it. Liberty, to a classical liberal, is absolutely fundamental.

The attacks on liberty in the national security legislation take two forms. First, they constrain freedom of speech. I've spoken and written about this a lot, particularly when it comes to freedom of the press. Second, they destroy liberty by undermining the rule of law.

In civilised societies, liberty dies without law – that's why classical liberals often spoke, historically, of an 'ordered liberty.' The 'order' in that phrase refers not to that infamous woman who appears at elections, Laura Norder, but to the idea that no-one is above the law – not the King, not his ministers, not the Church.

In England in 1215, that meant – to use a phrase common in the thirteenth century – 'the King is given for the sake of the Kingdom, and not the Kingdom for the sake of the King.'

Here and now, it means that the people who make the laws are also subject to those laws. There is no special 'parliamentary pass.'

And, at the heart of the rule of law lies the presumption of innocence.

For most of human history, we have believed that where there is smoke there is fire. When we accused people of wrongdoing, we considered our accusations true because we thought the accused 'had it coming to them.' That meant accused persons had to prove they were innocent – a 'presumption of guilt' was in force.

Many people do not appreciate, for example, that the conversation between Abraham and God in Genesis 18 concerning the fate of Sodom and Gomorrah could only have arisen in a society where behind every accusation was a presumption of guilt. Sodom and Gomorrah were to be destroyed for their wickedness, wickedness taken as a given.

Abraham pleaded for 'the Cities of the Plain' on the basis that he could prove a number of righteous people lived there. God started with 50. Abraham talked Him down to ten. But Abraham had to prove they were righteous. He failed. The cities went up in fire and brimstone.

If the world of Ancient Israel is now considered unrepresentative of Western Civilisation, then the world of Classical Athens is surely not. Yet Socrates' *Apology* – his speech to the jury at trial – reads oddly because Athens, too, was a presumption of guilt society:

> men of Athens, do not interrupt, but hear me; there was an agreement between us that you should hear me out. And I think that what I am going to say will do you good: for I have something more to say, at which you may be inclined to cry out; but I beg that you will not do this.

Socrates, too, had to prove his innocence.

It is from Roman and English lawyers and politicians that one first sees ringing declarations like, 'I would rather ten guilty persons should escape, than one innocent should suffer,' or 'a person ought not to be condemned on suspicion; for it is preferable that the crime of a guilty man should go unpunished than an innocent man be condemned.'

Both of these quotations are Roman, and we don't know who said them first. Worse, the ideal they enshrined disappeared for hundreds of years. By contrast, clauses 28, 29, and 30 of Magna Carta can not only be dated with precision, they still form part of our law – although, in light of our national security legislation since 9/11, I sometimes wonder whether that is still true in Australia.

Clause 28 provides:

> In future no official shall place a man on trial upon
> his own unsupported statement, without producing
> credible witnesses to the truth of it.

Clause 29 provides:

> No free man shall be seized or imprisoned, or
> stripped of his rights or possessions, or outlawed or
> exiled, or deprived of his standing in any other way,
> nor will we proceed with force against him, or send
> others to do so, except by the lawful judgement of
> his equals or by the law of the land.

Clause 30 provides:

> To no one will we sell, to no one deny or delay right
> or justice.

Of course, Magna Carta had antecedents in English thought.
As early as the ninth century, we find the Anglo-Saxon King
Alfred stating that 'in cases of doubt, one should save rather
than condemn.'

However, the presumption did not appear with real vigour
until Magna Carta, and once it appeared, it took root.

It is routine – and fair – to point out that Magna Carta
was wrung from a weakened King John by rebellious barons.
It is true that in 1215, it applied to a narrow caste of English
society: the rights it contains were granted as a series of conces-
sions to baronial families and the Church, with some benefits
for merchants, townsmen, and the lesser aristocracy. Serfs and
married women got nothing. It is also true that John repudi-
ated it within months, leading Pope Innocent III to annul it.

Nonetheless, the barons' particular grievances against the King were gradually extended to benefit an ever-larger proportion of the population. The greatest English jurist, Edward Coke, interpreted Magna Carta's clauses as they were written – which was in general terms. Not only did the presumption of innocence come to be the property of the whole English people, but the words 'free man' present in Clause 29 provided the foundation for Lord Mansfield's assertion in 1772 that 'England was too pure an air for a slave to breathe in.'

Why is the presumption of innocence so remarkable? Because it represents a decisive rejection of the 'just world' fallacy.

The 'just world' fallacy holds that a person's actions always result in fair and fit consequences, and it exists because people are uncomfortable accepting that suffering is random, that sometimes bad things happen for no reason at all.

It is common to believe people must have done something to deserve what they get, including being accused of a crime. If bad things only happen to those who deserve them, the argument goes, and I'm a good person, then I can be sure nothing bad will ever happen to me.

It's equivalent to, if you've done nothing wrong, you've got nothing to fear. We hear that all too often.

We do not live in a just world.

We ought not to ascribe characteristics to people before applying justice to them.

When we do ascribe bad things to people before rendering justice, we create a situation where people can be subject to raids, police harassment, inhuman treatment and injustice, purely for what they are.

Our society owes many of its liberties to Magna Carta. We need to remind ourselves of that from time to time, and not abandon them.

A new era in the Senate[3]

The first of July 2014 will be my first day as a Senator, representing NSW and the Liberal Democratic Party. I hope history will say it was the day we got to work putting Godzilla back in its cage.

Godzilla is that blundering monster that our governments have become, with their hands in our pocket and noses in every room of our house.

I am the first politician elected to an Australian parliament on a purely libertarian or classical liberal platform, with a mission to lower taxes, remove regulation, and put an end to the nanny state.

To see the challenge I face, you only need to stand at Canberra's War Memorial and look down Anzac Parade. From there you can look towards the modest building that was once our Parliament House and on to new Parliament House.

At the first sitting in Canberra's old Parliament House in 1927, taxation was less than 10% of GDP, with most of this directed to core government functions like defence, and only the Speaker of the House, the President of the Senate, the Prime Minister, the Leader of the Government in the Senate and Ministers had their own offices.

These days, taxation is around 30% of GDP, most directed to social security, health and education, and on sitting days there are 5,000 people in new Parliament House in more than 4,500 rooms. They are not there to produce anything; they are there to make legislation, tell others to make legislation or more likely, tell someone to do something entirely unrelated. Others are busy spending your money to let you know what a great job they are doing or what a bad job the people down the corridor are doing.

But of course, Parliament House is only the nerve centre of the monster. According to the latest figures, Australia has 1.9 million public servants – as many people as there are men, women and children living in Perth. Their salaries alone amount to $134 billion, or more than $100 dollars a week from each person in Australia. Much of this could be more prudently spent by individual Australians for their own purposes. It never seems to matter how much money is taken from us, it is never enough to satisfy the beast or those who believe they are entitled to some of it.

Public servants are mostly dedicated, well-meaning employees who spend their days in busyness. But the public service also tends to attract people who think they know what's good for us, and are intent on delivering it whether we need it or not.

When there are so many people being busy on our behalf, they start to encroach on our lives; drafting laws we don't need, spending money on things we can do for ourselves, spending money telling us what to do, and finding new ways to collect the money so they can do it all over again.

But if you corner any one of them at a barbecue, stories soon emerge about waste and mismanagement, the entanglement of bureaucracy, and how people in their organisation are cavalier with your money.

They might tell you why the Department of Industry spent $75,000 on coffee machines and a further $45,000 on a contract to service them; why Centrelink spent $4.6 million on a new logo; and why the Government committed $16 million to help a profitable corporation upgrade a chocolate factory in Hobart.

And these are just small examples that do not begin to explain the $10 billion we pay for government spending on corporate welfare or the tens of billions taken from us and then redistributed as welfare handouts to middle-class people who don't need it.

How does this happen? It is simply, as the economist Milton Friedman put it, what happens when people are allowed to spend money in the worst possible way – by spending someone else's money on somebody else.

In my term in Parliament, I want to convince Australians to reconsider whether handing their money over to the government is better than keeping it themselves. I want them to understand that disapproving of something does not justify it being prohibited or heavily regulated. I want them to understand the connection between the liberties they care about and the liberty of others, and to understand that individual freedom is universal, precious and must be fiercely protected.

We need more people in the Senate intent on putting Godzilla back in its cage, but in the meantime I will bring argument, reason, pleading and occasionally, blackmail, to the fight.

ECONOMIC LIBERTY

BALANCING
THE BUDGET

In 2014, 2015, 2016 and 2017 I published an alternative budget in the Australian Financial Review, to demonstrate that cutting spending, balancing the budget and lowering taxes was achievable. This is my alternative budget for 2016/17.

Alternative Budget 2016–17[4]

This year's budget provides an opportunity to return Australia to a path of fiscal responsibility. Rather than promising everyone some candy, the government needs to win back its credibility by demonstrating a clear plan to return the budget to surplus and pay down its debt. Credibility was lost when the Government went to the last election promising no cuts, only to propose cuts in the 2014 budget, and by promising responsible budgeting while presiding over a worsening budget deficit.

With Australia's taxes already internationally uncompetitive, the plan must be based on spending cuts. However, the only way to make cuts politically palatable is to share the load. The government must convince the community that if everyone takes a small haircut now, larger and more painful cuts will not be required in future.

Such a plan would set the agenda for the election, leaving Labor with the task of proving it is not irresponsible. An economic narrative based on curing the deficit disease before it becomes life threatening would be compelling. And unlike with the 2014 budget, obstructionist crossbench Senators would be irrelevant – the key vote would be at the ballot box, not in the Senate.

The government will never win the vote of those who care nothing for responsible budgeting, demand ever more government spending, and subscribe to tax-the-rich rhetoric. But if it can gain the support of the remainder, there are more than enough votes to win the election.

The responsible thing to do

In his budget speech, Treasurer Morrison should commit to paying off the Government's credit card, starting with a balanced budget in 2016–17. Our economy is growing at a healthy 3% and unemployment at 5.7% is as low as can be expected given our labour laws. And while commodity prices are lower than what we enjoyed over the last decade, they are higher than they were at any time between 1983 – when the Australian dollar was floated – and 2006.

An increasing debt burden does a disservice to the next generation. And a rising debt to GDP ratio, if not reversed, is a recipe for eventual Greek-style default and disaster.

A big job

Commonwealth Government revenue per person this year is around $16,500, while its spending per person is $17,900. Hence, we have a significant budget deficit.

Spending has been increasing relentlessly for decades and there has also been no letup in taxation. We now tax smokers, drinkers, high-income individuals, corporations, capital gains and retirement savings more than most other countries in the developed world. As a result our overall tax burden is high by international standards, even ignoring the tax-like nature of Australia's compulsory superannuation contributions.

Inflation-adjusted Commonwealth Government spending and revenue per person

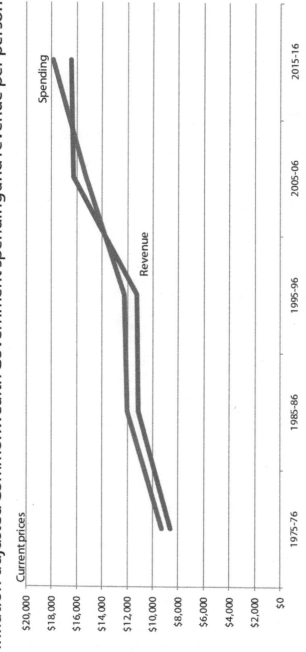

If we do nothing, bracket creep will boost revenue per person over the next three years to around $17,400, while spending will remain at around $17,900. Thus we would still have a sizeable budget deficit, spending would remain bloated, and our tax burden would be even heavier. This cannot continue. We need wholesale change, beginning with balancing the budget in 2016–17.

Spending cuts will be noticed

To balance the budget in 2016–17, the Commonwealth Government needs to cut spending by $1,400 per person. This amount could not be taken from you without you noticing. Everyone needs to take a haircut.

However, the cuts required should be put in context; real spending per person only needs to return to the levels of 2007–08, which represented the height of the big spending Howard era. 2007 was hardly a year when Australians starved in the streets.

All it requires is unwinding Kevin Rudd's spending splurge in response to the Global Financial Crisis.

Haircuts for welfare recipients

As welfare is more than a third of Commonwealth government spending, it cannot be immune from cuts. Government spending on welfare should be cut by $300 per Australian per year, noting that this would still leave $6,000 per Australian.

A third of this should come from freezing welfare payments and child care subsidies. The aged, families, unemployed and sick would all take a small haircut. Single age pensioners would miss out on a $20 boost to their fortnightly pension.

More than half of the cut should come by including the family home in the means test for the age pension. This would ensure that young people who can't afford a house don't pay taxes to fund older Australians with multi-million dollar houses.

The final contribution should come from consistently applying the income test for Family Tax Benefit Part A payments once a family earns more than $50,000. The impact of this would fall largely on families with incomes in excess of $90,000.

Haircuts for healthcare users
Government spending of $110 per person should be cut from the health budget.

A $5 Medicare co-payment for non-concessional patients should be reintroduced. This would represent a fraction of the cost of consultations. The Government's proposed $5 increase in copayments for pharmaceuticals for non-concessional patients should proceed as well.

Commonwealth Government subsidies for the training of future health workers – which represent a completely unnecessary intervention in state activity – should be stopped.

And programs to promote healthy lifestyles should be abolished, as how we live is none of the government's business. However, immunisation programs should be retained as these provide benefits beyond the individuals who receive the vaccine.

Haircuts for students
A budget boost of $150 should come from the education budget. Half of this boost could come by requiring graduates to repay their concessional student loans from their first pay check. Currently they don't start repaying their debt until their income exceeds $53,000, and the Government is planning to lower this threshold only slightly.

The other half of this budget boost could come by reducing Commonwealth funding for students in non-government schools, towards the level of Commonwealth funding for students in government schools. The only reason they are different is to counteract State discrimination against non-government schools. Ideally, only one level of government should fund schools using student-linked vouchers, making it irrelevant who owns the school.

Haircuts for public servants and the military

Government spending of $10 per person should be cut by implementing the Commission of Audit recommendation to remove excessive senior staff at Defence Headquarters, comprising the top brass of the Defence Force and senior executives from the Defence Department.

More broadly, public service wages have risen faster than private sector wages since the end of the Howard era. To restore relative wage rates, the wages of all Commonwealth Government employees should be cut by up to 2%, which would reduce government spending by $15 per person.

Haircuts to industry interference

Tourism, mining, energy, manufacturing, construction and agricultural industries should all receive a haircut by shaving 20% off their industry assistance, cutting government spending by $25 per person.

A similar haircut for university academics and other government researchers would cut government spending by around $20 per person. Philanthropic and business support is likely to increase in response, which would help fill the gap.

A 20% haircut for the ABC, SBS, arts and sports funding, heritage and national parks would cut government spending by around $25 per person. Taxpayers should not be expected to fund *The Weekly with Charlie Pickering*, the opera, or sporting events.

Suspending unnecessary spending

To round out the spending cuts, spending of $40 per person should be cut from the Commonwealth Government's environmental initiatives. The Abbott-era Direct Action Plan should be suspended until international commitments to reduce emissions become binding, and Abbott's Green Army should be abandoned as a Commonwealth frolic into State government affairs.

Government spending of $25 per person should be cut by abolishing regional development spending, which is code for porkbarrelling.

Spending of $130 per person could be cut by suspending foreign aid (except for short-term responses to natural disasters overseas, which often involve our military). Governments do not need to be involved in foreign aid so long as individuals are able to make charitable contributions to overseas causes they consider worthy. Government-funded foreign aid typically involves the poor in rich countries funding the rich in poor countries, or rich countries imposing first-world priorities on third-world countries.

Haircuts for the States

Government spending of $140 per person should be cut by discontinuing Commonwealth spending on affordable housing, which is a state responsibility. Similarly, government spending of $410 per person should be cut by discontinuing Commonwealth involvement in the provision of roads and railways. Road making is an important function of government, but it is a state and local responsibility. Commonwealth involvement is motivated by vote-buying. The State Governments have healthier budgets and balance sheets than the Commonwealth and can afford to fund roads.

	Annual spending cut per person
WELFARE	
Include the home in the age pension means tests	$180
Apply the income test for Family Tax Benefit consistently	$10
Freeze welfare payments	$110
HEALTH	
Introduce a means-tested Medicare co-payment	$45
Stop subsidies for training health workers	$55
Stop healthy lifestyle promotions	$10
EDUCATION	
Lower the income threshold at which graduates start repaying debt	$75
Reduce the gap between Commonwealth private and public school funding	$75
PUBLIC SERVANTS AND THE MILITARY	
Cut senior staffing at Defence headquarters	$10
Cut Commonwealth Government employee wages by up to 2%	$15
INDUSTRY INTERFERENCE	
Cut industry and agriculture assistance	$25
Cut research funding	$20
Cut funding for the ABC, SBS, sports, arts, heritage, national parks	$25
End the Direct Action Plan and Abbott's Green Army	$40

Stop Commonwealth spending on regional porkbarrelling	$25
Cut foreign aid	$130
RETURN RESPONSIBILITIES TO THE STATES	
Cut Commonwealth spending on roads, railways	$410
Cut Commonwealth funding for housing	$140
Total	**$1,400**

Cutting government spending by $1,400 per person is not dramatic. In fact, it would be hard to distinguish the proposed spending levels from the status quo (see chart). After making these cuts there would still be massive government spending.

If we were in Government, these spending cuts are a fraction of what the Liberal Democrats would pursue. Our policies include major reform to the big ticket items of welfare, health, education, and defence, and the abolition of all grants to the States, forcing them to manage their own finances.

The spending cuts the Liberal Democrats propose would not only balance the budget and repay debt, but would facilitate abolition of taxes on alcohol, fuel, tobacco and imports, allow the tax-free threshold to be lifted to $40,000, and allow personal income tax and company tax rates to be reduced to a flat 20%.

By comparison, the proposal outlined in this alternative budget – which achieves a balance simply by shaving spending – is very modest. There is no reason it could not be implemented.

A budget to set the election agenda

A balanced budget would set the agenda for months to come. We would continue to discuss the footy, traffic jams and the movie

Batman v Superman, but injected into these conversations would be comments about what the government is doing.

Over the weeks between the budget and the election, grudging acceptance that balancing the budget is the responsible thing to do would develop. A café manager may overhear a customer sticking up for the budget, saying: 'Why shouldn't the budget be balanced?' A publican may hear drinkers debate the budget across the bar, saying: 'What would you do instead?' And amid all the phone watching and thumb twiddling on the bus or train, one may even hear comments like: 'But we all have to pay off our credit card.'

The imperative to balance the budget is undeniable, and as my proposals demonstrate, it would not be hard to achieve. All it requires is some gumption from Turnbull and Morrison. Let's hope they have it.

Don't be like Greece[5]

There once was a country that enjoyed strong economic growth and had government debt of around 22% of GDP, a level not much more than Australia's expected debt in the next year or two. This country proceeded over the subsequent generation to have successive budget deficits, to direct workers into its burgeoning public sector, to raise the tax burden, and to produce a business environment characterised by red tape.

Voila. You end up with the basket-case economy that is Greece.

Is Australia treading down the path well worn by Greece? Or are we better than that?

If you think we are, then I invite you to confirm it.

My challenge is to everyone who thinks Greece has no lessons for Australia.

Tell me which spending cuts you support to stop the growth of the public sector, to stop the growth in the tax burden, and to deliver a balanced budget.

Tell me which red tape you are prepared to cut.

If you think we should deliver a balanced budget, but not right now, tell me why not now. What brilliant contortions in economics can justify us having a budget deficit now, when the global financial crisis was nearly a decade ago, and when the economy is growing at 3%?

If you don't think we should deliver a balanced budget now, then tell me when. We haven't had one since I was in my fifties. You can tell by the lines on my face that that was some time ago.

I previously requested the Senate to commit to a balanced budget by 2020. But my motion was voted down.

The Government now proposes to balance the budget in 2021. But on current trends, that's very unlikely to occur.

So I ask all Senators in this place, from all parties, if you won't agree to commit to a balanced budget within five years or so, by what year will you do so?

Or are you comfortable with perpetual budget deficits, ever increasing debt, and eventual default?

The current Liberal/National Government, and the previous Labor Government, signed up to a fiscal strategy of achieving budget surpluses on average over the course of the economic cycle.

This is fine, but we are now in the midst of an expected twelve-year stretch of budget deficits.

Twelve years is the upper limit of the duration of economic cycles, according to many economic estimates. So what we really have is a fiscal strategy of maintaining budget deficits on average over the course of the entire economic cycle.

The Liberal Democrats are alone in proposing an immediate balancing of the budget, and are alone in having a credible plan for spending cuts to achieve this.

For example, the Liberal Democrats have detailed plans to slash welfare, the biggest area of Commonwealth Government spending.

The Liberal Democrats would abolish Abstudy, the Pensioner Education Supplement, and the Assistance for Isolated Children Scheme. We would abolish Youth Allowance and Austudy for post-school study assistance. And we would abolish Family Tax Benefit Part B, the national paid parental leave scheme, the Child Care Benefit and the Child Care Rebate.

The Liberal Democrats would reduce Family Tax Benefit Part A and abolish associated newborn, energy, large family and multiple birth supplements. We would lift the age pension eligibility age. And we would freeze maximum unemployment payments for the duration of a recipient's unemployment.

The Liberal Democrats would means test all welfare payments and include the home in those means tests. We would limit welfare to citizens. And we would limit the growth of welfare payments to the rate of inflation.

This is just a taste of our spending cuts. Beyond the welfare system, the Liberal Democrats have extensive policies to cut spending in each other area of government spending. What's more, we have policies to avoid the red tape that has suffocated the Greek economy and is threatening to do the same here.

Key to this red tape reduction is the repeal of the Fair Work Act, which could more accurately be described as the *Keep Unemployment High Act*. This Act is not needed to allow unions to form, to ensure workplace health and safety, or to prevent workplace discrimination. But it bans work for less than $17.29 an hour and it bans work that doesn't conform to soviet-era 'award' regulations.

It bans the firing of workers who fail to attend work and the firing of workers without the approval of a tribunal, provisions which discourage businesses from hiring workers in the first place. And the Act requires businesses to negotiate with a union irrespective of whether the union enjoys support from workers.

Our first priority should be helping to get people into a job in the first place. Feather bedding those who already have a job, at the expense of those who want one, is exactly what Greece did.

These cuts to government spending and red tape proposed by the Liberal Democrats are necessary to avoid the path trodden by Greece over the last generation. No other party proposes anything like it.

Some politicians know we need to pursue such cuts, but they don't know how to do it and get elected. That's why we need a strong advocate of small government, holding the balance of power in the next parliament, to force whatever Government we end up with to avoid a future of big spending, more red tape and economic stagnation. In short, to avoid the slow path to Greece.

Angels and demons[6]

The Government's better angels are losing.

In last year's election campaign, the better angels encouraged the Coalition to offer some positive assurances about small government, with commitments to abolish the untargeted Schoolkids Bonus, cut corporate welfare for car manufacturers, slow the growth in taxpayer-funded foreign aid, reduce the company tax rate, and abolish the carbon and mining taxes.

But since the election, the Coalition's tax-and-spend demons have been winning. They've got the government to commit to some big spending projects like Direct Action, and to various tax increases. They want a levy to fund paid parental leave. They want to withdraw personal tax cuts scheduled for July 2015. (I managed to thwart their first attempt to withdraw these tax cuts, but they will surely try again.) And they have already succeeded in increasing taxes on businesses and superannuation as part of the mining tax repeal. As a result, they will gather billions more in revenue than the mining tax would ever have raised.

The angels did manage to inject plans into the Budget to reduce subsidies for GP visits, subsidies for university degrees, and middle-class welfare. But these savings have not made it into law. While this is mostly due to the tax-and-spend demons that dominate Labor, Greens and Palmer United, it is also a result of half-hearted support from within the Coalition.

The Coalition could have stood up for its plan to cut subsidies for GP visits, for example, by explaining that continuing to borrow money to pay for 'free' universal healthcare is a Ponzi scheme that will surely end in tears. But instead it was cast as a necessary evil to fund ever more government spending on medical research.

Meanwhile, the tax-and-spend demons are continuing to remodel the government in their own image.

They killed the election commitment to cut the public service headcount by an additional 12,000, they devised a plan to throw billions of dollars at medical research, and they snuck tax increases for banks, mature age workers and people with dependent spouses into the Budget.

The same demons also managed to increase the top marginal tax rate to 49 cents in the dollar. This discourages our most talented people from taking risks and pursuing more moneymaking opportunities. With top marginal tax rates of 17% in Hong Kong, 20% in Singapore and 34.5% in New Zealand, it also prompts talented people to leave and stay away. The government claims the 49% top tax rate is temporary, but there is nothing so permanent as a temporary tax increase.

Finally, the tax-and-spend demons have increased the tax on fuel, revealing the government's far greater commitment to raising taxes than to cutting spending. When it looked like legislation to increase fuel tax would be blocked, it simply increased the tax with a tariff that allows the tax to rise first and parliamentary approval to come later.

The Coalition views this as a cunning stunt – it thinks parliament won't invalidate the tax increase if it means giving money back to fuel companies rather than drivers. But I cannot think of any reasonable objections to refunding ill-gotten tax revenue to fuel companies.

It is true the Coalition is increasing the fuel tax in line with inflation, so the real level of the tax is maintained. But the fuel tax is damaging and it should be eroded. It hits businesses with vehicles under four and a half tonnes, like utes and vans – making deliveries and the services of tradies more expensive. The fuel tax also affects consumers in arbitrary ways, hitting the bush more than the city, outer suburbs more than the inner suburbs, and the owners of old cars more than the owners of new cars.

The dirty secret about the fuel tax is that it extracts more revenue than the combined spending of all levels of government on road construction and maintenance. Moreover, the Commonwealth Government doesn't even forward the revenue to the states – the entities responsible for road building.

The fuel tax cannot even be thought of as a reasonable proxy for a carbon price – it's equivalent to a price of more than $160 per tonne of carbon dioxide. The current carbon price in Europe is around $10.

There are small government angels in the Coalition, but they are overruled by its tax-and-spend demons, intent on keeping government at the centre of our lives.

It's not a fair fight.

TAKING OUR MONEY

Don't lift taxes to fix the Budget[7]

The Prime Minister has promised that his Tax White Paper will not be about increasing the tax take. This is heartening, because a look at the numbers confirms that the Government's Budget woes are not due to the Government forgetting to tax us.

After allowing for inflation, Commonwealth tax collections per person have increased by more than 15% since introduction of the GST. Moreover, the tax-to-GDP ratio is higher in Australia than in many countries with which we compete for investment and skilled workers, including South Korea and the United States.

And, although the Commonwealth tax-to-GDP ratio is currently below the post-GST average, the Government expects bracket creep to deliver an above-average tax-to-GDP ratio within two years, and a far heavier tax burden after that.

Yet Labor and the Greens want the tax burden to rise, and argue that some taxes can be increased without hurting everyday Australians. It's an appeal to the politics of envy, and it's false.

The Labor/Greens alliance wants to increase taxes on superannuation, the mining industry, rich individuals and large corporations. The problem is, heavier taxation of superannuation would penalise saving, a Commonwealth tax on mining would encroach on the States' tax base, the top marginal tax rate is already 49%, and our corporate tax take is the second highest in the world.

Each of these proposals represents an increase in income tax. Economists familiar with tax theory (like Shadow Assistant Treasurer, Professor Andrew Leigh) know that income tax is the worst tax of all.

Income tax represents more than two thirds of the Commonwealth Government's tax take. If there were any further opportunities to extract money via income tax without causing huge damage, you can rest assured that previous governments would have already figured them out.

Any increase in income tax would require us to employ more ATO staff to engage in the unproductive activity of chasing tax dollars, adding further complexity to a tax system that already drives Australian taxpayers crazy.

As well as rejecting calls to increase income tax, we should reject calls for a return to a carbon tax or an abolition of fuel tax credits.

A return to a carbon tax would hurt our economy and wages, as shown by the previous Government's modelling. Even the Garnaut review suggested that carbon pricing would be (slightly) in Australia's interest only if the world's major emitters adopted carbon pricing. As decisions on global emissions are currently made by the Chinese Government, Vladimir Putin, sundry Middle Eastern dictators and the US Congress, we shouldn't hold our breath.

Abolishing fuel tax credits would increase tax on heavy vehicles. This would add an arbitrary and hidden cost to the everyday products that heavy vehicles deliver. It would also increase tax on off road fuel use, such as generators. Taxing make-your-own electricity but not mains electricity makes no sense.

The GST causes far less damage than these taxes. As such, a case could be made to apply GST to currently-exempt items like food, healthcare, education and childcare – and even to increase the GST rate – so long as this was part of a package that clearly reduced the overall tax burden each year.

But a GST increase would still be damaging. It would exacerbate the inequity that occurs when some avoid GST through cash-in-hand transactions and small purchases from overseas. And it would discourage backyard businesses from growing to the point where they need to collect GST.

Rather than look to increase tax, we need to recognise that current Budget difficulties are driven by excessive spending.

After accounting for inflation, Commonwealth Government spending per person has increased by more than a third since the introduction of the GST. It is currently more than a quarter of GDP and well above the post GST average.

Growth in Commonwealth spending over the last decade has been fastest in the areas of health, schools and universities, housing, environmental protection, road and rail transport, and support for the arts and sport. Cuts need to be made in all these areas. And since public sector wages have grown faster than private sector wages over this period, a sustained period of public sector wage restraint is also in order.

A substantial improvement in the Budget position is required to sustain everyday Australians in the years and decades to come. This improvement needs to come through lower government spending, not higher taxes.

Labor 2013–14 Budget Savings (Measures No. 1) Bill 2014[8]

I rise to oppose the Labor 2013–14 Budget Savings (Measures No. 1) Bill 2014.

Under the law of the land, the Tax Office will start taking slightly less of your income in a fortnight's time. This is good news, but the Coalition and Labor can't stand it.

So today the Coalition and Labor will combine to pass a bill that cancels the slight reduction in income tax scheduled for July.

This bill proves that the Coalition and Labor are a unity ticket. If you want big taxes to fund a government that can spend your income better than you can, vote for either of them, they'll give you what you want.

The tax cut we are talking about is not huge. If you earn $66,000, the Tax Office currently takes away around $14,300. Next year they would take away around $14,220. So around $80 less would be taken from you.

The Coalition and Labor believe they can spend that $80 better than you.

In fact, as this Bill gets waved through the Senate, they will say that they can't afford to give you the $80, as if the $80 is theirs.

The mindset of the Coalition and Labor is that of someone who believes that all your income is owned by the government, and you get to keep some of it only because of government generosity or absentmindedness.

This mindset leads to tax increases being called 'budget savings.' We wouldn't put up with this abuse of language anywhere else. If a business claims that it is making savings, that means that it is spending less. It doesn't mean that they are jacking up their prices.

This mindset also leads some in the Coalition and Labor to treat tax deductions, offsets and exemptions as a government handout to be withdrawn when the going gets tough.

In reality, tax deductions, offsets and exemptions just represent instances where the Tax Office is taking less money than some imagined tax take. The approach of some in the Coalition and Labor is akin to a pickpocket skimming your wallet of notes, then expecting gratitude because this time they left the coins behind.

Yes, governments need to spend money and raise taxes. But our governments are spending more money and raising more taxes than ever in Australia's history. Fifty years ago, total taxes were around $5,000 per person after adjusting for inflation. This grew each decade until now the tax burden is around $19,000 per person. Those bleating about crashing revenues are on another planet. Their complaint, in essence, is that taxes ought to grow even faster.

There is no justification for the ever-expanding tax burden. Living standards for all groups of society have risen over the last 50 years, which means the need for government welfare services has declined. And we haven't uncovered new forms of effective government intervention either. To the contrary, the prosperity-promoting effects of free markets and the many failings of government involvement have been demonstrated time and again.

Yes, governments need to spend money and raise taxes. But our taxes are high even by the standards of the stagnant economies that make up the OECD. The average tax burden in the OECD is 30% of GDP. This average accounts for the different populations of OECD countries, as well as the social security contributions in many OECD countries that serve a similar purpose to Australia's compulsory superannuation guarantee payments. In contrast, Australia's tax burden, after including Australia's compulsory superannuation guarantee payments, is 31% of GDP. Having a higher tax burden than the OECD average is extremely concerning, particularly as the OECD average is high compared to prosperous and dynamic non-OECD countries like Singapore.

Yes, governments need to spend money and raise taxes. But every tax expert knows that income tax is the most damaging tax on the Commonwealth Government's books. It discourages working, saving, starting a business and taking risks. At times this Coalition Government has raised concerns about bracket creep imposing ever higher income tax burdens on middle Australia. But we've experienced considerable bracket creep since the last time there were income tax cuts, and when a scheduled income tax cut comes along that would return just a fraction of this bracket creep, the Coalition Government nips it in the bud. For the Coalition, this is akin to the cry of Saint Augustine: 'Lord, Give me chastity and continence, but not yet.'

The Liberal Democrats have a comprehensive plan to significantly reduce government spending, and an unshakable conviction that your income is yours, not the governments. That is why I am defending the $80 tax cut that is due to each Australian taxpayer in a fortnight's time. But sadly, the conspiracy of the big-government forces of the Coalition and Labor will cancel this tax cut through the Bill before us today. When the date of the election comes, the taxpayers of Australia will remember.

Tax and Superannuation Laws Amendment (2015 No. 5) 2015[9]

Season's greetings to you and all here in the Senate.

With the parliamentary year wrapping up (somewhat early) on the third of December, and with Christmas fast approaching, it's time to pause and look back on 2015.

And what a year it has been. The Government has been hitting home runs on tax reform all year.

There have been five – count them – five tax and superannuation laws amendment bills.

And I've loved every one of them. Well, a kind of love.

So in the spirit of Christmas, let me recite a little ditty about the five tax bills of Christmas. Given my warm feelings for all in this Chamber, I was tempted not to sing it. It's true I am not an undiscovered Pavarotti. But given its nature, I really have no choice. So here it is.

In the first Bill of Christmas my Treas'ur sent to me, a tax on the el-der-ly.

In the second Bill of Christmas my Treas'ur sent to me, slower deductions and a tax on the elderly.

In the third Bill of Christmas my Treas'ur sent to me, seafarers' tax, slower deductions and a tax on the elderly.

In the fourth Bill of Christmas my Treas'ur sent to me, more CGT, seafarer's tax, slower deductions and a tax on the elderly.

In the fifth Bill of Christmas my Treas'ur sent to me, m-o-r-e F-B-T! More CGT, seafarer's tax, slower deductions and a tax on the elderly.

Merry Christmas, everyone.

Tax and Super 2015 No. 6 Bill[10]

When we debated the fifth tax Bill of 2015 last December, I sang about the five tax bills of Christmas my Treasurer sent to me. If you recall, the five bills delivered more FBT, more CGT, seafarer's tax, slower deductions and a tax on the elderly.

Well, today we're debating the sixth tax Bill of 2015, which suggests I should sing something that sounds like 'six geese a laying.' But I can't, because with this bill, the Government is killing the golden goose.

Australia's prosperity is built on foreign investment, but with this bill, the Government makes it abundantly clear that foreign investment is no longer welcome in this country. The Bill imposes a tax on Australians who purchase Australian land, plant and equipment from foreigners unless those foreigners have obtained a certificate from the tax office. It's like requiring a note from the headmaster.

This will have the obvious effect of discouraging foreigners from purchasing Australian land, plant and equipment in the first place.

The Government justifies its new tax by complaining that it is difficult to get foreigners to pay capital gains tax when they sell Australian land, plant and equipment.

Foreigners are already exempt from capital gains tax when they sell other Australian assets, like shares. And such exemptions help Australians. If you tax the returns of foreign investors, you simply drive up the returns that foreign investors demand when they invest in Australia.

Australian businesses face a higher cost of capital as a result, and business expansion is stifled.

It is for this reason that successive Governments have reduced taxes on interest and dividend payments to foreign investors. But now we see a new tax on payments to foreign investors – a tax that pleases the xenophobes but hurts Australians. And a tax that sets out to rake in the revenue, when the Treasurer says that he's focused on cutting spending.

The solution is the exact opposite of what this Bill aims to achieve. The solution is to exempt foreigners from capital gains tax when they sell Australian land, plant and equipment.

The art of taxation is said to consist of plucking the goose to obtain the maximum amount of feathers with the smallest amount of hissing.

But we're not plucking the goose. We're strangling it because it flew in from overseas.

Taxing the rich is immoral[11]

Our government extracts huge quantities of tax from the rich. It does this for no reason other than that's where the money is, and it is addicted to huge spending.

The imposition of heavy tax burdens on the rich is inherent in our progressive income tax system. It is supported by each of the major parties in Australia, and it is commonplace in the developed world.

But this extraordinary taxation of the rich is immoral.

Some will instinctively disagree. They will defend tax attacks on the rich by referring to the so-called ability-to-pay-principle. But this is no more than the idea that the government should take what it can get. There is absolutely nothing principled about it.

Your next-door neighbour might have the ability to pay for your lunch, but that doesn't mean it is moral for you to take money from his wallet when you're feeling peckish.

Some will say that taking more money from the rich is justified by the idea that money in the hands of the poor boosts social well-being more than in the hands of the rich. But most government spending is directed to welfare, education and health handouts that aren't effectively means-tested, as well as to ad hoc interference with industry. When the government does direct money to the poor, it wastes billions on public servants along the way.

Taking money from the rich also depresses charitable giving, economic growth and employment – hardly a formula for boosting social well-being.

Some people may harbour the idea that tax attacks on the rich are moral because the rich enjoy ill-gotten gains. This is crude and wrong. It would be rare for a rich person's wealth to be a result of corrupt acts by the person, or their forebears. And corrupt acts should be prosecuted individually, directly and strenuously, rather than used as a justification to tar all rich people with the same brush.

Some may say that it is moral to tax the rich because their money is the result of luck. But by this logic it is OK to take money from someone who just won lotto. Regardless of the extent to which luck played a part in how much money rich people have, the simple point is this: it's still their money.

There is nothing moral about singling out the rich for tax attacks.

The only morally defensible tax principle is the benefit principle. This is the idea that people can be taxed if they benefit from the associated government spending. It means that government services from which we all benefit – like defence, police and the justice system – should be paid for by all. After all, these services don't particularly benefit the rich.

Our tax system is clearly not based on the benefit principle. It largely involves taking money from a rich person – well in excess of the cost of services the person benefits from, either directly or indirectly – to fund government services that the person will never use. I challenge each politician and commentator to explain how they think this is the moral thing to do.

The Liberal Democrats would replace the existing progressive income tax system with a flat 20% income tax in conjunction with a high tax-free threshold – and we have identified the spending cuts to fund it. This policy wouldn't completely remove discriminatory tax treatment of the rich, but it would be a huge step in the right direction.

In contrast, the major parties will adopt immoral policies that maintain high-income tax rates and increase tax on superannuation, capital gains and property investment. I will oppose all these immoral tax attacks on the rich, and any fellow Liberal Democrats who join me on these crossbenches after the next election will do the same.

Multinational Tax Avoidance Bill[12]

I rise to oppose the Tax Laws Amendment (Combating Multinational Tax Avoidance) Bill 2015. I suspect I will be the only parliamentarian to do so.

It is easy to throw stones at corporations. Even though a corporation is just a collective of individuals pooling their resources to make stuff, 'corporation' is still a dirty word.

It is even easier to throw stones at multinational corporations. To be multinational just means you sell your stuff to willing buyers in more than one country, but 'multinational' still serves as an effective dog whistle for those who do not like foreigners.

And it is easier still to rail against tax avoidance. After all, we should all pay our fair share.

The thing is, we've tried to define what a fair share is in tax law. And the multinational corporations have paid that fair share.

As it happens, we set the bar high when we defined what a fair share is. Australia gets more corporate tax as a share of GDP than any other OECD country apart from Norway.

We've passed tax laws that tell multinational corporations what tax rate they must pay, what revenue needs to be taxed and what expenses are to be deducted. So if our idea of what a fair share is has changed, we should enact changes to the tax rate, to what we mean by revenue, or what we mean by expenses.

The legislation before us today does nothing to change the tax rate, what we mean by revenue, or what we mean by expenses. It just says that – if you are a large multinational corporation who has paid the legislated tax rate – you've still broken the law if you've done anything with the purpose of getting a tax benefit.

The ATO and Courts will decide whether you've broken the law after the fact, in an unpredictable, arbitrary and ad hoc way. This is the justice of a kangaroo court.

What makes this even more farcical is that we already have a despicable rule that says you've broken the law if you've done something that is otherwise legal but that is done with the purpose of getting a tax benefit. It's called the general anti-avoidance provision. It applies to everyone, including multinational companies. No wonder the Government has struggled to identify any increase in revenue that will arise with the passage of the Bill before us today. It is nothing but grandstanding.

This Bill is targeted at companies like Google, Apple and Microsoft – businesses that generate ingenious goods and services from places that are as far away from Australia as you can imagine.

Even when their products came in plastic wrapping – which not many do now – Australia didn't even provide the plastic that surrounded the cardboard that encased the shiny product. And we have absolutely nothing to do with the science, marketing nous and entrepreneurship that made those products possible. The idea that anything more than a tiny fraction of the sales revenue should be treated as Aussie grown profits is jingoism worthy of the most embarrassing xenophobe.

It's obvious that companies set up their offices, base their intangible activities, and book their profits, in low-tax jurisdictions. Places like Singapore are teeming with business shirts, even though it's a place where the humidity never drops and your shirt sticks to your back.

The business-people of the world would much prefer to do their business in Australia, with its cool sea breezes and great coffee. So won't someone please think of the business people, and halve our corporate tax rate?

Making life harder for multinationals in a competitive market and expecting more revenue is like punching someone in the nose and expecting them to like you better.

Instead we should remember that big corporations are kept in check by competition – but there is no competition with big government, which has the unique power of being able to take your money by force.

Fuel Indexation and Road Funding Bills[13]

I rise to oppose the four fuel indexation and road funding bills before the Senate.

Fuel taxes are unjustified.

Taxes on goods and services should be limited to a broad-based GST. That way, the Government wouldn't interfere with people's choices about what to spend their money on – everything would be taxed equally.

The only reason we have fuel taxes is that taxing fuel used to be one of the few ways governments could reliably extract revenue, and once a government starts taxing something it finds it hard to stop.

Fuel taxes are not directed to funding road construction and maintenance, and fuel tax revenue exceeds spending on road construction and maintenance.

Fuel tax revenue last financial year was $19 billion, whereas total Commonwealth and State Government spending on road transport was $16 billion.

We should also remember that fuel tax is not the only way that governments extract money from motorists – we face registration and licence fees, insurance taxes, and road tolls. This is not just double dipping, it's triple and quadruple dipping. Road users should certainly pay for the roads they use one way or another, but not every way.

Fuel taxes are also not a proxy for a carbon tax. Our current fuel taxes represent a carbon price of over $150 per tonne of carbon dioxide. No emissions trading scheme or carbon tax proposes the imposition of such a carbon price, particularly when it is just on one product and not on the great bulk of products that generate greenhouse gas emissions.

More broadly, the Commonwealth Government should not fund roads. There is no Constitutional basis for Commonwealth involvement. And there is no policy reason for Commonwealth involvement – after all, roads are not like railway lines – we don't need to coordinate rail gauges.

Commonwealth transfers to the States should be abolished, including for roads. The States can reduce their spending, for example by means-testing access to government-run schools and hospitals. And if they don't want to do that, the States have the power to impose taxes that are less damaging than a lot of Commonwealth Government taxes.

If Commonwealth transfers to the States are not abolished, they should at least not come with strings attached. The idea that public servants in Canberra have any idea about how to divvy up spending between particular roads, particular schools and particular hospitals is ridiculous.

On Budget day I moved a motion calling on the Senate to express its opposition to the Government's fuel tax increase. The motion passed with support from Labor. Six weeks later, Labor has changed its mind.

Labor, the Coalition, and the Greens all support higher fuel taxes, provided the booty is spent to their liking. It is becoming clearer by the day to motorists, taxpayers and voters, that the only true small government, low-tax party in Australia is the Liberal Democrats.

SPENDING OUR MONEY

Spending addicts[14]

In the months since his appointment, Treasurer Scott Morrison has been telling the Australian public that the Government has a spending problem. At the same time, he and his Cabinet colleagues were making decisions to further boost spending.

Treasury officials would have told him government spending was rising automatically, at a rate that outstrips inflation and population growth; that government spending is nearly 26% of GDP – more than any year since the early 1990s except for Rudd's cash splash in 2009–10 — and that this automatic spending growth is happening now, before the baby boomer retirement tsunami hits the budget.

The Government's response has been to increase discretionary spending this year and next by $2.5 billion.

The Government has decided to throw an extra billion dollars at local roads and an associated advertising campaign. These ads won't be explaining why taxpayers in Cairns should fund roads in Fremantle.

It decided to throw more money at the National Disability Insurance Scheme, which has worthy intentions but intrudes into disability services run by State Governments. It hasn't bothered to explain what special expertise in disability services the Commonwealth Government brings to the table.

The Government has splashed more money on matters outside the Commonwealth's responsibility by increasing spending to 'enhance STEM education' in schools. The current push under Malcolm Turnbull to get schools to teach more science and maths (that's the 'S' and 'M' in 'STEM') follows the push a couple of years ago to get schools to teach more languages as part of Julia Gillard's 'Asian Century' policy. For the sake of some stability in our school curriculum, we might want to stop changing our Prime Ministers so often.

The Government's MYEFO update this week reveals other new spending plans over this year and next. There's a new taskforce on cities, even though the Commonwealth has no expertise or responsibility for any city other than possibly Canberra. There's new funding for Australia's synchrotron, an amazing scientific contraption that makes taxpayers' money disappear. And there's new spending on whale research, which is hard to view as a national priority.

What all this reveals is a spending addiction. When you're told you've got a spending problem, and you respond by spending more, it's pretty serious.

Like all addicts, the Government has a raft of excuses at the ready. For example, it will point to the decision to cut spending in the 'outyears' of 2017–18 and 2018–19. But spending now and hoping to cut spending in the future is like a priest saying, 'Lord, grant me chastity, but not yet.'

The Government will blame the Senate for blocking previous plans to cut spending. This has some truth, but while all non-Government Senators other than me have earned this blame, it is also true that the Government could readily reduce spending by making cuts to the 'supply' bills that Labor has promised – since the dismissal of Whitlam – to never block.

And as for genuine structural changes to restore the budget to surplus and allow tax cuts that would make Australian industry competitive with international rivals such as Singapore, forget about it. Reeling in middle-class welfare, reducing regulation of childcare to make it less expensive, reducing pension eligibility for those with valuable homes, and means-testing access to public hospitals and schools, are not even on the Government's radar.

This week's budget blowout was the least surprising announcement since Boy George told us he was gay. And yet, the only narrative we hear from the Government is that all options to increase taxes are on the table.

We cannot tax our way to a balanced budget. We already tax corporations, high-income individuals, capital gains and retirement savings more than most other countries in the developed world, and our overall tax burden is high by historical and international standards. Moreover, there is no magic wand that can elevate commodity prices or economic growth rates.

It's true that our budget woes are not of the Government's making, but came with the fiscal mess it inherited from the Gillard and Rudd governments and Treasurer Wayne Swan. But it's also true that the Government has failed to convince the Australian public that when you're in a deep financial hole, it's a good idea to stop digging.

The cure for an addiction is often cold turkey. With Christmas approaching, perhaps that's more than usually appropriate.

The ghost of Julia Gillard[15]

The ghost of Julia Gillard has returned to our TV screens, and her tales of past glories and dramas fill the pages of a recently released memoir. But the ghost of Julia Gillard is also haunting another set of recently released books, called the Budget Papers.

And in these you will find some truly scary reading.

In 2012, Gillard made the politically-popular decision to allow universities to offer as many government-subsidised courses as they wish. This enabled them to increase student numbers and, in turn, the number of government subsidies and concessional student loans. Gillard made no attempt to pay for this increased burden on the taxpayer. It was a matter for the years beyond the end of her budget reporting period, and after the 2013 election.

The chickens have now come home to roost, with the Budget Papers outlining sky-high government university subsidies and concessional loans next financial year.

When Christopher Pyne's plan to reduce university subsidies per student returns to the Senate, I suggest to my crossbench colleagues that we should not see this as a disruption to a long-standing system that has stood the test of time. Instead we should see it as fixing a system that was tinkered with only a couple of years ago and is heading for the skids.

Gillard also applied her penchant for unfunded feel-good politics to schools funding. Her Gonski reforms can be criticised for their Canberra-centric meddling, their proliferation of bureaucracy, and their failure to deliver on the goal of fairness. But they can also be criticised for their astronomic impact on the Budget.

The reforms they bring will increase real Commonwealth Government funding per school student by 4.3% each year for the next decade. Like the tertiary funding issue, Gillard transferred its funding into the never-never. So when the Coalition committed to only four years of Gonski-esque funding growth, the ghost of Gillard could be heard in the moans of protest that followed.

Gillard's cash splash on matters educational also extended to toddlers. She invented a new role for the Commonwealth

Government by funding State Government preschools. The non-means-tested child care rebate was increased from 30 to 50% of child care costs. And she ramped up these child care costs by requiring child care centres to hire only certificate, diploma and degree-qualified child care workers to look after the kids.

Another long-term, federation-eroding and bureaucracy-inducing promise was made in relation to funding of hospitals. Gillard's desire to concentrate spending just beyond her budget reporting period is plain to see – she committed the Commonwealth Government to fund 45% of the growth in public hospital costs to 2017, but then ramped up this commitment to 50% thereafter. The Coalition Government's decision to undo this arrangement from 2017 drew predictable cries of protest. Now, its decision to merely increase hospital funding in line with CPI and population growth is being characterised as the height of austerity.

But Gillard's piece de resistance must surely be the National Disability 'Insurance' Scheme – a welfare plan that adds Commonwealth public servants and red tape to existing State-based bureaucracies and expects an outcome different from the chaos we have seen from Commonwealth takeovers in health and education. Once again Julia Gillard put the spending beyond her budget reporting period, such that the cost of NDIS implementation has only become apparent in this year's budget.

Over the next four years Commonwealth Government spending on the NDIS will exceed $21 billion. Only $2.5 billion of this will be funded by the NDIS levy, which Gillard tearfully introduced as if it were a significant step towards sustainable care for the disabled. So even with the pretence of funding her promises, she fell well short.

Like a bitter army retreating from the field of battle with no regard for the civilians left behind, Gillard buried land mines throughout the Budget for future Ministers and tax-payers to negotiate.

The Abbott Government has a responsibility to extract the country from its budget hole. It should not make excuses and say that it is all too hard. Regrettably, that is exactly what it is now doing.

But we need to remember who got us into the Budget hole in the first place. Bill Shorten's windy Budget reply speech – heavy with spending on free university degrees and increased research and development – shows us how well the ghost of Julia Gillard lingers on.

Malcolm's spending problem[16]

On the night he seized the Prime Ministership, speaking about Australia's economic problems, Malcolm Turnbull extolled the importance of 'explaining what the problem is, making sure people understand it … presenting a path forward and then making a case for that path forward.'

He is failing his own test.

There is no bigger problem facing his government than the budget. But because this has not been explained, most Australians think the most important issues of our time are rowdy behaviour, match fixing, and gambling in sport. The Prime Minister and his government have neither presented, nor made a case for, bringing the budget under control.

Quite simply, we have a spending problem. The Commonwealth Government spent 18% of GDP in 1970 and spends 26% of GDP now. And of course, taxes are rising accordingly.

The Government is spending $17,850 per person this year, up from $17,750 last year and $6,350 in 1970 (all adjusted for inflation). This growth has occurred despite all cohorts of society becoming richer, so there is less need for welfare. And it has occurred despite us knowing from the collapse of socialism that centrally planned service provision is highly inefficient.

It gets worse when we include the other levels of government. Our national, state and local governments together spend 35.6% of GDP. In more prosperous countries like Hong Kong, Singapore and Switzerland, governments spend less (17.6, 18.2 and 33.5% of GDP respectively).

One reason the government dithers on whether to cut spending is thanks to stupid advice from public servants. They tell it not to touch spending because that would push the economy over a cliff. This is simpleton economics. Our current budget deficit is injecting 2% of GDP into the economy, but this is funded through foreigners buying government debt. This boosts our exchange rate, which in turn hurts our trade-exposed industries like tourism, education, agriculture, mining, and manufacturing. The deficit simply helps some at the expense of others.

Even if a budget deficit could be justified, this would be best delivered by cutting spending in Canberra (to free up resources currently mired in unproductive activities) and concurrently cutting taxes (to free up business activity and employment in the real world outside Canberra).

Another reason the government dithers is it is not being urged to cut spending by the community. Many people find it inconceivable that the government would dare to cut anything.

Huge swathes of the population benefit from the status quo in the short term. More than half of all households receive government cash handouts. More than 80% of the population pay less in tax than they receive from the government, including 'in-kind' benefits such as public schools and hospitals. That means less than 20% of the population pay for the collective goods we all benefit from, like defence, police, footpaths and street lighting. And only these Australians are providing the funds to pay interest of a billion dollars a month on our growing public debt, more than what we spend on unemployment benefits, foreign aid and the ABC combined.

Many in our community are urging the government to leave spending alone, either in the belief that the economy can continue to remain in deficit indefinitely or it can be remedied by yet more taxes imposed on those who are already 20% carrying the load. They are wrong.

What we need is a new economic narrative from the Prime Minister, using his renowned charm and powers of persuasion. He must convince the public we have a spending problem, that it cannot continue, and that the burden of fixing it must be shared. That includes families and pensioners, welfare recipients and corporate welfare recipients, public servants and defence force personnel, uni students and school teachers. Adjustment need not be painful if the burden is shared, but the notion that nobody should be worse off must be demolished.

As to where expenditure can be cut, there are numerous opportunities. Middle-class welfare and the duplication of state and commonwealth departments are good places to start. But unless the community can be convinced there is a problem, no solution will be acceptable.

Appropriation Bills 2015–16[17]

I rise to speak to the various Appropriation Bills before the Senate. I will not be calling a division on the second reading, because the major parties support their passage. But I have grave concerns about these annual Appropriation Bills that I want to put on the record.

Commonwealth Government spending is at record levels. Figures for last financial year indicate that real Commonwealth Government spending per person is at its highest level on record.

Real government spending per person across the federation is also at its highest level on record.

There is no hiding the rise of government spending, even when you compare government spending with GDP. Commonwealth government spending is 25.9% of GDP. Since 1970, the ratio of Commonwealth Government spending to GDP was above this for just four years under Bob Hawke, for two years under Keating, and for one year under Rudd. In all other years since 1970, Commonwealth Government spending relative to GDP was lower than it is today.

There is no justification for the ever-expanding Commonwealth Government spend. As I have said before, living standards for all groups of society have risen inexorably over the past decades. This means the need for government welfare services has declined. And we haven't uncovered new forms of effective government intervention either. To the contrary, the prosperity-promoting effects of free markets and the many failings of government involvement have been demonstrated time and again.

The annual Appropriation Bills authorise Commonwealth Government spending. They provide line by line authorisation for spending on specific items. They also set limits for some general categories of spending.

The Senate is empowered by the Constitution to reject any Appropriation Bill. This reminds us that Senate scrutiny into Appropriation Bills does not represent sticking our noses into other people's business. Indeed, the Senate has a responsibility to scrutinise.

The Senate is also empowered by the Constitution to amend any provision in Appropriation Bills that does not relate to the 'ordinary annual services of Government.' That means the Senate can amend any provision relating to loans, capital equipment, assets and depreciation, any provision relating to grants to the States and Territories, and any provision relating to new policies.

So the Senate has a particular responsibility to scrutinise capital spending, grants to the States, and spending on new policies.

This leads me to the first of my grave concerns.

The Government is asserting that the Senate cannot amend provisions relating to new policies. The Government is doing this by placing provisions relating to various new policies in those Appropriation Bills that should exclusively house provisions relating to the 'ordinary annual services of Government.'

These are the odd-numbered Appropriation Bills, like the Number 1 and Number 5 Bills before us today.

For example, the Number 1 Bill includes provisions for Australia's contributions to the Asia Pacific Project Preparation Facility and to the World Bank Global Infrastructure Facility. These are new policies, but because they fall under an existing, broad departmental outcome, the Government is asserting that they represent the 'ordinary annual services of Government' and are immune from Senate amendment.

I reject this assertion, and reserve the right to amend provisions relating to new programs and projects, even if the Government places these provisions in odd-numbered Appropriation Bills.

Another grave concern relates to the even-numbered Appropriation Bills. These are the bills that should contain all the provisions that the Senate is empowered to amend, including grants to the States under section 96 of the Constitution.

Section 96 of the Constitution provides that 'the Parliament may grant financial assistance to any State on such terms and conditions as the Parliament thinks fit.'

This is a very strong power provided to the Parliament, but the Number 2 Bill before us today contains a clause – clause 16 – that delegates this power to the relevant Minister. In particular, it provides the Minister with the power to determine the amounts and timing of payments to the State, Territory and local Governments. It also provides the Minister with the power to determine conditions under which those payments may be made.

The Government asserts that these payments to the States and Territories can be made without a written determination from the Minister. And the Government asserts that, if there is a written determination, the determination may not be made public, and it will not be disallowable by the Parliament.

It is bad enough that the Commonwealth uses section 96 of the Constitution to undermine the federation, but it is unforgivable that this occurs at the whim of a Minister, without Parliamentary scrutiny. This is a centralisation of power that would put the Soviet Union to shame.

My final grave concern relates to the massive blank cheques provided in the Appropriation Bills. Take for example the issue of National Partnership Payments. These are payments of tied grants to the States and Territories that are authorised under the *Federal Financial Relations Act 2009*, so they don't need to be individually specified in annual Appropriation Bills.

But the annual Appropriation Bills need to set a limit on the total amount of National Partnership Payments in a year. The Budget papers outline Government plans for $10.6 billion of National Partnership Payments next financial year. But the Number 2 Appropriation Bill sets a limit on National Partnership Payments next year of $25 billion. This represents a $14.4 billion blank cheque. It would allow the Government to make National Partnership Payments that it has not outlined in any document.

Such a blank cheque is completely unnecessary. For instance, if the Government increased its planned National Partnership Payments in later months, it would be able to outline these increased payments in updates to the Portfolio Budget Statements, and to seek authority for a higher spending limit in follow-up Appropriation Bills, which are routine.

That the Government seeks authority for National Partnership Payments without even outlining them in Budget documents is the height of authoritarian swagger.

I have a simple amendment to the Number 2 Appropriation Bill, to reduce the authority for National Partnership Payments next year from $25 billion to $11 billion. This is still well above the planned level of National Partnership Payments.

This is the most modest of amendments. It is an amendment to a Bill that the Senate is clearly empowered to amend. And it is an amendment that defends the limited rights of the Parliament. So if any Senator opposes this amendment, I would appreciate an explanation in the committee stage as to why.

I have outlined three grave concerns with the Appropriation Bills before the Senate. But these are not the paranoid concerns of a solo libertarian.

The first two of the concerns arose from the Senate Scrutiny of Bills Committee – a cross party committee of which I am not a member.

The third concern arose from the Parliamentary Library's briefings on the Budget.

If individual Senators don't take the time to personally scrutinise these bills, then surely it is our responsibility to listen to those people who do take the time – that's the Senators on the Scrutiny Committee, and the Parliamentary officers that prepare their Committee reports and that undertake research at the Parliamentary Library.

There are five Appropriation Bills before the Senate, with more than $97 billion of specific spending proposals in its Schedules, and with spending limits applying to general spending areas in excess of $30 billion. Even if you do not share my concerns about the magnitude of government spending, there is a case for applying more scrutiny to these bills than to the other bills that pass through this place. Unfortunately, the scrutiny is far less.

I believe it is a dereliction of duty to let government spending drift. But, through a failure to scrutinise these Appropriation Bills, that is exactly what this Parliament is doing.

Privatise hospitals[18]

Imagine if a libertarian like me had his way with health policy and nobody died. It would be a disaster. Not for the public, but for the thousands of public servants and lobbyists who would be out of a job.

The Commonwealth Government employs more than 5,000 public servants in the Health portfolio, yet it runs no hospitals and employs no doctors or nurses who care for the sick. Under a Liberal Democrats government, the Commonwealth Government would employ a few hundred health officials to coordinate health service standards, health statistics, immunisation, and biosecurity. That's it.

For the dozens of interest groups that hang around health issues, this would be catastrophic. Almost all of them oppose change of any sort, not because the status quo is the best approach, but because they are experts at negotiating the existing bureaucratic maze. Defending this maze keeps them in their well-paid jobs.

Any whiff of change would prompt a huge scare campaign from the Pharmacy Guild, which represents the owners of pharmacies, the Australian Medical Association, which represents a minority of doctors, and the Health Services Union, which represents a minority of other health professionals.

But it is easy to conceive how change would make individual pharmacists, doctors and nurses better off. Currently, governments regulate numerous healthcare decisions, commonly via the Medicare Benefits Schedule, so that notionally private sector operators make the 'right' decision. It controls what services GPs provide, what they can charge patients, and how often they refer patients to specialists.

When a patient needs a prescription, governments regulate how far they must walk to the nearest pharmacy. By owning public hospitals, governments regulate the procedures that hospitals may provide and how long the wait will be. Governments subsidise insurance for certain health services but not others. And they limit the private health insurance market by preventing insurers from covering gaps between actual and scheduled fees and offering lower premiums to low-risk people like non-smokers.

If we did away with this hands-on intervention and redirected just half of current government spending on health into a medical expenses subsidy for individual Australians, the average subsidy would exceed $2,000. If we then allocated this subsidy according to need, taxpayer-funded support for the poor and chronically ill would exceed support provided under current arrangements. This subsidy could also be used to pay private health insurance premiums for the poor and chronically ill, offering the peace of mind that comes with such cover.

Everyday Australians could be encouraged to save for their own future healthcare needs in accounts similar to superannuation accounts, except that they would be tax-free and withdrawals would be allowed to cover the costs of medical emergencies and health insurance premiums.

Subsidising individual Australians directly, and helping them save for themselves, would then allow public hospitals to be transferred into non-government ownership and compete for patients on the basis of quality and price.

Getting the government out of hospital ownership would improve healthcare. Private hospitals have repeatedly proven themselves to be overall safer, more effective and more efficient than public hospitals. As the regulator of health service standards, the government would no longer be regulating itself. And the restrictions and burdens of red tape – which hinder doctors and nurses helping their patients – would be slashed.

These measures would not solve all problems in healthcare. For instance, doctors would continue to know more than patients about which expensive procedures are really necessary, so the risk of over-medicalisation would remain. But this risk exists under the current system, where patients pay nothing for expensive procedures and bureaucrats tasked with restraining money-hungry doctors have no expertise or motivation to do so. At least under a privatised system, agents for patients like private health insurers have a better chance of taking the fight to doctors.

For those who see socialised medicine as an article of faith, the arguments for privatising healthcare are probably not convincing. They typically rely on the private sector to maintain their houses, pets, computers and cars, but see the maintenance of their bodies as somehow different. And while they maintain their bodies with private sector food, and exercise at private sector gyms, relying on private sector health services is a bridge too far.

That is a shame, because healthcare is better when it is between a doctor and a patient, rather than between a doctor, patient, and bureaucrat.

Budget cuts[19]

I made history in the Senate last December.

I am the first senator to introduce a Bill that received only one vote in its favour. On the other side of the Chamber, 45 senators were herded together by their whips, while the remaining Senators decided not to turn up for the vote.

So what was the content of this outrageous, history-making Bill that united the Coalition, Labor, the Greens, the PUPs and other cross benchers?

Was it a suggestion that we should use nuclear weapons to mine coral from the Great Barrier Reef? Was it perhaps a Bill allowing school children a free cigarette every morning, or to allow hunters to use National Parks for koala culls?

It turns out my history-making unpopular Bill was a modest proposal to cut middle-class welfare – a Bill to limit entitlement to Family Tax Benefit A, mostly affecting families with an income over $90,000 per annum. While so many politicians talk about their dislike for middle-class welfare, when it came down to it, none of them was willing to take action against it.

I have repeatedly challenged cross benchers in the Chamber to explain what they would do to fix the budget. If forced to write an essay on the subject some might be able to wrangle a pass, but all (with the honourable exception of Senator Day) would fail the practical component on account of not having done a damn thing about it.

Senator Cormann was right when he said that for all of the complaints about budget fairness, it is unfair in the extreme to saddle our children with debt. So what would I do?

One quarter of the Commonwealth Government's spending is payments to the States, Territories and local governments. These payments should be abolished. Abolition would prompt the States to means test access to public hospitals and schools, and to put tolls on arterial roads and highways. Even if they reacted by increasing taxes, which I would not encourage, the States have access to substantial tax bases, many of them more effi-cient than the Commonwealth's income tax. The abolition of Commonwealth payments to States would increase the autonomy and accountability of the States, allow greater competition and experimentation, and end a system where funds are effectively taken from rich State Governments and given to poor State Governments.

I support ending industry assistance such as spending on agriculture, tourism, mining, manufacturing, and construction industries. But not to be forgotten is funding for the arts industry, the sports industry, and the communications industry, including the ABC and SBS. Corporate welfare doesn't stop being corporate welfare when the corporation is government-owned, or when it's a corporation you like, such as a renewable energy business.

We need to bring back a central support role for family and community, focus tax-paid support on the least well-off and revisit the Commission of Audit report, which suggested the removal of the Schoolkids Bonus and Family Tax Benefit Part B.

We need to include the family home in the assets test for the aged pension. So long as only the home's value above a high threshold is taken into account, and so long as there is always access to a pension equivalent payment through a reverse mortgage or something similar, there is no reason for the family home to be excluded.

Finally, the salaries of the 1.9 million Australians who work for one tier of government or another have grown more quickly than salaries in the private sector over the last decade. A 10% cut to these salaries would be reasonable.

As I have explained to the Senate, I support just about all of the spending cuts brought forward by others. The only exception has been the plan to temporarily remove the dole for unemployed youth, which is bizarre when the Government prices them out of jobs through the minimum wage. While we hear complaints about 'dole bludgers,' the truth is that spending on family payments is more than three times larger than unemployment benefits.

For all of the talk from the Government and others about a budget crisis, my attempt to make a modest cut to middle-class welfare was a telling moment. It suggests that perhaps what we face is not so much a budgetary crisis, as a shortage of testicular (or ovarian) fortitude in our legislative chambers when it really matters.

Middle class welfare[20]

There is no government today that restricts itself to the provision of law and order, justice, and national defence. We have all become accustomed to the state providing an array of services.

Some of these are more justified than others. Well accepted is support for the truly poor and needy – nobody wants to see anyone starving or children missing out on health care or an education through no fault of their own.

Prior to the welfare state, in prosperous societies, private philanthropy undertook such tasks. That's obviously changed, with various adverse effects. There is an inverse relationship between the size, scope, and number of private voluntary charities and the size of the welfare state. Governments tend to be inefficient, spending about 70% on bureaucracy to get 30% to the poor, whereas the ratio is reversed for the private sector.

State welfare and intervention also tends to undermine the spirit of voluntarism, which is still strong in Australian culture. The Victorian government's efforts to impose union rules on the Country Fire Authority, a volunteer and community based organisation, is likely to have serious implications for its future for example.

But our sense of compassion, of extending a 'helping hand,' comes to a shuddering halt when we are forced to assist those who don't need help but are receiving aid merely because someone wants their vote.

This is the situation in Australia today. Millions of people who do not need welfare are receiving it. Millions who are quite capable of supporting themselves are being supported by others.

I am not merely referring to Disability Support Pensioners who are not disabled, or those on Newstart who refuse to work. A far bigger problem is welfare paid to people who have good jobs and are not even remotely poor. This is known as 'middle-class welfare.'

One of the most egregious examples is childcare support. This comes in two forms: the Child Care Benefit is paid to families with incomes up to $178,023 (or higher if you have more than three children), while the Child Care Rebate is not means-tested at all.

From July 2018 the Government wants to combine these into a single payment which will fall to $10,000 per child if family income reaches $340,000, then continue regardless of a family's income. Those on million dollar incomes will still receive it.

Another example is Family Tax Benefits. Families with six children, depending on their ages, are eligible for this, until their income reaches $242,000. There is no assets test either; a family with assets of over $5 million, a level most Australian households will never reach, can be eligible to receive tax money paid by a single person on a modest income.

Yet another is student loans. All Australian citizens, regardless of their household income or assets, have access to loans for higher education that are extremely concessional. No interest rate applies and the value of the debts is simply indexed to the CPI. Again, some students with high household net assets or income will inevitably be subsidised by those who are far less prosperous.

Finally, a retired aged couple that owns their home can have an annual tax-free income over $75,000 before eligibility for the age pension ceases. Moreover, pension eligibility is not influenced by the value of the family home. There are people living in multi-million dollar homes receiving pensions funded by the taxes of people who are never likely to own a home.

Some disabled people are also very well off too, yet their principal residence is also exempt from the assets test for the disability support pension.

Australia currently has a $40 billion dollar deficit and a public debt of $285 billion. Neither the Liberal government nor Labor opposition has a credible plan to address this. Both are content to pretend that debt and deficit can be ignored for at least the next four years.

This is not something we should tolerate. With our tax rates already high by both regional and global standards, and with so much wasteful spending, the elimination of middle-class welfare should be a high priority for any new government.

We can easily afford to support the poor and genuinely needy while reducing taxes for those battling to get ahead if we stop handing out money to those who don't need it.

Pensions are charity[21]

To my fellow mature Australians, I'd like to explain something. We are not entitled to an age pension merely because we have paid taxes all our life. Pensions are not for everyone; fundamentally they are welfare, reserved for the poor.

Like many others, I have been in continuous employment since 1974 and paid my taxes each year, increasingly fairly considerable sums. But governments have not saved my taxes to pay for my retirement. Instead, those sums were spent each year. In fact, our taxes haven't even covered each year's government spending. Over the past 40 years, budget deficits have been the norm, with the country now in debt to the tune of $245 billion. If anything, I and my fellow baby boomers should pay the rest of Australia a lump sum when we retire, to cover the debt we are leaving.

And it's not as though my taxes have been devoted to buying assets that will be in service for decades to come. Successive Commonwealth Governments have been selling off these assets for much of my taxpaying career. Rather, my taxes have been devoted to providing services to the voters of the day, including many from which I've benefited, such as medical services, university studies and opera performances.

It is true my taxes have also funded the welfare state. But that doesn't represent a downpayment on a pension. The welfare payments were primarily to parents, the sick, the disabled and the unemployed.

It is also true that my taxes funded age pensions, but this has been a small part of my tax bill. When I started in the workforce, there were more than seven working age Australians for every Australian aged 65 or over. There are around five working age Australians for every older Australian now. But at some point during my retirement, this ratio will probably fall to less than three.

More to the point, my taxes have not helped every older Australian, because the age pension has never been a universal entitlement. Eligibility has been income tested since 1909, and asset tested from 1909 to 1976 and then since 1985. This is different from the UK and New Zealand, where pensions are not means-tested and funded from special tax contributions.

Given the debt we will leave behind, baby boomers like me have a duty to make the asset test comprehensive. Those who own million dollar houses shouldn't rely on welfare when they can draw on their own wealth, especially knowing they can take out a reverse mortgage and avoid the need to move. A desire to leave the family home to dependents is no justification for receiving welfare funded by the taxes of people who don't even own a home.

We also need to increase the eligibility age for the age pension. Current law will lift this to 67 by 2023 and the

Commission of Audit recommends a glacial increase to 70 by 2053. We actually need to get to 70 by 2027. This would mean fewer baby boomers escaping the burden of debt we've helped create. And it would also mean we don't defer fiscal responsibility forever.

Such a change would also belatedly reflect the reality of our lifespans. The eligibility age of 65 was introduced in 1909 when male life expectancy at birth was 55. Now a 65-year-old is likely to live to eight-six. Many will remain active and healthy over this period, and those unable to work will be eligible for the disability support pension. Taxpayers should not be required to pay people of sound body and mind not to work.

Finally, before anyone complains about hypocrisy from a politician, I should point out that the scheme giving retired federal politicians a generous life pension was closed in 2004. New politicians like me contribute to a superannuation fund, the same as everyone else who has a job. And, like everyone else, whether we will need welfare in the form of a pension depends on how much super we manage to save, not how much or how long we have paid tax.

What Australians have an entitlement to is the assets we own; our houses, our superannuation, our savings. If we give in to the notion that everyone is entitled to government hand-outs when we are not poor, then our assets will surely suffer the death of a thousand taxes. Let's save for our retirement and keep pensions in the charity basket.

Think of the childless: No Jab No Pay Bill[22]

Since it is about time somebody did, I rise to ask: won't someone please think of the childless?

Politicians seem to be obsessed with families, so it may come as a surprise to many that most households in Australia are childless.

A quarter of all households consist of an individual, and more than a quarter of all households consist of an adult couple. There are also hundreds of thousands of households where unrelated adults live together.

Childless households are also on the rise in part because kids have grown up and moved out of their parents' home, and thanks to the increasing propensity of couples to remain childless.

To the childless people of Australia I want to say, on behalf of this parliament, thank you for being childless.

You work for more years and become more productive than the rest of Australia. You pay thousands and thousands of dollars more tax than other Australians. You get next to no welfare and your use of public health services is minimal.

But you pay when other people get pregnant, you pay when they give birth, you pay when they stay at home to look after their offspring, you pay for the child's food, clothing and shelter, you pay when the child goes to child care and you pay when the child goes to primary and secondary school. And then you pay when it goes to university.

Thank you for all you do for others. I am sorry that rather than receiving thanks, you are often ignored, pitied, considered strange, or even thought of as irresponsible.

For your sake, I hope the children you are forced to support don't end up as juvenile delinquents, and I hope that they get immunised so that you don't end up getting sick, because you'll pay then too.

For this reason, amongst others, I support the Social Services Legislation Amendment (No Jab, No Pay) Bill 2015. This Bill concerns parents who, on religious or conscientious grounds, refuse to immunise their children. The Bill makes such parents ineligible for child care subsidies and family assistance end-of-year supplements.

This is as it should be. It is bad enough that people continue to bring wave upon wave of these little blighters into the world.

The least they can do is immunise their bundles of dribble and sputum so they don't make the rest of us sick.

Withholding welfare payments from parents who fail to immunise their kids is entirely legitimate from a libertarian perspective.

Immunisation generates a significant social benefit, and parents do not have a right to welfare payments. Such payments are, fundamentally, a gift from their fellow Australians. No work is done for the money, so there is nothing wrong with placing conditions on it.

Most welfare payments to parents should be abolished, because people without children should not be forced to subsidise people with children.

Children generate great joy, warmth and meaning for their parents. They are a precious gift. What more do you want?

It is unfair that people without children are forced to pay money to those people who have received the gift of a child.

Some people are childless by choice and are happy with that choice. There is no moral case to make them subsidise other people's choices.

For some people, childlessness is not a choice; it is a great sadness. Forcing them to hand over money to more fortunate people is like charity in reverse. It's like making people in wheelchairs pay for other people's running shoes.

People without children are not freeloaders; they can look after themselves throughout their life through working, saving, and engaging in voluntary, mutually beneficial exchanges.

It would be weird to suggest that you need to pay for the upbringing and training of a baker just because one day you will want to buy bread. It is equally as weird to suggest that a childless person needs to pay for the upbringing and training of children just because they might want to buy services from those children in the future.

Some argue, when taxpayers fund subsidies for today's children, this is a proxy for paying back the subsidies the taxpayers received when they were children. But this ignores the fact that some taxpayers received little or no subsidies when they were children. They have nothing to pay back. And forcing money on today's children, need it or not, does not create any special obligations on them in the future either.

And there are plenty of adults right now who pay little or no tax, so if they received subsidies when they were children, they aren't paying them back now.

Overall, intergenerational wealth transfers are best achieved within families.

The Liberal Democrats support the abolition of childcare subsidies, coupled with deregulation of the childcare sector – including its excessive credentialism – to cut the costs of childcare.

The Liberal Democrats support the abolition of taxpayer-funded paid parental leave, which is an arbitrary payment provided only to those new parents who were in employment in ten of the prior 13 months.

The Liberal Democrats believe that Family Tax Benefit Part A should be limited to low-income families, and that family tax benefits should end its march through the alphabet right there.

Family Tax Benefit Part B should be abolished and instead we should have a flat income tax rate to ensure that families are not penalised if one member of a couple makes more money than the other. Parenting Payment would remain only for low-income families with children who are not yet in school.

Some people may say that, if this policy platform came to pass, they would not be able to afford to have children. In response let me make this very clear – people do not have a right to expect or force others to pay them to have children.

The government is not your parent or your spouse. Get over it. In fact, don't just get over it, be thankful for it. The

Government does not make a good parent – just ask any ward of the state.

What's more, when you allow the government to become a de facto parent, it encourages the breakdown of traditional family units – something many politicians claim to support.

And mark my words, when you treat the government like a parent, it will soon enough treat you like a child.

The passage of the current Bill before us, the Social Services Legislation Amendment (No Jab, No Pay) Bill 2015, should help. I commend the Bill to the Senate.

Welfare for the states[23]

Most Australians support some degree of welfare for the needy, where a taxpayer effectively transfers money to a non-taxpayer. But many do not realise there is a bizarre welfare system sitting on top of this, in which taxpaying states effectively transfer billions of dollars to non-taxpaying states.

This welfare system involves two states – Western Australia and New South Wales – transferring funds to the other states and territories. WA transfers $20 billion a year, equivalent to more than $8,000 a year from each West Australian, while NSW transfers more than $2 billion a year, over $300 per person.

Out of this system Tasmania and the Northern Territory draw nearly $4 billion a year each. That means each Tasmanian, rich or poor, gets nearly $8,000 per year from the people of WA and NSW while Northern Territorians get more than $16,000.

The state-to-state welfare system is complicated and to unravel it is no easy task. Some think it simply involves the GST, but that only plays a small part. Of the $8,000 a year that each West Australian transfers to the east, only $600 is a result of paying GST to Canberra.

The real cause of the system is the Commonwealth government's collection and use of income tax revenues.

The workers of WA and NSW tend to earn higher wages than other Australians, and thus pay more personal income tax – particularly because of the euphemistically named 'progressive' system, where the taxman takes a higher and higher share of your income as your income rises. The businesses of these states also tend to earn higher profits than businesses elsewhere and pay more company tax as a result.

These higher wages and profits are partly a result of some natural or historical advantages enjoyed in those states, but they are also the result of hard work and risk-taking. In addition, the state governments in WA and NSW play a role through building the infrastructure that underpins business activity, and by approving developments despite political opposition.

The income taxes disproportionately paid by the people of WA and NSW tend not to find their way back to those states. For instance, the Commonwealth government uses the revenue to fund unemployment payments. As unemployment is relatively low in WA and NSW, these states get little benefit. The government's failure to require recipients of unemployment payments to move to places with better employment prospects, like WA and NSW, serves to entrench the problem.

The Commonwealth government also uses the income taxes paid by the people of WA and NSW to scatter grants across the country for public housing, public schools and public hospitals. These grants are insidious. Not only do they result in bureaucracies in Canberra that duplicate those in the state capitals and undermine the states in carrying out their own responsibilities, but they also discourage people in economically-depressed states and territories from moving to where economic prospects are brighter.

In addition, they discourage people in those states from supporting local economic development. After all, if there are public services funded by economic growth generated elsewhere, why bother trying to generate economic growth at home?

For many reasons the state-to-state welfare system should be abandoned. But this will not occur by simply tinkering with the distribution of GST revenues. It requires a marked reduction in Commonwealth income taxes, a rejection of 'progressive' taxation and unconditional unemployment benefits, and the withdrawal of the Commonwealth government from areas best managed by state and territory Governments.

Australia was established as a federation in the expectation that the states would compete with each other to create the most jobs and prosperity, and most pleasant environment in which to live. The steady concentration of powers in Canberra, especially the power to levy taxes, has seriously undermined their ability to chart their own course.

If this is to change, it won't be led by the states that benefit from state-to-state welfare. It will be up to the people of WA and NSW to return Australia to genuine federalism.

Tasmania: a province of Victoria[24]

Having once lived there, I know Tasmania is a pleasant place to live. But so is Greece. And if Tasmania was an independent country, it would be in more trouble than Greece.

There was quite a lot of discussion about this in 2013. A good summary came in an article by Jonathan West, director of the Australian Innovation Research Centre and a resident of Tasmania, who described the state as follows: 'Tasmania ranks at the bottom among Australian states on virtually every dimension of economic, social, and cultural performance: highest unemployment, lowest incomes, languishing investment, lowest home prices, least educated, lowest literacy, most chronic disease, poorest longevity, most likely to smoke, greatest obesity, highest teenage pregnancy, highest petty crime, worst domestic violence.'

Tasmania is also a mendicant state, highly reliant on the rest of the country. It generates about a third of its state budget, the rest being GST allocations and specific purpose payments from the commonwealth. GST and income tax originating within the state fall well short of what it receives, meaning the government effectively receives welfare from the rest of the country. When the NSW economy goes into recession, one of the consequences is less money for Tasmania.

This is on top of the higher proportions of welfare that Tasmanian individuals receive.

None of this is new. Tasmania has been a claimant state since the inception of the Commonwealth Grants Commission in 1933. Apart from brief spurts of growth due to mining, Tasmania's income has rarely lived up to its aspirations since federation.

Every year, many of the state's best and brightest move away. Between 1900 and 1935, Tasmania's population grew at less than 0.7% per year, about the same as its current growth rate. It nonetheless has politicians in abundance. In addition to local government and an upper and lower house in the state parliament, it is constitutionally guaranteed five seats in the House of Representatives and 12 seats in the Senate. And while each federal electorate in NSW has about 95,000 voters, in Tasmania there are less than 70,000.

It also has a long history of anti-development policies. Indeed, rather than offering a low tax and less regulatory environment to attract investment and generate jobs, it has repeatedly done the opposite. Among many examples: utility charges since 1998 have increased on average 6.1% per annum, electricity 6.4% and property rates and charges 5.5%, compared to the CPI in Hobart of 2.7%.

So what should be done about Tasmania? I have four suggestions.

First, the federal government should provide fewer transfers to state governments. There is no need for 'special purpose payments' that come with strings attached, as if Canberra knows how to run hospitals, schools and the like. With reduced commonwealth taxes, states should raise their own taxes to fund their spending, creating a far more effective discipline on it. If the federal government were to treat the states less like children, they might start behaving like grown-ups.

Second, to the extent that the federal government still transfers money to state governments, such as GST revenues, it should return the money to the state where the revenue was generated. This would immediately prompt states like Tasmania to introduce growth-promoting policies.

Third, subsidies for shipping to and from Tasmania should be abolished. If islands such as Hong Kong and Singapore can become wealthy without them, so can Tasmania. Bass Strait is not a cruel plot for which mainland Australians should compensate Tasmanians. The solution is cheaper shipping, such as by abolishing industrial relations laws introduced specifically for the shipping industry.

Finally, respect for the principles of equality before the law and one vote one value should be embedded in the constitution, giving Tasmania the same representation as other Australians. Such a reform would reflect the proud egalitarian spirit of Australians on both sides of the Strait.

Of course, if it ever chose to get really serious about its situation it could become an unincorporated territory as part of Victoria, like French Island. Eliminating all those state and local politicians along with thousands of bureaucrats would save a fortune.

WA secession[25]

WA should secede from Australia. If policies affecting Western Australia were decided by the 2.5 million Western Australians, rather than by 23.5 million Australians, those policies would better reflect the needs and aspirations of Western Australians. Government is nearly always better when it is more local.

There are no efficiencies coming from policy being delivered for the entire Australian landmass. Most of the government services that Western Australians actually value are delivered by the WA State Government, for example by WA doctors, nurses, principals, teachers, social workers, police officers, judges and prison wardens.

By contrast, it is national arrangements that will deliver Western Australians submarines and frigates built in marginal electorates in South Australia at lower quality and greater cost than those on offer overseas. National arrangements also deliver subsidised freight across Bass Strait for Tasmania, small-scale tariffs to support Victorian manufacturing, subsidised opera at the Sydney Opera House, and bans on imported bananas to protect Queensland farmers. There is no efficiency in this for Western Australians.

Secession would stop the bureaucratic duplication that result in 5,000 employees in the Commonwealth Government's health portfolio on top of more than 30,000 health staff employed by the WA Government. With the Commonwealth not running a single hospital, it is not clear what the 5,000 Commonwealth employees actually do.

Secession would also stop the conveyor belt of money from West to East. Most of us support some degree of welfare for individuals in need, but the idea that an entire state can be needy is ridiculous. Western Australia transfers more than $25 billion a year to needy states, equivalent to around $10,000 a year from each West Australian.

Around $5 billion of this goes to Tasmania. That means each Tasmanian, rich or poor, gets nearly $10,000 per year from the people of Western Australia. No wonder successive Tasmanian Governments are so reluctant to approve progress and development – Tasmania has outsourced moneymaking to the West.

And don't be fooled into thinking that fairness for Western Australians would come simply from adjusting the distribution of GST revenues. Western Australians also pay more personal, company and fuel taxes to Canberra than other Australians, and with its long history of lower unemployment, receive less back from Canberra through spending in areas like welfare.

Some argue that from the 1930s to the 1960s the flow of money went from East to West. But this ignores that, over this period, Western Australia was held back by policies designed to protect manufacturing jobs in the East, including high tariffs, heavy wage regulation and the White Australia Policy. So, overall, Western Australia has given more than it got throughout the history of the federation.

Secession wouldn't undermine the relationship between Western Australians and Eastern Australians. Just as travel and migration with New Zealand is unrestricted, so it could be between Western and Eastern Australia. And as the Republic of Ireland and Northern Ireland choose to play together in sports when it suits them, Western and Eastern Australia could do the same.

Suggesting that Western Australia should secede is not a parochial thought bubble prompted by the Canning by-election. The Liberal Democrats have long maintained a policy respecting the right of people – whether in Tibet, Quebec or Western Australia – to form their own sovereign government. (Indeed, this long-standing policy led me to accept the Taiwanese President's invitation to visit his wonderful sovereign country, from where I wrote this article.) Other politicians, by contrast, say one thing when out West, then the complete opposite when in Tasmania.

A key question is how Western Australia could achieve secession. After all, a large majority of Western Australians voted to secede in 1933 but the King and Canberra wouldn't allow it. Obviously it requires widespread support in the West. But political support from the East is also a necessity, lest we repeat the futility of 1933.

What we need is politicians and political parties who value the West but don't want to control it. In other words, we need a groundswell of support for the adage: if you love someone, set them free.

South Australia needs an intervention[26]

If we can think of Australia's Federation of states being like a family, there is one family member that needs more than a good talking to – it needs an intervention.

South Australia needs intervention because its problems are self-inflicted, and because too many South Australian politicians have developed a monstrous sense of entitlement.

If the South Australia Government was a person, it would be an obese 40-year-old man with awful body odour who lives with his mother, refuses to work, and plays Xbox all day. He pauses only to demand more Cheezels and iced coffee, or to complain when the lights go out.

It really is that bad.

Over the last five years, every category of private investment in South Australia has fallen.

While population and employment growth in other states have risen steadily, the graph for both indicators in South Australia is as flat as the Nullarbor Plain. And it's heading for a cliff, as thousands of young South Australians follow the jobs interstate.

Unless its course changes, South Australia risks becoming one big, barren, candle-lit retirement village.

The economy of Western Australia left South Australia far behind years ago, and now it appears the tiny ACT could overtake South Australia within 20 years. And the ACT can achieve this despite its primary products being bull-dust and hot air.

The only economic competition left open to South Australia will be the race with Tasmania to the bottom. Sadly, the lone positive influence that South Australian politicians are having on Australia right now is to make politicians from other states feel better about themselves.

It's hard to say exactly why South Australian legislators are so consistently terrible. But there seems to be a sizeable voting bloc of Whingeing Wendys and Doctors' Wives who like to be represented either by doe-eyed Greens who have never grown up, or shameless populists and protectionists.

They are professional virtue signallers. They might fly economy and wear cheap suits, but they are costing us billions with the most irresponsible approach to governance imaginable.

They claim to be servants of the people, but they are every bit as dodgy with Other People's Money as the shonkiest crony capitalist.

Even the most reasonable South Australian politicians these days seem to believe their constituents will be unable to stand unless propped up by elaborate government schemes. They insult them with their low expectations.

If all they did was turn their own state into an economic basket case, perhaps we could live with it. But the dysfunction of the state now affects us all.

This week, I was visited by Louise Burge, who is still counting the cost of floods on her property near Deniliquin in southern New South Wales. The damage was greatly exacerbated by releases from the Hume Dam as part of the Murray–Darling Basin Plan. You can understand why she is outraged by suggestions from South Australia that yet more water should be sent down the river.

As Chair of the recent Senate inquiry into the Basin Plan, I heard testimony from dozens of people in Queensland, New

South Wales and Victoria who have suffered greatly, losing their jobs, businesses and regional communities, because of water buybacks in their area, turning productive irrigation farms into dryland farms.

And yet the primary concern of some South Australian politicians appears to be that people visiting holiday houses in Goolwa might miss out on watching gigalitres of fresh water flow into the ocean every day.

Likewise, the submarine contract is no joke to the rest of us. While we need submarines, it will cost every Australian thousands of dollars to let South Australians have a crack at making them – despite the sorry history of the Air Warfare Destroyers. If you recall, in 2007 we ordered three such ships to be built in South Australia. Even now, not one ship has been delivered and costs have blown out by more than a billion dollars.

I should at least acknowledge the South Australian Premier, Jay Weatherill, for recognising something has to be done about his economy, and opening up the debate about nuclear technology.

Initiatives in the nuclear field could pull the state out of its malaise. A large-scale waste repository alone could attract billions for the state, with little or no risk.

Thousands of my constituents in southern Sydney currently live within a few kilometres of nuclear waste held temporarily in a shed at Lucas Heights. Because of the laws of physics, there is no increase in radiation beyond the gates of the facility.

However, creating a permanent repository in South Australia, much further away from people than the deposit in Sydney, sends South Australians and their representatives into paroxysms of rejection. With the recent backtracking from the South Australian Opposition Leader on the issue, I can confidently predict a large-scale permanent nuclear waste repository won't happen in South Australia.

If South Australia is to become a useful member of the Federation, it needs to change.

Like other Australians, South Australians would be better off concentrating on areas where we have natural advantages, such as agriculture, mining and tourism.

No taxpayers' money is needed to support these. Simply reducing red tape would go a long way to encourage more investment.

The potential expansion of Olympic Dam should have South Australian politicians bending over backwards to help the project proponents make the necessary cuts to their costs. And they should be bending over backwards to ensure that future approval processes will be less arduous than the processes of the past. But instead we have South Australian politicians promising that approval processes will be more arduous and costly.

Allowing farmers to grow genetically modified crops, like in WA and Victoria, would also be important. Genetic modification can help us feed the world's poor. Pandering to thoroughly debunked, anti-scientific fear mongering about genetic modification is a luxury that South Australia, and the rest of Australia and indeed the world, cannot afford.

South Australia desperately needs to reform its electricity industry. Poor electricity policy burdens its citizens, has made manufacturing in the state unsustainable, raises the operating costs of all businesses including tourism, and leaves the state dependent on others.

It should allow all forms of power generation, including nuclear power, on equal terms and without subsidy, so that the lowest cost suppliers succeed.

The South Australian Government should cut its spending, such as by abolishing the wide range of subsidies it irresponsibly doles out to home owning pensioners. These subsidies just reinforce South Australia's status as the world's biggest retirement home.

The South Australian Government should reduce taxes so as to make South Australia a place where at least some people want to live and do business. And it should make it easier to establish and operate a business in South Australia than in any other state.

Meanwhile, the best thing we can do to help South Australia get over its addiction to Other People's Money is stop giving it to them.

The Federal Government should provide fewer transfers and special payments to all states, and tax them less, but allow them to raise their own taxes.

It would concentrate the minds of South Australians wonderfully if we started to return GST revenues to states based on what they generate, or at least if we doled revenue out on an equal per capita basis. But currently, when an average Australian gets one dollar of GST revenue, each South Australian gets $1.42.

We should respond less to all of their bleatings – their bleatings for money, for water, for power, and for anything else, until such time as they can demonstrate they can behave like responsible adults in the Federation.

Build the submarines in Western Sydney[27]

The Liberal Democrats accept that national defence is a legitimate role for the Commonwealth Government. The navy comprises part of that defence.

Furthermore, because there are only two kinds of ships – submarines and targets – we support the need for submarines.

However, we know that unnecessary spending means excessive taxation, and that putting Australia further into debt only makes us less secure.

Unfortunately, so far the Collins Class Submarine Replacement Project appears to consist mainly of unnecessary spending. The Government insists on building submarines here, so it's the most expensive defence procurement project in Australian history.

If the Government were taking advice, I'd tell them to buy second-hand nuclear-powered submarines. These would halve the cost, they are already proven, and would be much safer than gas belching diesel subs forced to the surface on a regular basis.

However, I know that nothing I say here will make the Government change its mind, because none of this is about good submarines.

I also know that my colleagues such as Senators Xenophon, Lambie, Lazarus and Madigan have all made a case to get a piece of the spend for their states.

I can't say I blame them for this. Let's face it, vocational options for people in some of the states they represent are limited to working for a senator, or picking up road kill.

So I have decided to make a bid on behalf of the people of New South Wales.

Mr Acting Deputy President, today I call on the government to shift its $50 billion submarine project to Western Sydney. You know it makes sense.

If you want truly Aussie submarines, you need to build them in Western Sydney.

As we all know, there are only two kinds of Australians: people who live in New South Wales, and people with a chip on their shoulder.

When Australia was first settled by Europeans, everything in Australia consisted of New South Wales, until some people started camping out, and decided to form other states. Now some of them want to build submarines.

This is a risk that none of us should be forced to take. Who among us doubts that if we put submarines into the wrong hands, Senator Lambie may try a sneak attack on Bondi Beach, or South Australia become the Republic of Xenophonia?

Western Sydney is the home of Eastern Creek. This venue has the benefit of being both a magnificent waterway, and the centre of Australia's motoring expertise.

The proprietor of a Penrith Muffler Shop by the name of Ferret advises me that he could custom-make plenty of submarine shaped vessels at Eastern Creek for much less than a billion dollars and weld them so they are pretty much water tight.

He further advises we could generate considerable savings for taxpayers if we were willing to take the aluminium option, rather than stainless steel.

The proprietor of a Blacktown engine reconditioning shop, Raylene, tells me she can source any number of Australian-made V8 engines to power the submarines. She's willing to charge taxpayers 'mates' rates.

But because it's important that submarines are quiet, and V8 engines in the western suburbs are not usually quiet, we may have to look elsewhere in NSW to find a muffler manufacturer. However, I'm in no doubt at least one will be found.

Nothing could be more Aussie than that.

Some might argue that a submarine powered by V8 engines would not be especially stealthy, but I doubt it would be any noisier than an unmodified WB V8 Caprice or Statesman. And seriously, who can argue with that. Especially when you recall they'll be Aussie, and will leave all other ocean vessels behind in a cloud of smoke.

There is one vexing question, however – and that is, should the engines be Ford or Holden?

Since I do not wish to marginalise half my voter base, I propose that this sensitive question be decided by plebiscite.

In addition, New South Wales can provide everything else we need for the submarines. This includes furry dice made from premium Goulburn Merino wool, knitted by Slim Dusty's daughter, and hung up in the control room.

Of course, an Aussie sub would not be complete without some bumper stickers, commemorating various B&S balls, and reminding foreign invaders to 'eff off, we're full.'

To make it completely Aussie, I propose that the whole Eastern Creek Submarine Corporation be overseen by Dick Smith.

But the most important reason to adopt my modest proposal is that western Sydney is home to around one million voters. And isn't that what all this is about?

Renewable Energy (Electricity) Bill[28]

I rise to speak against the Renewable Energy (Electricity) Amendment Bill and the life support it provides for the Renewable Energy Target.

This Bill is the result of negotiations between the Government and Opposition. Its rationale was flawed from the beginning.

The Warburton Review found that $9.1 billion in cross subsidies have been spent since the commencement of the Renewable Energy Target.

A further $22 billion is expected to be spent by the end of the scheme in 2030.

That's money largely paid by electricity consumers to renewable energy generators, in addition to the unsubsidised cost of electricity.

Quite rightly, the Warburton Review described the Renewable Energy Target as nothing more than a transfer of wealth to large energy companies.

Fairly obviously, it would be far better for our economy to leave billions of dollars in the pockets of Australians, through lower electricity bills.

Households and businesses, large and small, will pay the cost. Deliberately legislating measures that raise electricity prices and make industry less competitive should have no place in this country.

The cry of the left, people before profits, should absolutely apply. The jobs and prosperity of people should come before the profits of renewable energy companies.

This bill's efforts to patch up the Renewable Energy Target will do for Australian manufacturing what wind turbines do for wedge-tailed eagles.

Compared to this bill, I would prefer that nothing was done to the Renewable Energy Target, with the result that the target of 41,000 GWh would not be reached, penalties would apply, and the resultant increase in electricity prices would lead to a public backlash against the lunacy of the RET.

Instead, it is set to become no more than a wind industry support fund.

Already, for 15 years we have been throwing money at this uncompetitive form of electricity generation.

This new target of 33,000 GWh will more than double the number of wind turbines being subsidised by Australian families and businesses. That's around a couple of thousand new turbines.

Nowhere in the world does electricity generation by wind survive without subsidy. Wind turbines are only profitable when subsidised or sold for scrap.

As much as Big Wind — and let's keep in mind the vast majority of new renewable energy generation is wind — likes to say wind energy is driving down the cost of wholesale electricity, business and households pay retail electricity prices, which of course includes the direct subsidy they are paying.

If artificially high electricity prices were not reason enough to oppose this bill, then the very high cost of emissions abatement from wind energy, again identified in the Warburton Review, should be.

The Select Committee on Wind Turbines, of which I am a member, has heard convincing evidence that the contribution of wind energy to emissions reduction is less than significant.

Importantly, the cost is wildly disproportionate to the reduction in carbon dioxide emissions.

And as we have all heard recently, Australia is on target to meet its emissions reductions target without any additional wind power.

If we are to retain a Renewable Energy Target – and in my view it is such poor policy we should not – then the target should be no more than 27,000 GWh. That at least would meet the original target of 20% of renewable energy.

And we must remember that a 20% Renewable Energy Target would set a minimum – if additional wind turbines were profitable without subsidies, then wind turbines would account for more than 20% of electricity generation.

This Bill is flawed. For years to come, it will make wind energy companies rich, and electricity consumers poor.

I oppose it.

GETTING A JOB

The minimum wage[29]

Thousands of Australians would love to have paid work. They include those just out of school, just out of jail, age and disability support pensioners, sole parents and refugees.

Thousands of Australian businesses would be willing to take a chance on these job seekers and pay them more than the $5 to $10 an hour they currently receive on welfare.

But they are forbidden from doing so. It is against the law to offer or accept any such arrangement. To take on a new starter and pay them even double their welfare payment is illegal. No matter how poor their resume or how willing they are to work for rates of pay and/or terms and conditions that suit them and their families, they can only be employed if they are paid the minimum wage, notionally about $16.40 an hour but over $20 an hour for some casuals.

Such bans on low paid work create unemployment. Before he entered Parliament and became Labor's Shadow Assistant Treasurer, Dr Andrew Leigh was a professor specialising in labour economics. He found that reducing the minimum wage in Western Australia by 10% would increase employment by around 3% within three months.

Over a longer period, the employment gains would expand. And a reduction in the federal minimum wage would have an even greater employment impact, as the WA minimum wage in Leigh's study covered very few workplaces.

In a separate study Dr Leigh found that most of the people on the minimum wage are in middle income households. By contrast, low-income households are typically in that position due to unemployment. Abolishing the minimum wage, by creating employment, would help them the most.

Other studies have shown that most people on low wages move on to higher wages after about a year. This shows that low wage jobs are an opportunity for people to start at a bottom rung and work up. The problem is, Australia's regulated minimum wage is so high that many cannot even reach the bottom rung and begin to climb.

In fact, Australia's minimum wage is one of the highest in the world. Australians start paying income tax once their annual income exceeds $18,200, but they are not allowed to get a full-time job unless it pays more than $32,000 a year. In the OECD, only Luxembourg and France have a higher minimum wage.

The minimum wage in both New Zealand and the UK is 84% of ours; Canada's is 78%, Japan's 58% and South Korea's 42%. Other countries with which we might compare ourselves, including Austria, Germany, Finland, Sweden, Switzerland, Italy and Singapore, have no minimum wage at all.

Despite the weight of evidence, Dr Leigh has an uphill battle to convince his colleagues of the futility of minimum wages. While in office Labor was proud of its disability policy but struggled to see that the minimum wage was a key impediment to a better life for many disabled Australians.

The Greens similarly take pride in their advocacy for refugees and opposition to the recent reduction in sole parent payments, but cannot see that a truly caring policy for both refugees and sole parents would be to allow those who want to enter the workplace to do so. The high unemployment rate for refugees is staggering and raises concerns for the future.

The Coalition faces a similar dilemma. The Employment Minister, Senator Eric Abetz, is from Tasmania, where unemployment is persistently higher than the rest of Australia and youth unemployment is over 40% in some areas. Even though living costs are markedly lower there, the minimum wage is the same nationally. It is this fact that drives such a sorry statistic.

Australia's minimum wage runs counter to the Australian credo of giving everyone a fair go. It is time sensible voices in the Parliament agreed to help the underdog by removing the barriers that prevent them from getting a job and improving their lives.

Penalty Rates Bill reintroduction[30]

This week I reintroduced a Bill to remove requirements to pay weekend penalty rates in hospitality businesses.

This would help cafes and shops that currently struggle to be open on weekends to stay open. This is good for workers.

It would also lead cafes and shops to open more on weekends and to hire more staff. This is also good for workers.

The idea that this change would hurt workers is fanciful. The idea relies on the fantasy that huge numbers of workers currently get as many hours of weekend work as they want in cashed-up cafes and shops, but that these cashed-up cafes and shops would slash wages the split-second they are allowed to.

In reality, this change would mostly hurt unions, whose business model revolves around charging workers for their expertise in lobbying for complicated workplace regulations.

Removing the requirement to pay weekend penalty rates in hospitality will help the proprietors of our cafes and shops. These small business owners receive next to no public sympathy but work extremely long hours at low rates of pay. I am unapologetic that removing the penalty rate requirement would sometimes serve to boost the pay and conditions of these people, because that is exactly what they deserve.

Finally, removing the requirement to pay weekend penalty rates in hospitality will help our community. Lively shopping, café and entertainment districts draw us out of our homes, and promote weekend catch-ups and activities with families and friends.

Defenders of penalty rate requirements are doing the work of the fun police. They hate small business. They are the enemy of our young workers. And they are in the pocket of the unions.

The time to break their callous hold on our weekends is now.

Fair Work Amendment Bill 2014[31]

There are 761,350 Australians who are unemployed.

Hundreds of thousands of these people are in this position because of the *Fair Work Act*.

If an external force were threatening the survival of hundreds of thousands of Australians we would declare war on it.

But in this instance, we are doing it to ourselves.

The Fair Work Act should be repealed.

People should be free to form a union, even though this essentially involves workers engaging in collective agreement, which would be otherwise called collusion if it was done by business people. This freedom is assured through an exemption contained in the *Competition and Consumer Act*. As such, the Fair Work Act is not needed to allow people to form a union.

People should be protected from harm to their health, safety and welfare through the minimisation of risks at work. This protection is provided by workplace health and safety law. Therefore, the Fair Work Act is not needed to deliver workplace health and safety.

And people should not be denied employment just because of the colour of their skin, their gender, or their membership of a trade union. Anti-discrimination law combats this and other forms of discrimination, so again, the Fair Work Act is not needed.

But above all, people should be free to offer jobs, and others should be free to accept them. The Fair Work Act is in no way necessary for these voluntary agreements to occur. And all too often it actively prevents these voluntary agreements from occurring.

The Fair Work Act bans agreements where someone agrees to work for less than $17.29 an hour. Removing this ban would lead to more jobs being offered and more jobs being filled by unemployed Australians. Based on a conservative reading of the Shadow Assistant Treasurer's research, more than 200,000 unemployed Australians would be employed within months.

The absolute kindest thing we can do for the unemployed is to make it easier for them to reach the first rung on the working ladder. Once they do, they invariably move up further.

The Fair Work Act also bans employment agreements that involve paying more than $17.29 an hour, if those agreements don't conform with prescriptive employment regulations called 'awards.' The widely acclaimed move to enterprise bargaining saw the share of workplace 'awards' fall away over the Hawke, Keating and Howard era. But with the 'award modernisation' process brought in by the Rudd/Gillard Government, we have witnessed a concerning increase in the share of the workplace subject to these command economy-style 'awards.' Where once awards set the wages of 15% of the workforce, now 19% of workers have their wages set by government. That this re-centralisation of wage fixing is not widely known shows that parliamentarians, lobbyists and economic journalists are asleep at the wheel. Even if our system of government is unable to pursue further reform, we must at least defend the reforms of the Hawke, Keating and Howard era.

The Fair Work Act prevents a business-person from firing an employee who fails to attend work, under provisions euphemistically referred to as a right to strike. And the Fair Work Act prevents a business-person from firing an employee without the approval of a tribunal, under provisions euphemistically referred to as unfair dismissal laws. If business people can't rely on staff attending the workplace, and can't fire staff without navigating a bureaucratic maze, will they want to hire them in the first place?

Many lament the rise of the machines, but don't lament the laws that continue to promote their employment at the expense of human beings.

Finally, the Fair Work Act grants privileges to unions – including rights to enter private property against the will of the owner, and rights to be a party in employment agreements negotiations – irrespective of whether the union enjoys support from employees.

The Fair Work Act is a creation of the unions, by the unions, and for the unions. And the Bill before us shows the continuing handy-work of that ever-diminishing sect.

Part One of the Bill seeks to prevent an employer from refusing an employee's request for an extension to unpaid parental leave unless the employer has given the employee a reasonable opportunity to discuss the request. As it stands, the Fair Work Act simply requires that refusals must be based on reasonable grounds.

The Fair Work Act Review recommended inserting this requirement for there to be a discussion, but it did so with next to no explanation, after having outlined that there was no problem with the existing provision. This is change-for-change's-sake. It would generate unnecessary compliance and administration. It would also create the possibility of litigation based simply on the inadequacy or absence of a discussion, even if a refusal to extend leave was reasonable.

The only people who benefit from this circus of compliance, administration and litigation costs are the thousands of lawyers in government and the private sector who make labour law their living.

The remainder of the Bill represents a baby step in the right direction. But the 761,350 Australians who are unemployed need more than timid baby steps. They need the Fair Work Act to get out of the way, and they need it now.

Business Services Wage Assessment Tool[32]

Michael has a moderate intellectual disability and cerebral palsy. A business owner in Coffs Harbour offered Michael a job shredding documents, despite the fact that Michael couldn't prepare the equipment, ensure he had the right documents, or record the work he had done.

The owner offered Michael $1.85 an hour – which Michael and his guardians accepted. Michael gained the personal pride and social camaraderie that comes with paid employment, while continuing to receive graduated income support from the government. If he had not been given the job, he would have spent his days sitting around in an institution. And no other employer offered Michael a job, at any wage.

Gordon has a mild to moderate intellectual disability and is legally blind.

A business owner in Stawell offered Gordon a lawn-mowing job. He would be constantly supervised, because he was unable to carry out necessary safety checks and preparatory steps, and had difficulty correctly interpreting instructions.

The owner offered Gordon $3.82 an hour – an offer Gordon accepted. Again, Gordon had much to gain from paid employment, and no other employer was offering Gordon a better deal at the time.

I have nothing but praise for the business owners who employed Michael and Gordon. After all, I didn't offer Michael or Gordon a better paid job. It would be rank hypocrisy for me to complain that the business owners didn't do enough for Michael and Gordon, when I did nothing.

Nonetheless, some people did complain that the business owners didn't do enough for them. They argued in the Courts that Michael and Gordon should have been paid more. The first judge rejected this argument, but in an appeal to a 'full bench,' two of the three judges agreed.

In light of the Court's judgement, the Commonwealth Government now advises business owners that if they employ disabled people, they need to pay them more.

We will never know how many disabled people now spend their days in an institution rather than a workplace because of this. I am pretty certain the number isn't zero.

It is also unknown how many of the people who campaigned for higher wages for the disabled have put their money where their mouth is by employing more disabled people. I strongly suspect the number is zero.

These campaigners believe that their utopian vision – in this case, a world where vast numbers of disabled people are remunerated generously in jobs tailored to their needs – can be achieved by decree.

But they are oblivious to the real-world consequences of their decrees. Their behaviour is akin to banning bread and then responding to hunger by declaring, 'let them eat cake!'

To save the business owners in Coffs Harbour and Stawell from further harm, the Commonwealth Government stepped in and paid the Court-ordered costs to Michael and Gordon. And now the Government is offering back pay to other intellectually disabled people who were paid under arrangements like those of Michael and Gordon. This would save the Government and the disabled workers going to court, where you can never predict whether your judge resides in the real world or utopia.

But the utopian campaigners love the drama of a day in Court, and are furiously campaigning for the Senate to block legislation that would authorise the Government's back pay offer.

It is time to stand up in support of business owners who are willing to employ and supervise disabled people in the workplace. And it is time to stand up against holier-than-thou campaigners, for whom ever higher minimum wages for the disabled will never be enough.

For work that was done in the past, we should let the Government make its offer of back pay. But looking forward, we must let employers offer wages as they see fit. And we must similarly let disabled people and their guardians accept or reject such offers as they see fit, safe in the knowledge that, regardless of their decision, the safety net of the Disability Support Pension and other government services remains.

A famous public figure once confronted a mob of holier-than-thou campaigners who were about to set upon a sinner. He said, 'He who is without sin among you, let him be the first to throw a stone at her.'

Let's insist that the campaigners provide generous employment to the disabled before we allow them to cast stones at employers who provide more meagre wages. And until such time, let's be grateful for small mercies.

FREE TRADE

Free trade[33]

Hot on the heels of the free trade deal with China there is clamouring for further deals with the likes of India and Indonesia. But if we want higher wages, cheaper stuff, less red tape and a better deal for the world's poor, we needn't bother with more free trade deals. We just need to get rid of our tariffs.

Many believe we now only have tariffs on cars and clothing. In fact, we impose tariffs on nearly all categories of imported products, in an absurd and scattergun way.

There's a 5% tariff on margarine, a 4% tariff on dairy spreads, but no tariff on butter. There's a 5% tariff on pasta, a 4% tariff on bulgur, but no tariff on couscous. There's a tariff on almonds but not walnuts, strawberries but not raspberries, maple syrup but not golden syrup, biscuits but not crispbread. And when you paid for Christmas lunch, there was a tariff on the ham but not the turkey.

Beyond the world of foodstuffs, there's a tariff on guitars and drums, but not violins and pianos. On calendars but not diaries. On towels, but not tea towels. There's a tariff on granite and sandstone if it's in blocks, but not if it's 'roughly trimmed.' A tariff on flat steel if it's coated with zinc, but not if it's coated with tin. A tariff on umbrellas, except those with a telescopic shaft. The list goes on and on.

Administering this list requires hundreds of customs officials to check that the correct tariff is imposed on each product. It drives importers crazy and discourages potential importers from even bothering to offer their products to Australians.

Customs officials not only have to determine what sort of product they have in front of them, but also its country of origin. There are different tariff rates depending on whether a product originally comes from a least developed country, a developing country, or a country with which Australia has made a deal.

Having different tariffs for different countries messes up our trading. When we reduce tariffs on products from a high cost country while retaining them on products from a low-cost country, imports from the high cost country increase at the expense of the low-cost country. Australians end up paying the same price for the same sort of product while our customs officials gather less revenue.

Whenever Australian businesses use imported products or materials on which tariffs are imposed, they pass on the costs. Overall that leads to lower sales, fewer workers and lower wages. Other local businesses divert their production away from what they are good at in order to produce a local version of the imported products, and Australia is poorer as a result.

And whenever we impose tariffs, we hurt the world's poor. Tariffs make us buy less of the stuff that the world's poor are good at making. This not only hurts them in the short term, but is crushing over the long term as it reinforces their dependence on aid. We substitute paying them for working with giving them money for nothing.

Following the recent free trade deals with China, Japan and South Korea, two thirds of our trade is now with the 13 countries with which we have a deal. The remaining third is with hundreds of countries. We should unilaterally remove tariffs on products from these countries too. This would not only give us access to some of the world's best products at the cheapest prices, but would help the world's poor regardless of what country they are in.

Seeking deals with these hundreds of countries is not the way to go. It would cost millions to fly Canberra bureaucrats to negotiations around the globe, and any improvement in market access would have little impact on our export prices and volumes. The next 22 countries being targeted for future deals, such as India and Indonesia, account for just 6% of our current trade.

And holding out for more deals would require us to retain our self-destructive tariffs for longer, when we have the option to rid ourselves of them right now. It amounts to saying, we won't stop harming our economy until you stop harming yours.

Tariffs (excluding special tariffs on fuel, alcohol and tobacco) contribute just $3 billion towards the Commonwealth Government's annual budget of around $400 billion. Compared to the significant nuisance cost they impose, this is a small revenue contribution. We should get rid of this nuisance without delay.

The TPP[34]

What do the Greens, Nick Xenophon Team and One Nation have in common with Hillary Clinton and Donald Trump? As it happens, quite a lot, and at the top of the list is their declared hatred of the free trade treaty known as the Trans Pacific Partnership (TPP).

Later this century it is likely to become clear that western civilisation has fallen into decline. When historians look for an event that signifies the turning point from progress to paralysis, rejection of the TPP may well be that event.

The TPP is about trade; as in facilitating more of it. It will allow Australian producers to sell more dairy products, wine, steel and automotive parts at better prices. Nick Xenophon has said he supports each of these producers, yet he opposes the TPP. Sugar, beef and wheat producers will also benefit, but somehow the One Nation Senators of Queensland, New South Wales and Western Australia still oppose the deal.

The TPP is also unashamedly about empire. It is a plan orchestrated by the leading countries of the free world that are not yet drowning in a culture of entitlement, including Australia and New Zealand, the US and Canada, Japan and Singapore. Together we represent an empire of liberal democracy which has allowed its people to build great wealth and, through the example it has provided to poor countries, helped pull a billion people out of extreme poverty.

The TPP would serve to cement this empire in the face of the bureaucratic behemoth of China. And it would further enrich our liberal democratic empire, so that China's only option to emulate our strength would be to become more like us.

The Greens, Nick Xenophon Team, One Nation, Clinton and Trump each have a pathological fear of China, and yet they oppose the TPP that excludes China. Chinese Communist Party leaders must be chuckling in their chow mein.

The opponents of the TPP are willing to throw farmers, miners, manufacturers and workers under a bus – just to pander to a rabble of anti-everything voters. And they are a weird, eclectic rabble.

The TPP is a thick wad of paper, yet they want it to be even thicker. They want the TPP to add some magical rules to stop countries from printing more money so as to devalue their own currencies. Some of them want it to morph into a deal to save the world from climate change.

They want the TPP to force Vietnamese bosses to provide first world pay and conditions to their workers – a recipe for impoverishing an already poor country.

They want to reject the TPP because its 'country-of-origin' rules aren't mean enough to non-member countries like

China, even though rejecting the TPP would be a massive free-kick for China.

They want to reject the TPP because it obliges the government to choose the bidder offering the best value for money in many of its purchase decisions. This would save taxpayers a lot of money, but the rabble doesn't care – probably because they don't pay tax.

The rabble wants to reject the TPP because it requires member countries to enforce royalty payments when using intellectual property from another member country. While it can be argued the new intellectual property protections are excessive, the rabble want to decimate intellectual property protections, somehow assuming new medicines will still be invented even if they can be immediately copied and are therefore unprofitable.

Finally, the rabble object to the TPP because it requires member countries to impose the same laws on foreign investors as are imposed on domestic investors, protects foreign investors from an uncompensated seizure of their property or a denial of justice, and allows foreign investors to complain if this is not the case. This helps prevent the promulgation of arbitrary regulations, and is a requirement that Australia currently meets anyway, so it would do no harm in Australia. However, it would certainly help Australians investing overseas.

The TPP isn't perfect. We'd get an even bigger boost if we simply abolished tariffs on imports from all countries, or if we achieved a deal covering more countries. But there is no doubt the TPP offers net benefits for Australia. Its adoption in both Australia and the US should be a no-brainer. Unfortunately, the decision is in the hands of no-brainers.

Foreign Investment Bills[35]

I oppose the Foreign Investment Bills before us today.

These bills will hurt Australians who want to sell their property, by scaring away potential buyers. All Australians who will one day want to sell property should see these bills as a violation of their property rights that will make them poorer.

The bills scare away potential buyers by raising the hurdles that foreign investors need to jump to invest in Australia. There is no valid reason for this. Indeed there is no valid reason for the existence of the hurdles at all.

The Government's explanatory memorandum states 'there is a need to review foreign investment proposals to ensure they are consistent with Australia's interests.' But the explanatory memorandum fails to identify one cost or risk of foreign investment. The lack of costs, and the preponderance of benefits from foreign investment, suggest that foreign investment is always consistent with Australia's interests, and the entire foreign investment review process is a farce.

We don't need to hinder foreign investment for national security reasons. If there is a risk from a Chinese Government investor owning a shipbuilding or internet company operating in Australia, then the same risk is present if a disloyal Australian investor owns the same shipbuilding or internet company.

Thinking that we can achieve national security by keeping out Chinese Government investors is naïve. If a shipbuilding or internet company operating in Australia needs to be managed in a specific way to protect our national security, then we should regulate the company accordingly, regardless of who owns it.

For similar reasons, we don't need to hinder foreign investment to achieve industry development. The Australian Government may hope that key companies in Australia expand their operations, use local suppliers and sell to local distributors. But an Australian-owned company is just as likely to disappoint on this front as a foreign-owned company.

Foreign investment has nothing to do with food security or energy security. A company may want to export its products rather than service the domestic market regardless of who owns the company. This is fine, as Australia is not at risk of going without food or energy. We are a net exporter of both food and energy, and both are readily imported.

Some people are concerned that foreign companies could sell Australian-made food or energy back to their home countries for below-market prices. But the ATO's transfer pricing rules are designed to ensure that this practice would have no impact on the contribution that foreign companies pay to us in tax.

We don't need to hinder foreign investment to ensure a competitive market. The ACCC can rule out acquisitions it deems to be anti-competitive, regardless of whether or not the prospective acquirer is a foreigner.

Finally, the idea that we should restrict foreign investment in housing in order to suppress house prices is absurd. Foreign investors help Australian sellers, and their investment encourages an expansion of housing supply.

So there is no valid reason to put any hurdles in the way of foreign investors. Instead, it boils down to xenophobia.

There is as much logic in restricting foreign investors as there would be in restricting gay investors or black investors.

These bills will raise the hurdles foreign investors need to jump, in a number of ways.

The bills introduce foreign investment application taxes.

The Government is calling them 'fees,' but the legislation makes it clear that they are taxes.

The taxes are substantial, ranging from $5,000 to $100,000. The taxes apply to each purchase, and can also apply when an attempted purchase falls through.

These taxes, like all other taxes on international capital flows, will have two effects.

Firstly, they will reduce the supply of foreign capital to Australia, making us poorer. That some foreigners will be dissuaded from investing in Australia because of these taxes is undeniable.

Secondly, these taxes will hurt the Australians wanting to do business with foreign investors. The taxes will be physically paid by the foreigners buying assets in Australia. But because foreigners literally have a world of investment options before them, they won't cop any attempt to make them pay more than the going rate for an asset. So the taxes will be effectively paid by Australians because they will have to accept a lower price when selling their asset, to compensate for the new tax.

The Government estimates that this tax hike will generate more than $700 million by June 2019. This will far exceed the costs of regulating foreign investment. So there is no avoiding the conclusion that this is a blatant and economically-irre-sponsible tax grab.

The bills provide the Treasurer with the discretion to waive the payment of these taxes. The Treasurer will be effectively unconstrained in the use of this discretion, as he need only be satisfied that a waiver is not contrary to the national interest. No guidance on the circumstances in which a waiver should or should not apply is provided. This is astonishing. It is a licence for arbitrariness and uncertainty, for favourable treatment of mates, and for corruption.

Another way these bills discourage foreign investment is by facilitating more rigorous enforcement of the ban on foreign investment in existing residential real estate.

This ban is nonsensical, particularly as real estate can't be shipped off like the family silver.

The Government justifies the ban by saying it wants to promote Australia's housing stock. But allowing foreigners to buy existing residences would encourage the building of new residences.

The bills facilitate more rigorous enforcement of the ban by making the ATO responsible for enforcing it.

Fans of *The Untouchables* might find it romantic to empower our own internal revenue agency to bring down gangsters, but a foreigner who buys residential real estate is no Al Capone, and prohibition was, and always will be, a terrible policy.

The bills before us today raise the hurdles foreign investors need to jump by extending foreign investment restrictions to a broader range of agricultural investments.

This means that foreigners will need to get the Treasurer's approval before buying an agribusiness or a certain amount of agricultural land.

Foreigners will be charged taxes of up to $100,000 each time a decision from the Treasurer is sought, and decisions can be delayed for up to four months.

Any foreigner who buys an agricultural asset without the Treasurer's approval will face penalties including:

- fines of up to $135,000,
- jail of up to three years,
- orders to sell the asset in question to certain buyers, or
- the seizure of the asset by the Commonwealth.

All of this will send a very clear signal to prospective foreign investors in Australian agriculture – you are not welcome.

An agribusiness will be defined as a business where a currently unknown share of its revenue, profit or assets relates to agriculture, forestry, fishing or food manufacturing. However, manufacturers of cured meat, smallgoods, ice cream, cereal, pasta and confectionery will be excluded. Also, those businesses lucky enough to be classified as manufacturers of 'other' foods will be excluded. This is all as clear as mud.

Similar clarity applies in relation to which agricultural land transactions will be subject to the foreign investment restrictions. The details are not included in the bills, but the Government suggests that they will regulate to exclude agricultural land transactions where the foreigner ends up with less than $15 million worth of agricultural land. The Government has provided no detail on how and when holdings are to be valued.

The upshot of this is that foreigners who already own agricultural land will be able to bid freely for agricultural land only up to a vague range. Once bidding reaches this vague range, foreigners will presumably have to withdraw from bidding. Only if they get a valuation for their existing holdings, pay a tax to the Treasurer and get his eventual approval – will the foreigners be able to re-enter the bidding.

A more sure-fire way to scare away buyers is hard to imagine.

The Government estimates that 125 agricultural land transactions a year will be threatened by this extension of the foreign investment restrictions. And the Government estimates that complying with these restrictions will cost foreigners $10,000 per transaction, over and above the new taxes that need to be paid. Not only will this scare away buyers, but it will ensure that the prices that Australian farmers receive will be severely depressed.

This is policy that hurts rather than helps farmers. The only potential beneficiaries are hangers on in farming communities who want nothing to ever change. But pandering to these fuddy-duddies will only condemn our farming communities to a slow, grey decline into backwardness.

Labor has an amendment to exclude agribusinesses from this regulatory nightmare, and to lift the threshold on the value of agricultural land, beyond which the screening processes kick in. Labor should be congratulated for this amendment, although I wish they didn't support the rest of the Government's Bill.

These bills ramp up criminal penalties for the sin of investing in Australia. This is completely unwarranted, as existing penalties have never been imposed.

The bills also introduce civil penalties. For instance, a foreigner who commits the sin of buying residential land from a willing seller can be hit with a civil fine equal to 10% of the land's value.

Some of the civil penalties can be imposed through the issuing of infringement notices. This means that if people believe they have done nothing wrong, they will have to prove their innocence.

The fines set out in these bills are well in excess of the levels recommended in the Government's own Guide to Framing Commonwealth Offences. The Government justifies this by saying that the fines must counteract the large financial gain a foreigner can get from holding an Australian asset without approval. But the financial gain is marginal. The foreigners aren't stealing multi-million dollar assets, they're paying for them, from willing sellers.

These bills also discourage foreign investment by requiring foreign holders of agricultural land to report to the ATO, so it can create a register.

The Government does not explain why we need to keep a list of foreigners who own a parcel of land. Perhaps we should need to know when a foreigner is walking down the street, perhaps by passing a law requiring them to wear a yellow badge.

Or how about a register of land owners who are female, or gay, black or disabled? This would be no more idiotic than having a register of foreigners.

The Government intends to separate the register into a basic part and a published part. There is no requirement to confidentialise the part to be published.

The Government will demand the contact details of the foreigner, the value of their land, and the purpose for buying the land. Such prying into private affairs is far from welcoming.

The Government has also left open the option of seeking and publishing the nationality of the foreigners. This would seem a distinct possibility, given that pandering to fears about a Yellow Peril is surely what this register is all about.

Foreigners will need to report to the ATO the agricultural land they hold, and also report their purchases of agricultural land.

It is not hard to envisage how this register might be used. Imagine an increase in foreign ownership from say 8% to 10%. It will be said this is a 25% increase, and the country will soon be overrun by foreigners. To which the aborigines have an obvious rejoinder.

And of course, nobody mentions that many of those foreigners are from New Zealand rather than a country where the people don't look or speak like most of us, like China.

Determining whether land is deemed to be agricultural land will be a bureaucratic mine field of arbitrariness and uncertainty. Land not currently used for agriculture – but that could reasonably be used for agriculture – will be covered, even if the land could only partially be used for agriculture.

So if you could put a beehive on your land, it might be covered. Even a mine site could be deemed to be agricultural land if you expect the land to be eventually remediated.

If you think your land somehow ceases to be agricultural, or if you think it somehow becomes agricultural, you'll need to report the change to the ATO.

People will need to report their agricultural land holdings to the ATO if they become a foreigner. When this will occur to an Australian citizen who is living overseas is not clear. When this will occur to a non-citizen permanent resident is also not clear – perhaps on their 165th day out of the country.

Foreigners who hold agricultural land will also need to report to the ATO if they cease to be a foreigner. When this will occur with an Australian citizen is not clear – perhaps once they come back to Australia for good. For a non-citizen, they will cease to be a foreigner on their 200th day in the country, so they'll need to mark off their days on a calendar – just like a prisoner etches the days on their cell wall. This is not the most welcoming way to treat the skilled migrants we need for our twenty-first century economy.

If you fail to report any of this to the ATO, you'll be hit with a fine.

It may come as a surprise that Australian citizens living overseas are treated as foreigners under our foreign investment restrictions. Aussies like Mark Webber could easily be wrapped up in the red tape.

When Malcolm Turnbull announced his push to become Prime Minister, he said:

- That a change in leadership was needed for our country's sake.
- That we cannot be defensive.
- That we need to respect the intelligence of the Australian people.
- And that we need to seize the enormous opportunities the world offers.

I agree.

We cannot be defensive, and we must reject the politics of fear surrounding foreign investment.

We need to respect the intelligence of the Australian people, which means that if we cannot list a single cost from foreign investment, then we should not argue for foreign investment to be restricted.

Above all, we need to seize the enormous opportunities the world offers. And one of the greatest opportunities the world offers is the opportunity of foreign investment, to:

- add to our capital and infrastructure,
- improve competition and consumer choice,
- introduce new technology and global access, and
- boost jobs and skills.

I end my speech with an appeal. To all Senators, I urge you to let these foreign investment proposals of the former Prime Minister quietly slide into your huge pile of un-enacted bills.

They do not serve an Australia of free enterprise, individual initiative and freedom.

SUPERANNUATION

Superannuation changes[36]

It's rather nice when people queue up to give me money. Of course, the money isn't for me – it's for the Liberal Democrats – but the warm inner glow is still just as satisfying.

In the last week, we've received a touch over six figures in donations, many of them tied to a single issue: superannuation.

The IPA's John Roskam has pointed out repeatedly that Malcolm Turnbull and Scott Morrison do not appreciate the depth of disquiet over this issue, and Turnbull's intransigence on Alan Jones's radio program in which he simply ruled out any change to the budget announcement of a $1.6 million cap on tax-free super savings in retirement, or the $500,000 life-time cap on after-tax contributions, only served to drive more 'rusted on' Liberal voters in our direction.

I've appeared at multiple fundraisers all over Australia, many arranged by Liberal Party members, and my office has been besieged with calls from grumpy superannuants offering assistance.

In truth, I don't think the people coming to the Liberal Democrats have become libertarians overnight. Nor is super-annuation their only concern. Rather, it is the proverbial straw that is breaking the camel's back. They are furious with their own party's abandonment of liberal values and looking to vote strategically. That is, they'll vote Liberal Democrats in the Senate and preference the Coalition, while sticking with the Liberal Party in the House of Representatives in order to ensure Labor does not have the numbers to govern.

Why are they furious? Since 1992, Australians have been compelled to park money in superannuation so they can fund their own retirement, justified on the basis that it would be taxed a lot less than other savings to compensate for the fact that it cannot be used until retirement.

Raising super taxes is shirking on the deal. The changes suggest the government is less serious about reducing the number of people receiving the pension than it is about increasing taxes.

Furthermore, the fact that the increase in taxes applies once a superannuation fund reaches $1.6 million, and that contributions from after-tax income are now limited retrospectively, suggests the government believes we are not entitled to a particularly prosperous retirement. For those on middle incomes who look to wealthy retirees for inspiration, this is deeply discouraging.

Moreover, no matter how often Mr Turnbull says his superannuation policy will only affect a small number of individuals, the door is now open to raiding the super honey-pot. If the Liberals get away with it this time, the temptation for future governments of either persuasion to once again stick their greedy paws in all that lovely honey will be irresistible.

If the government was to ever get serious about reducing the numbers receiving the age pension, it would cease taxing contributions and earnings in superannuation funds entirely. This would provide a huge incentive to all wage and salary earners to maximise their savings. It would also rid us of triple taxation, where money is taxed when we work for it, when we save it, and then when we use it for consumption. Once in retirement, withdrawals of previously-untaxed savings could be taxed as income.

However, the proposed changes to superannuation are only part of the wider concerns of traditional Liberal voters. They are concerned that the budget increased discretionary spending, despite Mr Morrison's acknowledgment we have a spending problem. It increased tax on multinationals and smokers, despite various Coalition spokespeople ridiculing Labor when it earlier made similar suggestions. And it dropped the limp commitment to deliver a budget surplus equal to 1% of GDP by 2023–24, despite rhetoric that government must 'live within its means.'

Then there have been numerous blocks on foreign investment, new spending programs renamed as 'initiatives' or 'investments,' and constant sneaky attempts at revenue-raising, all in the context of a chronic budget deficit of around $40 billion which the Liberal government apparently regards as no more urgent to correct than Labor.

I recognise many of the people now donating to and supporting the Liberal Democrats disagree with us on other issues. That's all right. Perfect political congruence doesn't exist, which is probably a good thing.

However, I am confident that a vote for the Liberal Democrats in the Senate is an appropriate response for disaffected Liberal voters. Irrespective of who wins government, neither the Liberals nor Labor will have a majority in the Senate. Indeed, because of the double dissolution, a crossbench of between 6 and 12 is almost certain. The election of a sensible crossbench comprising several Liberal Democrats would help drag the Liberal Party away from its addiction to spending other people's money.

Using forced savings for more than retirement[37]
Two wrongs make a right.

It is wrong that we are forced to deposit a prescribed amount of our earnings into a particular type of account and are prevented from withdrawing it until we reach a certain age. It is also wrong that people who are able to save prior to retirement, but who choose not to do so, get an age pension funded by others.

If the first wrong (forcing everyone to save) reduces the second wrong (the irresponsible receiving tax-funded age pensions), then it's worth doing. That's the logic of our super-annuation regime.

Such logic can and should apply more broadly.

It is wrong that people who are able to save to prepare for future ill health, but who choose not to do so, receive public health services. This wrong could be reduced by obliging people to save and use the money to cover future health costs.

Some think we already do this through the Medicare levy, but they are wrong. The levy is not an insurance premium and only covers a small fraction of public health costs. It is really just another tax on income.

We already have forced saving through the superannuation regime, with bipartisan agreement that the compulsory rate of saving should rise. Given this, it would make sense to compel people to draw down these savings before they are granted access to public health services.

Singapore has had a similar scheme for many years, where it is considered a great success.

Such an approach would not affect the poorest in society who are unable to accumulate superannuation savings. They would continue to have immediate access to benefits in instances of ill health and remain eligible for the age pension upon reaching the appropriate age.

It would only affect those who are able to save but who currently choose not to, and might prompt some of these people to undertake additional precautionary saving, to reconsider any unhealthy practices, and to avoid unnecessary visits to the GP. Any of these changes would reduce costs on taxpayers.

Alternatively, it would simply put off the day that tax-payers are required to cover the health expenses of the irresponsible.

Like many developed countries, Australia has a massive and growing budget problem because of health and social welfare commitments. In 2013, federal government expenditure on health was $61 billion and social security and welfare $132 billion, of which assistance to the aged comprised $51 billion. Combined, they account for over 50% of total federal government expenditure, far exceeding defence or any of the other big ticket items normally associated with governments.

Future demand for age pensions will be limited by superannuation savings, but state and federal budgets will be overwhelmed within a generation unless there are major changes to the funding of health.

Already a common topic of discussion among the baby boomer generation is whether they have accumulated enough super or will be forced to rely on the pension in retirement. This is as it should be. The age pension, while modest, whittles away at the natural incentives to save for retirement. As such, it is important that only those who absolutely need it are eligible.

Using our system of compulsory savings accounts to achieve independence from taxpayers makes sense. But for those in their twenties and thirties, saving for a distant retirement is not a high priority. Using the funds to cover health expenses is far more relevant.

Of course, this would require a phase-in period. Compulsory superannuation, which began in 1992, is only now starting to make a real difference. Funds managers should also compete more transparently on cost and performance than they do now, so account holders can choose a fund that suits them. Earnings in the savings accounts should ideally be tax-free, and insurance should play a part for those who have not accumulated a high balance.

But if it is wrong to force people to save, it is also wrong that others pay for the health and retirement of those who refuse to save. Two wrongs can make a right.

REGULATION AND OTHER ECONOMIC INTERFERENCE

Childcare[38]

Every time I make comments critical of childcare subsidies, the internet explodes with abuse about the evil, childless, cat-owning libertarian who doesn't understand that bearing children requires lashings of other people's money.

The internet outrage always misses my main point: childcare needs deregulation to bring down costs.

Over the past decade or so, subsidies for childcare have grown continuously and rapidly to the point where they now pose a real threat to long-term budget sustainability.

The main reason for this is the increased credentialism and regulation that pervades the sector. Whereas childcare workers were once just sensible, caring people, most with children or grandchildren of their own, these days they are expected to hold post-school – and sometimes even university-level – qualifications. There has also been a ratcheting up of regulation of the physical environment in childcare centres, the programs and routines offered, plus staff ratios.

For the most part this has been driven by middle-class parental guilt. That is, parents seeking to justify the decision to place their children in childcare are demanding standards that allow them to believe their little darlings are receiving a better start in life than if they stayed at home. It makes them feel better about leaving the kids with someone else.

The problem is, in the case of children from the middle-class families, there is no evidence that these standards are enhancing children's outcomes. This was conceded in the Productivity Commission Inquiry Report into Childcare and Early Childhood Learning.

More to the point, ramped up regulation and credentialism has put the cost of childcare out of reach of the poorest parents – many of them single mothers – who have a strong need to return to work and whose children are more likely to benefit from childcare.

Currently, there are two payments to subsidise childcare fees – a means-tested childcare benefit and a non-means-tested rebate in which all families, regardless of income, receive 50% of their fees to an annual cap of $7,500. The Government's Budget proposal will boost childcare fee assistance by 54%, after accounting for inflation, from this financial year to 2018–19.

The wealthiest families, earning more than $185,000, will be able to get $10,000 in subsidies per child each year, representing a $2,500 gain per child. There is absolutely no evidence to show that well-off parents need prompting to re-enter the workforce, nor evidence suggesting that well-off parents will change their childcare decisions if they receive even more subsidies. The increase amounts to unprincipled vote-buying by the Coalition, which views well-off parents as a natural constituency it must retain to be re-elected.

A low-income family that sends two kids to child care full-time, costing $115 a day, will receive $50,830 a year in subsidies. Fairly clearly, payments like this are so generous that many families will receive more in childcare subsidies than they earn, making it very attractive to put kids into care.

Doing this for the most disadvantaged families may make sense. However, what the Government proposes – affecting decisions of low and middle· income families – amounts to social engineering on a vast scale. Mothers who prefer to stay at home will come under enormous pressure to go to work.

Ignored in all this is the obvious point that subsidising a particular good or service increases its price. Even other failed subsidy experiments – like the First Homebuyers Scheme – weren't as bad because only a subset of buyers were eligible. With childcare, everyone with young children will qualify.

Before we hit taxpayers for more money to pay for additional subsidies, the sector needs to be substantially deregulated. Middle- and upper-middle-class families who expect gold-plated, diamond-encrusted childcare – with its university educated workers and low staff ratios – should pay for it themselves. While it is legitimate to screen childcare workers to ensure those who present a danger to children are excluded, the ratcheted-up regulation and credentialism should be scrapped.

Moreover, existing subsidies should be aggressively means-tested to ensure they are not directed towards parents who would work regardless of the presence or absence of a subsidy.

I support payments for the poorest parents so that kids can be raised with good nutrition, shelter, clothing, and care. But my support is on welfare grounds, not because it is legitimate to impose middle-class child-rearing preferences on the rest of the population. Having children is not a reason to help oneself to other people's money.

An unhealthy approach to health[39]

Popular thinking about the role of government is all over the place. Nothing exemplifies the muddle more than the wide-spread support for massively increased government spending on medical research, and the noisy opposition to the proposed reduction in Medicare rebates to doctors.

Everyone supports medical research. What's not to love? But that fact is the very reason governments shouldn't fund it. People give freely and generously to medical research charities every day. They direct their money to the fields of research they care most about. They give when they know where the money is going. And they give to organisations that they trust.

According to research by the National Australia Bank, nearly a third of Australian tax-deductible donations last year went to cancer charities (like the National Breast Cancer Foundation), health and disability charities (like Diabetes Australia) and medical research charities (like the Heart Research Institute). This suggests that Australians freely donate more than $700 million dollars to these organisations every year.

The proposed Medical Research Future Fund aims to add a billion dollars to annual government funding of medical research in a decade's time. But as government funding for good causes goes up, private donations go down. One study estimates that for every $100 of government funding, private donations fall by $73.

We should not ask the government to do what we can do ourselves. It robs us of our direct connection with those we want to help and makes politicians believe they are angels when being generous with other people's money. It also generates public sector jobs in which bureaucrats serve as unnecessary middlemen rather than working in the private or not-for-profit sectors where they could add real value to people's lives.

It is no secret that the Government's Medical Research Future Fund was supposed to be a Trojan horse that would allow the Government to sneak in a reduction in Medicare rebates. But a reduction in Medicare rebates is not something the Government should be ashamed of, or something that could be snuck in anyway.

A reduction in Medicare rebates, and the associated increase in the prices doctors will charge patients, is good policy. The Government should be proud of it and ought to directly argue in support.

We pay mechanics to service and fix our cars, and we pay tradespeople to maintain and repair our homes. This arrangement works. Many mechanics and tradespeople compete for our custom by developing a reputation for good work, honesty, and good value. Those that don't, risk going out of business.

Our bodies are more valuable than our cars and homes, and the services provided by doctors, based on at least a decade of training, are more valuable than the services of mechanics and tradespeople. As such, there is no more important place to encourage good work, honesty and good value than the doctor's surgery.

Various arguments are made to oppose the introduction of charges for a visit to the doctor. Rather than hide behind the Medical Research Future Fund, the Government should rebut each of them.

It is said the introduction of charges will hurt the poor and chronically ill. But there is a generous cap; concessional patients and children under 16 years will only have to pay $7 for the first ten services each calendar year, a total of $70. Opposing the Government's proposal in its entirety will only maintain a situation where the well-off and healthy receive the same level of medical support as the poor and chronically ill, a level that is inadequate for those most in need.

It is said the introduction of charges will discourage people from visiting the doctor. But some visits to the doctor should be discouraged. We cannot afford to waste the limited and valuable services of our doctors on consultations that are more social than medical. Over-servicing can worsen health outcomes.

And the mindset that good health hinges on the services of doctors rather than exercise, nutrition, sleep, social networks and low stress is a harmful mindset of dependency that free consultations only serve to reinforce.

In an ideal world we would shop for health services based on quality and price, protected from unaffordable costs by insurance. The government's role would be limited to ensuring that the poor and chronically ill are insured, and collecting and publishing information about the providers to help us make better choices.

In that world the most needy would receive all the support they required, and private support for medical research would not be discouraged.

The Pharmacy Guild[40]

It is night, a fever takes hold and a mother starts to worry. A bathroom cupboard is raided, but it is full of medicine past its use-by date. A child is bundled into a car. A waiting room is endured. Then a GP provides a prescription.

With child in arms the mother returns to the car, then scratches her head. Where is a chemist that would be open at this time of night?

The mother scrounges for her mobile phone, but it is out of charge. Should she drive around in the hope of finding a chemist that's open, or trek back home to look one up?

Driving past the lit-up supermarket, the mother wonders, 'Why is it so hard to find a chemist?'

Meanwhile, the enthusiasm of a young pharmacist slowly seeps away. She's at home, twiddling on her iPhone, passing the time. She had a short shift today. They're always short shifts. She's just a temp.

She used to dream of running her own pharmacy. The dream took hold during her years of business and pharmacy studies. It lingered on after graduation as she did stints – in pharmacies far and wide – working for the man. But now the dream of working behind her own counter, building her own reputation, in her own neighbourhood and community, is gone. It was a silly dream.

Over at the Pharmacy Guild headquarters on National Circuit in Canberra, David Quilty, the Guild's Executive Director, reclines in his office chair. His late-night meeting with the Health Minister went well. The Guild's members – the owners of pharmacies across Australia – will be pleased.

All going to plan, the next Community Pharmacy Agreement – a five-year deal between the Guild and the Government – will be much like the last one, and the one before that. The deal should see pharmacy owners continue to enjoy regulations to protect them and subsidies to enrich them.

Mr Quilty recalls how he had to explain to the Health Minister his own regulations. 'They ban new pharmacies within ten kilometres of an existing pharmacy. Of course, this exclusion zone is reduced to 1½ kilometres if the new pharmacy is to be near a GP or supermarket, 500 metres if the new pharmacy is to be in a large medical centre or small shopping centre, and 200 metres if the new pharmacy is to be near four GPs and a supermarket. And two pharmacies are allowed in large shopping centres with more than 100 shops; three are allowed if there are more than 200 shops. Naturally, pharmacies directly accessible from a supermarket are banned. And the regulations require any new pharmacy to be approved by an authority that includes incumbent pharmacy owners nominated by the Guild.'

Mr Quilty chuckles as he recalls the Health Minister's bemused look.

As the Commonwealth car drives off into the night, the Health Minister shakes his head in the backseat. He ponders the numbers thrown around in the meeting just gone. More than $15 billion from taxpayers to around 5,000 owners of pharmacies over five years. He does the maths in his head – that's around $600,000 per owner per year. Nice work if you can get it. And well above the tens of thousands of dollars that the Pharmacy Guild provides in political donations.

A wry smile passes his face as he heads back to the comfort of Parliament House, a place where deals usually involve the Government getting something in return for giving something away.

He's philosophical. No previous Health Minister has been able to cut the taxpayer funds flowing to pharmacy owners, or remove the anti-competitive regulations that grant them protection. And perhaps no Health Minister ever will.

He resolves to get the deal done with the Guild – the most feared lobby group in Canberra – as soon as possible, before the Government-commissioned Review into Competition Policy reports.

As the Commonwealth car pulls up at Parliament House, an image pops into the Health Minister's tired head. A granny hobbles to the nearest chemist, then smiles at the owner in the white coat. The owner smiles back, thinking of the margin provided by the taxpayer – up to $148 – for each prescription filled. He asks the granny to sign a petition while she waits. She scans the petition – something to do with keeping some regulations. She signs her rickety signature as the man in the white coat passes over the medicine.

Such a nice man.

Profit from education[41]

While schools are not the only way for children to get an education, they are a central one. And even libertarians like me, who argue the government is too large and intrusive, accept there is a role for governments in ensuring all children are educated. Nobody wants children to grow up without the skills necessary for them to become productive members of society due to poverty or parental failure.

That means making schooling compulsory for ages 6 through 16, enforcing minimum standards and, at least in some cases, spending taxpayers' money.

Schools receive taxpayer funds in a convoluted fashion. For the most part government schools are allocated money by state governments, while non-government schools are funded by the federal government. Overall, government schools receive more taxpayer funding per student. In addition, there's a system of government grants for various projects. This is not new, but became prominent thanks to Kevin Rudd's 'school halls' program.

This system is needlessly complex and bureaucratic. A better funding approach would be to allocate taxpayer funds to children based on their circumstances and those of their parents, with parents free to choose the best school for their children and contribute extra if they think it will help. Provided the level of taxpayer funding for the poorest parents and children is sufficient to ensure a sound education, and takes account of children with special needs, this approach can be equitable.

Such an approach is often referred to as a 'voucher system.' With funding attached to children rather than allocated to schools, it results in schools competing for students on the basis of quality and price. There is no real need for governments, state or federal, to own schools or employ teachers. Subject to meeting standards, a school run by a church or community group could compete on equal terms with a government-owned school.

Unfortunately, the politics of education are fraught, which means this goal is some way off. There may be a need for intermediate steps before the community is comfortable with the idea that the government's role is to ensure all kids receive an education, rather than to provide that education.

One such step would be to counter the notion that schools should not operate as businesses, with the intention of making a profit. A truly competitive educational market, with all the benefits that competitive markets deliver, is far more likely if for-profit schools vie for students alongside not-for-profit providers.

Currently, state governments do not permit for-profit schools, either explicitly or by denying them funding. Moreover, federal funding of for-profit schools is expressly prohibited. Even if they were permitted to operate by the states, they couldn't do so on the same terms as other schools.

If they were permitted and could attract funding, for-profit schools would offer a service that is not currently available. While government schools offer free education, religious schools offer religious education. Many other not-for-profit schools cater to parents for whom high fees are not a barrier; indeed some compete on the basis of how high their fees are.

Given that for-profit childcare centres are important contributors to early education, and for-profit universities are increasing options at the other end of the educational process, it seems reasonable to expect that for-profit schools would offer a quality education at fees below those of established not-for-profit schools, particularly for those not keen on a religious education.

There seems to be little reason for an effective ban on for-profit schools other than an anti-profit mentality among policymakers. Private investment in school education is stifled by the inability to apply the profit motive.

The current fee-charging, not-for-profit schools use their surplus funds to deliver generous remuneration to the people who run the school and to gold-plate their playing fields. For-profit schools would be more likely to use surplus funds to expand their market share, by lowering fees and investing in outcomes sought by parents.

Allowing for-profit schools, and extending existing subsidies to them, would cost the taxpayer nothing. It would have no impact on the total number of students being educated and subsidised. And if students moved from government schools to for-profit schools, taxpayers would actually see a modest saving under current funding arrangements.

Schools run on a for-profit basis should be free to participate in the education sector on a level playing field. It would give parents and students greater choice and governments less need to be educators themselves.

The Reserve Bank[42]

During the Global Financial Crisis there was a splash of taxpayer's funds bigger than school halls, pink batts and $900 cheques combined. But it was a cash splash that no-one knows about, because it was done by a part of government that has zero accountability to ministers, the parliament or the public.

From September 2008 to July 2009 the Reserve Bank agreed to borrow US dollars from the US Federal Reserve so it could on-lend them to local traders on concessional terms. The purpose was to boost US dollar liquidity in the East Asian time zone. At its peak, the Reserve Bank provided A$41 billion to the US Federal Reserve under this agreement.

In acquiescing to the US Federal Reserve in this way, the Reserve Bank chose not to invest taxpayer funds to maximise returns relative to risk. A conservative estimate suggests this may have cost taxpayers half a billion dollars compared to the alternative returns available.

It is possible the Reserve Bank's actions were in Australia's interests. Alternatively, they may have been nothing more than industry assistance or even a favour for the US Federal Reserve. The point is, the Reserve Bank never outlined the cost, nor provided a lay explanation of its actions. It never needed to; the Reserve Bank answers to no-one.

With the power of the printing press, the Reserve Bank pays its staff as much as it pleases, then chooses whether or not to pass on any excess funds to the government.

The Senators on the Senate Economics Committee are too intimidated to ask it to turn up to Senate Estimates to be quizzed on its activities. And when the bank appears before a House of Representatives Committee, we see officials speaking in complex terms and fawning politicians nodding soberly rather than asking for answers than can be understood.

The Reserve Bank and our politicians should bear in mind what Einstein said: 'If you cannot explain it to a six-year-old, you don't really understand it.'

The Reserve Bank is also subject to no real legislative constraints. Even though the *Reserve Bank Act* of 1959 requires it to target currency stability, the bank (wisely) chose to target price inflation in 1993. Even when the government declared in 1996 that the Reserve Bank should indeed target inflation, it didn't bother to update the Reserve Bank's legislation to this end.

This is a concern, because the Reserve Bank's ability to create inflation is akin to a power to tax. After all, inflation reduces our purchasing power just like tax. The Reserve Bank's legislation should be updated to set out how much inflation the government and parliament expects.

The Reserve Bank's legislation should also ban it from undertaking activities beyond inflation targeting. We don't need the Reserve Bank to have a standing power to bail out banks. It is scandalous that the Reserve Bank has the potential to bail out a bank, at a cost to taxpayers of hundreds of billions of dollars, without prior approval from the elected government or parliament.

We also don't need the Reserve Bank to play with the exchange rate, which is supposed to float. Nor do we need it to regulate banks – APRA, ASIC and the ACCC already do this.

And we don't need the Reserve Bank to invest funds on behalf of the government – we have the AOFM for that.

We should set the rules for the Reserve Bank as if it were staffed by its fair share of lazy and stupid bureaucrats. While the officials currently in control of the Reserve Bank seem conscientious and smart, this will not always be the case.

We should make the Reserve Bank accountable through legislation. Moreover, it would be best if the Reserve Bank sought regular budget funding from the parliament to pay for its staff and overheads.

This wouldn't threaten the independent implementation of monetary policy. We get independent tax administration by the Tax Commissioner, and independent collation of statistics from the Australian Statistician, even though they both lead agencies subject to legislation and a budget appropriation.

And we should insist the Reserve Bank justify its actions to taxpayers, whose money it lends to others without informing them.

Coastal shipping[43]

Just before it lost office, Labor did a sweetheart deal with maritime unions on coastal shipping. It passed the Coastal Trading Act, which was meant to revitalise the shipping industry by protecting coastal trade for Australian ships and seamen.

Since the Act took effect, coastal shipping users have seen significant cost increases leading to a serious decline in the amount of coastal freight loaded at our ports, a reduction in Australian-flagged vessel capacity, fewer voyages and fewer Australian vessels. Worse, the deal has spread the misery around – there are now two million tonnes less freight being moved by foreign vessels and the number of major Australian registered ships with coastal licences fell from thirty in 2006/07 to just thirteen in 2012/13.

The importance of a productive and competitive shipping industry cannot be overstated. Australia is enormously dependent on shipping, with 99% of international trade volume carried by ship and Australian ports handling 10% of the world's sea trade.

What we have now is definitely not the revitalised shipping industry Labor promised. Its deal with the unions is costing our industry money and markets by entrenching poor workplace practice and restricting competition.

Some of the regulations are simply bonkers. For example, one of them requires a vessel to sit in port for a day before it can start loading. This costs up to $10,000 a day for foreign ships and $20,000 per day for Australian ships. And even though there are no Australian ships currently capable of carrying bulk liquids between Australian ports, companies chartering shipments of liquids must still allow time for an Australian shipper to tender. The cost of waiting has caused at least one company to lose business.

Gypsum Resources, a CSR/Boral joint venture, supplies and ships bulk gypsum from a mine in Thevenard, South Australia, to plasterboard factories in Melbourne, Sydney and Brisbane. The business had lost substantial volume to imports because it is more attractive to import product from Thailand than to supply from Thevenard.

Because it is almost entirely reliant on shipping, Tasmania has been more severely affected than any other state. The *Coastal Trading Act* was one of the reasons the AAA international shipping service left Tasmania. Now all Tasmanian exporters must ship their products to Melbourne for unloading and reloading onto international ships.

During the first year of the Coastal Trading Act, Bell Bay Aluminium saw its shipping freight rate from Tasmania to Queensland increase from $18.20 per tonne to $29.70 per tonne. This compared with $17.50 a tonne being charged by foreign vessels in 2012. The increase added $4 million per year in extra costs to the Bell Bay smelter.

Another Tasmanian business, Simplot Australia, had an additional $550,000 per year added to its annual costs and has lost markets as a result. This is a crushing burden at a time when the company, the last vegetable processor in the country and an important regional employer, is considering the future of its Devonport plant.

Yet another major company says it is cheaper to ship product from New Zealand to every port in Australia – except Melbourne – than to ship product from Tasmania. And that's after taking into account the benefit of the Tasmanian Freight Equalisation Scheme rebate, which the Kiwis don't receive.

Australian Peak Shippers, which represents companies like SunRice and Bega Cheese, said in a submission to the Parliamentary Inquiry on shipping:

> When it is cheaper to buy product in New Zealand and land it in Brisbane for blending than it is to purchase the equivalent Australian raw material from Victoria and ship it to Brisbane, or indeed when it is cheaper to ship product from Melbourne to Singapore than it is to ship the same from Melbourne to Brisbane, it is not hard to realise that our Australian exports, which are competing with Singapore based companies for the same market, are finding it tough to do so.

Labor and its union allies created this mess. The effect on manufacturing and agriculture is completely contrary to Labor's claimed support for the two industries and their workers. The Coastal Trading Act is facilitating the replacement of Aussie made products with imported products. Australian companies are not competitive in their own market due to excessive freight costs.

Tasmania's economy is in bad shape and needs help. What would help most is not more handouts from taxpayers in other states, but removal of the hurdles that prevent it from helping itself. Chief among these is a crying need to make our logistics more competitive by deregulating coastal shipping.

Electoral funding[44]

Various people, the Greens among them, are cheering at the defeat of former Newcastle Lord Mayor Jeff McCloy in the High Court. He had sought to overturn a New South Wales law banning property developers from making political donations. The same law also prohibits donations by gambling and tobacco interests to state political parties.

This cheering is misplaced. The ruling provided no endorsement for similar proposals for a federal ban including mining and alcohol industries. It merely upheld the NSW government's right to make this kind of law. It says nothing about whether banning people from doing what they want with their own money is good law.

Nonetheless, the Greens are working on banning donations from everyone whose activities they dislike, while continuing to receive donations from people who support their policies. Fairly obviously, this is a game anyone can play. It could just as easily lead to bans on donations from wind farms, Greenpeace, and NGOs lobbying to close down the coal industry.

There is a simple solution to concerns about donor corruption – the disinfectant of sunlight. Anyone should be able to donate to any political party of their choice, but we should all be able to find out who donated. Making it easy and fast – so that donors can be identified in a week, not months – will ensure both donors and recipients are held to account. The media will have a field day, and this would be a good thing.

Risks regarding the political influence of donors, real or perceived, are also countered by regular elections. If you don't like what politicians have been doing, you can kick them out.

In the interests of disclosure, here is my contribution to donor transparency.

Because we have received donations from tobacco companies, the Liberal Democrats are sometimes accused of being in thrall to Big Tobacco.

This is regrettable. We would like it known that we are equally in thrall to Medium and Small Tobacco. Furthermore, I cannot in good conscience say that my party would knock back donations from the fast growing illicit and chop-chop tobacco sectors either – on a strictly don't ask, don't tell basis, of course. In fact, I look forward to the day when we are accused of being in thrall to Big, Medium, and Small Weed. As for developers, alcohol, gambling, and mining companies – we welcome them all.

To explain this, it should be understood that we have a long and glorious history of supporting the right of smokers to enjoy their habit, provided they do no harm to others. Ten years before we ever saw a cent of tobacco money, one of our founders decided to take up smoking as a publicity stunt.

That said, anyone who thinks donations influence my vote doesn't know me well. The belief that people should be free to make their own choices so long as they are not hurting anyone else is fundamental to classical liberalism, the philosophy that underpins Liberal Democrats policies.

But when political parties take donations from organisations where there is no obvious connection, public scrutiny could make a big difference. An example of this would be the Greens accepting donations from the CFMEU, while at the same time proposing anti-forestry and anti-mining policies that would put many foresters and miners out of a job.

Such donations look curious at best, but at least only CFMEU members are paying. Those members who don't want to fund the Greens can presumably opt out of membership if they so choose.

By contrast, we cannot opt out of paying taxes. That makes giving taxpayer funds to political parties much more of a concern.

The Liberal Democrats benefited from the current policy at the last federal election, qualifying for $1 million of taxpayers' money. But this is small change compared to the major parties, which received a total of $58 million from taxpayers. Most of this was used to pay for those annoying television and radio ads and leaflets in our letterboxes. Knowing we all paid for such drivel doubles the annoyance.

Wouldn't it be better if individuals, corporations and unions voluntarily paid for that electioneering with their own money? And for it to be all in the open, where it can be scrutinised?

In seeking to ban donations from those they consider bad people, the Greens make two grave mistakes. They fail to appreciate that plenty of folks consider Greens donors to be equally bad; and, in an endless cycle of tit-for-tat banning, they will leave taxpayers footing the bill.

Coal is king[45]

To the many Australians who are the silent majority in the debate about the value and benefits of coal to this country, I think it is time to acknowledge the 55,000 men and women employed in the Australian coal industry. They keep the lights on.

I'd also like to thank the coal industry itself for the $6 billion in wages paid to those workers.

We need to reaffirm the positive contribution coal makes to this country and to our lives.

Coal is our second biggest export, earning $38 billion in 2013. The coal industry directly provided $3.2 billion in royalties to state governments, and $10 billion more in company and employee taxes. That money pays for schools, hospitals, pensions and all the other services we expect governments to provide.

This money does not fall from the sky, we must earn it. Coal mining does that for us. It is indisputable that every Australian benefits from the use of and export of coal.

Nobody in their wildest green dreams has any expectation that we will ever earn export dollars by sending renewable energy overseas.

Our high standard of living is underpinned by the wealth and energy created by coal, which is by far the greatest contributor to the generation of the electricity that powers industry, heats and cools our homes, cooks our food and charges our smartphones.

This is not so for 1.4 billion people on this planet who have no access to cheap energy. For many, their days are spent unproductively gathering firewood and animal dung for heat and cooking and washing.

No flick of the power switch relieves them from poisonous fumes from cooking fires – one of the third world's biggest killers. They are almost pre-destined to poverty through lack of cheap energy, something they realise and are desperate to overcome.

The world's biggest democracy currently has 300 million people who have no access to electricity at all. India is rich in history and culture, but its poorest people live in grinding poverty where life without electricity is hard and dirty, with dim prospects for immediate improvement.

India is a very big consumer of Australian coal: it seeks to lift its people out of poverty. Energy, like water, is a wealth generator. The energy provided by Australian coal is an important part of ending poverty in India.

In praising the virtues of coal I am stating the obvious, but it would appear that is necessary, because some people seem to have entirely lost the plot.

It is bizarre that well-fed, well-paid activists in Australia campaign for an end to coal mining. The consequence of this, if it were to succeed, would be to deny the most economically viable energy source to the world's poorest people.

Not only is it a gross understatement to characterise this stance as economically illiterate when it comes to Australia's well-being. It is also morally repugnant for the future prospects of the world's poor.

So to that pious minority who oppose coal, I say – don't stop at divestment of your shares in coal.

Turn off your coal powered computers, air conditioners, lights, fridges and entertainment systems, then book a plane ticket to a country that does not have access to reliable electricity to live out your convictions.

But I don't expect they will do that. Those opposing coal are happy to deny the benefits of coal to those who need it most, but don't have the strength of their convictions to practice what they preach.

By all means let's welcome viable renewable energy.

And while we're at it, let's cast off last century's ideological thinking opposing nuclear energy.

There's also no question we should continue improving the way in which we use coal.

Because, of necessity, we will be using it for decades. And that's good.

Until there is a better solution for the world's energy needs, one that provides 24/7 baseload electricity, whatever the weather, at a price the world's poorest can contemplate purchasing, it is unreasonable to expect us to live in the dark, fantasising about a world without coal.

The NBN is a mess[46]

In the time before Kevin Rudd, what customers were willing to pay determined our internet speeds, the technologies employed and the companies that wanted our business.

Then we had Kevin 07. He promised fast, affordable internet speeds for everyone, delivered by a new wholesale internet company owned by the Government, using fibre-to-the-premises technology in towns and cities. The total cost to the government was going to be $4.7 billion.

A trailblazing government monopoly to replace the chaos of the market – it was all so simple. It was amazing no one had thought of it earlier.

But then Telstra was paid billions to never compete with the NBN, an early sign of trouble. If the NBN was going to be so good and affordable, why did it need to eliminate potential competitors? Fairly obviously, the Government wanted everyone to sign up to the NBN so that their financial projections looked more credible, like a despot eliminating other candidates and 'encouraging' voters to vote before claiming a landslide election victory.

By the end of Labor's six years, less than seven percent of the population could access the NBN, and it was estimated that its final cost would exceed $70 billion.

When the Coalition came to office in 2013, there were expectations the plan would be abandoned or at least hived off to the private sector. After all, the Coalition purports to be the party of business. But no, the new government (with Malcolm Turnbull as Communications Minister) decided writing it off was too difficult and in any case the NBN wasn't such a bad idea. It said it would build it cheaper and faster.

So fibre to the premises and 1 Gb per second speeds were replaced with everyone having at least 25 Mb per second no matter where they are located in Australia. In the cities the technology would be fibre to the node, greater use would be made of fixed wireless in towns, and satellites would be used for everywhere else. The fastest speed was dropped to 100 Mb per second.

Things have not gone particularly well. According to the latest figures the cost of the NBN is estimated at $49 billion, far in excess of what it will be worth either in value to customers or the price it could fetch when privatised. Accumulated losses are in excess of $8 billion, equal to more than $300 per Australian. This money will never be recovered.

Astonishingly, the Government's continued borrowing so as to make repeated injections into the loss-making NBN is classed by Treasurer Morrison as 'good debt'. No sensible investor in the private sector would dare make such a claim.

Moreover, the NBN is nowhere near completed and some of those connected are complaining that the promised speeds are not being delivered. Unless mobile phone-based services are an option, those people have no way of moving to a different service.

Unless something changes the NBN will result in higher taxes, higher internet charges and poor service. Reminiscent of Telecom in the bad old days, it will display the typical characteristics of a government monopoly. Not being a private business, it lacks the imperative to pursue profit, offer good service at low prices, or limit borrowings by funding capital expenditure from cashflow. On the latter point, consider the fact that it gave top priority to rolling out its least profitable component, the satellite service. Only a government-owned business is that crazy.

There is no way of unscrambling the egg. However, a bad situation can be improved. Probably the best option is to restructure the NBN into three divisions, based on its technologies. This would result in three internet wholesalers – a fibre-to-the-node business, a hybrid fibre coax business, and a wireless/satellite business, competing with each other wherever their services are capable of overlapping. This would result in better service and lower prices, and give customers an option when one technology fails to deliver.

In due course, if not immediately, the divisions could be privatised so that taxpayers recovered some of their money.

If this left the bush at a disadvantage, it could be addressed through subsidies, which are at least transparent. The current approach amounts to seeking to achieve equity for the bush by screwing all Australians equally while keeping them blindfolded.

When Kevin Rudd offered us something for nothing, Australians believed him and jumped at the chance. Now we're all paying the price. The quicker we return to the real world of customers paying for what they get, and businesses competing for their custom, the better.

Aboriginals: Higher Education Support Legislation Amendment (2016 Measures No.1) Bill 2016[47]

The disadvantage suffered by Aboriginal Australians and the dysfunction in some of their communities continues to be Australia's greatest policy failure.

And yet, according to the latest figures from the Productivity Commission, this failure is not caused by a lack of funding.

Total expenditure in 2012–13 on services for Aboriginal and Torres Strait Islanders was more than $30 billion, or $43,449 per person. This is roughly equivalent to the average wage in Japan, Italy and South Korea. And this spending is on top of the general government spending that is supposed to benefit all Australians.

And yet the Annual Closing the Gap Report tells us every year that the gap is barely closing.

Nearly everyone agrees that education is the key – so this Bill authorising higher education grants to Aboriginal people should be an issue of the utmost importance.

And here I am, the only person who wants to talk about why our education policies are failing to address Aboriginal disadvantage.

Everyone else in this place considered this Bill to be non-controversial. That throwing even more money at the problem is somehow a solution, despite past experience.

If I can borrow an Americanism – go figure.

To understand Aboriginal disadvantage, it helps to understand Aboriginal communities.

According to the 2011 Census, 550,000 indigenous Australians – or 65% – were employed and living lives much like other Australians; 22% were welfare dependent and living in urban and regional areas; and 13%, or 70,000, were welfare dependent and living on Aboriginal land where education and work opportunities are often limited.

Many of these people in the third category are amongst the most disadvantaged in Australia and live in third-world conditions.

This third group needs a policy response that differs from that provided to the first and second groups of aborigines, and yet our indigenous education policy treats them as all the same.

Someone from a comfortable, middle-class family on the north shore of Sydney who identifies as Aboriginal will scoop up the grants and the scholarships, and fill in the quotas when it's time to get a job.

They will continue to be middle-class, and their lives will not change significantly, except for perhaps an ever-expanding sense of entitlement.

However the people living in remote areas who cannot read will not apply for university places or leave their dysfunctional communities, particularly given our policies to keep them there.

And that's why the gap is not closing.

Ironically, this demonstrates why schemes to help people should be based on need, and not race. If all university grants were based on need, they would better serve Aboriginal people who really need the grants.

What's more, it would help prevent a disgraceful situation where a refugee from Africa, who comes from the most impoverished background and suffers from racism, can be beaten to a university place by someone from a middle-class background who identifies as Aboriginal, but suffers only from sunburn.

I lived in South Africa for a time during the apartheid era, and I know what racism looks like. I abhor it in all its forms.

I am proud to represent the Liberal Democrats, who believe that all poor people should have access to a good education, but race should have nothing to do with it.

I am proud to take a stand against racism today.

Immigration tariff[48]

Most of the people attempting to come to Australia on fishing boats are economic refugees seeking a better life. Moreover, they are from families with the means to pay for passage. They are neither the poorest nor the most vulnerable from the societies they leave behind.

The Government's current approach to stopping them is expensive, vulnerable to developments in partner countries outside our control, and distracts the Navy from its primary purpose. Moreover, it lacks compassion and treats foreigners as something to be feared rather than as potential contributors to our society. There is a huge opportunity for mutual benefit for economic refugees and incumbent Australians.

The solution is to open the front door and allow them legal entry upon payment of a fee.

This idea originates from the recently deceased Nobel Prize laureate Professor Gary Becker, who recommended it as a solution to the problem of illegal immigration in America and the UK.

What he proposed is for the government to set a price according to how many people it wished to admit, then allow everyone who can pay that price to come in apart from obvious exceptions like terrorists.

In the Australian context the fee should be set at a level that makes it more attractive than paying a smuggler after taking into account the risk of drowning at sea, detention upon arrival and being deported. While an auction may be the best way to discover the right price, around $50,000 seems about right.

Becker argues that as well as being a revenue raiser for governments, the policy would ensure that only the most productive and skilled immigrants would be attracted. Having paid the fee, the immigrants would be committed to their adopted country and keen to make a go of it.

He also suggests the program would reduce opposition to immigration by eliminating the sense that immigrants were getting 'a free ride.' Fees would contribute to the cost of maintaining and renewing infrastructure that others had paid for. Indeed, at the current level of immigration, a fee of $50,000 would generate about $10–15 billion annually.

Fees could be reduced or waived for a number of bona fide refugees fleeing persecution, while those who support the entry of more refugees could raise funds to pay their entry fees. Under this approach, rather than lose your voice at a rally in support of refugees, you could put your money where your mouth is and solve the problem yourself.

Businesses that are looking for specialist skills could also cover entry fees to ensure the supply of highly-skilled workers.

However, the system would only work if payment of the fee entitled people to permanent residence, not welfare payments (unemployment, etc). Such payments should be reserved for citizens, with citizenship restricted to those who had established themselves over a number of years, share our values of freedom and democracy, and have demonstrated their desire to build a long-term future in Australia.

The system would ensure intending migrants were well aware of the need to gain employment on arrival. The most qualified and employable person in a family would be first to pay the fee and take up residence, working to save the funds for other family members. Over time, families would be reunited in Australia as they are now, except that each member would have made a valuable contribution to the economy.

Those unable to find work may have their permanent residence cancelled and be subject to deportation. Short-term assistance could be justified on the grounds that it was covered by the fee they paid.

Allowing immigration subject to payment of a fee would also provide a more moral basis for detaining and deporting illegal and unauthorised arrivals, should they still occur. For economic refugees, the obvious message is to stay home and save until you have the money to come legally.

This proposal would not disrupt our relationship with New Zealand, which allows Australians to live and work in New Zealand and vice versa. Indeed, there is a good case for establishing similar agreements with other countries that share our values, such as the UK, Canada and Japan.

It also need not disrupt working holiday agreements or temporary residency for skilled workers and tourists. The only people affected would be those who seek to live in Australia permanently.

It is time Australians recognised the significant contribution that immigrants make to our country and the prosperity that accompanies free trade and the free movement of people. It's time to open the front door.

Pay for refugees by cutting foreign aid[49]

Having won life's lottery, most Australians understand we have a responsibility to share some of the spoils.

When we share our luck with refugees, we profoundly improve the lives of people and their children for generations. It's an unambiguously great thing to do. I consider helping to negotiate an increase in our refugee intake from 13,750 this year to 18,750 in 2018/19 as one of my proudest achievements.

Now, by some measures, we lead the world in resettlement of refugees. But there are currently millions of refugees seeking asylum around the world, not just in the Middle East. There are plenty from our region – like Burma, Vietnam, Sri Lanka and China – who we could make into great Australians.

It's also well known that the religious minorities in the Middle East – Yazidis and Christians – face severe persecution.

There is a broad consensus in this place that our refugee intake should continue. The only question then is how many refugees we should take, and at what cost?

The problem is that taking refugees is expensive.

I am advised by the Immigration Department that the current refugee intake costs Australians about $1 billion a year, including language and training courses, social services and welfare.

The Australian Government does not have surplus money for charity. Just as a family that is deeply in debt should not be giving their money away, neither should a government.

What's more, there are storm-clouds on the economic horizon.

If the economy heads south, as it just might, an overly generous refugee intake could cause resentment.

It can be far too easy for middle-class parliamentarians, who can expect never to have a refugee as a neighbour, to be blissfully ignorant of the potential costs to social cohesion.

However, Australia has proven itself as a great absorber of people from many backgrounds over many decades. I believe it is possible both to double our refugee intake, and to pay for it.

We can achieve this by cutting foreign aid.

Foreign aid is accurately described as money taken from poor people in rich countries and given to rich people in poor countries. The money we spend on resettling refugees does far more good to people who need our help.

The American writer Bob Lupton described the problem with foreign aid in this way: 'When you give something the first time, there is gratitude; when you give something a second time, there is anticipation; the third time, there is expectation; the fourth time, there is entitlement; and the fifth time, there is dependency.'

That is where we stand with foreign aid – where something designed to do good, ultimately causes harm.

This might also explain why foreign aid has proven itself to be a poor diplomatic tool. At the height of tensions regarding the executions of Australian drug smugglers in Indonesia, mentions of our generosity to Indonesia were treated with contempt.

Doubling our refugee intake would cost around a billion dollars a year, while abolishing foreign aid would save around three and a half billion a year.

We are better able to look after people here than we are at making foreign aid effective overseas. So my proposal would do more good overall, while sparing the taxpayer.

Labor, the Greens and parts of the Coalition have called for more refugees, without calling for spending cuts to pay for this. This is not a responsible approach by adults.

I challenge all those proposing an increased refugee intake to accept that there is a trade-off between spending money on refugees and spending money on foreign aid. I challenge them to accept that refugee resettlement does more good than foreign aid. And I challenge them to commit to an increased refugee intake, even if it is funded by cutting foreign aid. If they cannot make such a commitment, then their effort to appear compassionate will be exposed as a fraud.

Citizenship[50]

Earlier this year, 'Reclaim Australia' and various counter-protests were in the news as people hurled abuse at each other and engaged in punch-ups. And since both sides had a fair sprinkling of the great unwashed, we all got to admire some unfamiliar tattoos and body piercings.

Much of the outrage by 'Reclaim Australia' concerned halal certification, about which my office has been bombarded with emails. Many are from people who do not appreciate the difference between voluntary and mandated certification schemes. Like kosher, halal certification is entirely voluntary. I would strongly object if the government got in on the act, but a voluntary scheme allows us all to choose what to buy ourselves.

But not all of Reclaim Australia's claims are so easily dismissed. There is a problem with child marriage among some Muslims, as there is with misogyny, homophobia, and support for terrorism. However, the protestors make a dreadful mistake in viewing all Muslims as a group, represented either by violent Islamists or the conservative 'community leaders' that governments and the media persist in treating as spokesmen.

As others have noted, people of Muslim faith have lived in Australia since the 1800s; they only make up 2% of our population; halal certification has no measurable impact on our daily lives; and people waving Israeli flags marching side-by-side with others brandishing swastika tattoos is 'cognitive dissonance' at its best.

And yet, Reclaim Australia's 'progressive' opponents are just as guilty of cognitive dissonance. Not only did they burn the Australian flag – which isn't illegal, but is rather unpersuasive – they engaged in more violence than those they were criticising for their, er, violence. They too sought to treat all Muslims as an amorphous mass – in this case, as uniformly benign and politically progressive.

As I see it, Australia doesn't need 'reclaiming.' While a bit of patriotism is fine, nationalism is little more than pride in an accident of birth. However, the concept of citizenship – particularly citizenship in a liberal democracy – does require reclaiming. Its value in Australia has been substantially diminished.

My party, the Liberal Democrats, has a policy of restricting citizenship to those who have established themselves in the community over at least ten years, who share our values of freedom and democracy, and who have demonstrated their desire to build a long-term future in Australia.

We would seek to confirm this with a citizenship test, not about historical trivia or tricky definitions, but liberal democratic values – values we share with lots of other liberal democracies. Our test would be outward-looking and our concept of citizenship cosmopolitan, exploring values such as women's rights (particularly suffrage), free speech, freedom to divorce, freedom of association, and freedom of religion – including the right to leave a religion or have no religion at all.

In our view, prospective citizens need to accumulate an employment history rather than a criminal one. While we have a somewhat relaxed approach to permanent residence, we would restrict welfare payments to citizens (apart from genuine refugees). Indeed, that's a conversation I hope to start via the Productivity Commission's inquiry into our policy of using tariffs, rather than quotas, to manage Australia's immigration intake. If we can decouple immigration from welfare, people are much more likely to appreciate its positive benefits.

Increasing the value of citizenship is not radical in the rest of the world. For example, Switzerland requires residency for ten years, support from the canton and local area, integration into the Swiss way of life, and compliance with the rule of law. The Swiss system makes it clear that citizenship is about values, not real estate.

To the extent that religious or cultural beliefs and practices conflict with basic liberal democratic values, then it is reasonable for Australia to demand that those cultural or religious practices be given up by those who seek to become citizens. If people are to integrate into a liberal democracy, they should at least share its core values.

Australia neither needs nor wants to import illiberal values, whether from Sharia or any other value system. Indeed, we are far too accepting of those who come to Australia with its respect for liberty, only to seek to transform it into something like the illiberal, authoritarian country they left behind.

Australian citizenship is precious, and should not be granted lightly.

PERSONAL LIBERTY

THE NANNY STATE

The true history of the nanny state[51]

I would like to clear up some confusion. First, I'm going to answer a question that has come my way a lot in recent times – 'what is the "nanny state"?'

Next, I'm going to outline the origin of the phrase.

At its core, the nanny state involves enacting laws and enforcing policies that interfere with or manage personal choices, when the only consideration is the individual's own good.

This is distinct from public health interventions that address public problems, such as product safety, sanitation, vaccines and water quality. These are not nanny state laws. They are not directed at making individuals live their lives according to a certain set of rules or to a certain standard.

A good example of nanny state intervention can be seen in the case of obesity. If you eat too much and get fat, that is your problem. It may be unwise, but it is not the government's business whether you eat too much and get fat. You are the one affected, and the costs you incur are private.

The distress and grief of those who choose to be around you is a consequence of that choice. It is a private matter between you and your loved ones.

And if governments make an unconditional and unsolicited commitment to pay your healthcare costs, that simply indicates that governments are reckless with the money of taxpayers.

This recklessness does not justify further incursions into our lives. Two wrongs do not make a right.

The Senate Economics References Committee Inquiry into Personal Choice and Community Impacts, of which I am chair, has adopted 'nanny state' as a short-hand phrase to describe its focus.

Last week, during the course of the first hearing, and then during an interview on Lateline, Mr Michael Moore – CEO of the Public Health Association of Australia – spent a great deal of time deliberately confusing nanny state issues with non-nanny state issues.

He was aided and abetted by the ABC's Emma Alberici, who kept asking me questions about guns. Firearms ownership is not a nanny state issue. If it were, it would have been included in the terms of reference for the inquiry. It is not a nanny state issue because the legal regime pertaining to the licensing of firearms owners has the aim of protecting others from harm.

Why does this matter?

I am a classical liberal, like John Stuart Mill. And it is John Stuart Mill's 'harm principle' that is at the core of the political philosophy I espouse.

That is, 'the only purpose for which power can be rightfully exercised over any member of a civilized community, against his will, is to prevent harm to others. Over himself, over his own body and mind, the individual is sovereign.'

During the first hearing, Senator Dastyari pointed out that it was in Australia's interest for people to be honest about their ideologies. Senator Dastyari is correct. The unwillingness of politicians – and many others – to admit to having an ideology allows confusion to arise.

You will never be in any doubt about my ideology.

Mr Moore is hot on the idea of 'stewardship,' developed by the UK's Nuffield Council on Bioethics in a lengthy policy paper called Public Health: Ethical Issues.

'Stewardship,' I'm given to understand, means that 'the state has a duty to enable people to lead healthy lives.' It emphasises reducing what the Council calls 'unfair health inequalities.'

While I do not agree with the notion of stewardship, the arguments advanced in the Council's paper are nuanced. They take John Stuart Mill's 'harm principle' seriously and treat those who oppose coercive public health intrusions with respect.

That said, public health advocates conflate the sort of regulation needed to protect children, with regulation intended to protect adults from harming themselves through personal choices.

The Nanny State Inquiry is not about children, and attempts to make it so are a strawman. No-one disputes that children must be treated differently from adults. While I absolutely prefer decisions about children to be left to parents, without state interference, there are circumstances – like child abuse – where the state must become involved.

Public health advocates also purport to speak on behalf of the poor, less educated and less sophisticated. This looks superficially compassionate, but it is not. It is arrogant and elitist, and assumes moral and intellectual superiority.

Its effect is to hector people about unhealthy lifestyle choices, controlling their purchases, and punishing those who maintain 'impure' behaviours. Regressive taxes on cigarettes and alcohol, for example.

In the Public Health Association's submission – and on Lateline – Mr Moore also made claims about the origin of the phrase 'nanny state.'

He said it was coined in 1965 by the Conservative British Health Minister, Iain MacLeod, writing under the name of Quoodle, who in 1954 famously smoked through a press conference on the dangers of smoking, and who died of heart attack at age 57.

There's only one problem with this story. It isn't true.

In fact, use of the word 'nanny' to describe state interference in individual choices is at least 13 years older and came from the left.

In 1952, American journalist Dorothy Thompson (and one time wife of Sinclair Lewis, the Nobel Prize-winning socialist writer) used 'nanny state' to describe British imperialism in the Middle East. 'Western empires,' Thompson wrote in her syndicated column, 'have filled the role of headmaster, or Nanny-governess. The West does not treat the inhabitants of its colonies as equals.'

She continued, and I quote:

> It is an amusing notion that comes to me that, with the retreat of empire, Britons are turning Britain itself into a nanny state, perhaps out of a long habit in persuading or coercing natives to do what is good for them.

In a 1960 article in the New Statesman, the magazine established by the Fabian Society, 'nanny' was used to attack the British Board of Film Censors. 'Novels and the Press get along, not too calamitously, without this Nanny; why shouldn't films?' asked columnist William Whitebait. 'Nanny exercises a crippling drag on the growth of a serious and healthy British cinema.'

Any attempt to discredit the nanny state term by linking it to Iain MacLeod will fail. He was a smoke-like-a-chimney-health Minister who voted for the legalisation of abortion and homosexuality; supported the immigration of all races into Britain, and advocated decolonisation. He also had a serious war wound and ankylosing spondylitis, such that it is unlikely smoking killed him at 57. It is also likely he was a classical liberal. Mr Moore thinks that the phrase 'nanny state' was coined by a fool. Iain MacLeod didn't coin it, but he was certainly no fool when he used it.

In fact, his opposition to illiberal laws and racism was drawn from the same anti-paternalism that drives modern resistance to public health regulation. MacLeod believed that a powerful class should not impose its own values on the rest of society. Colonial masters told their subjects how to live their lives – lessons given force by military domination.

Every time people in love with their own expertise – including many public health advocates – seek to regulate what people buy or how they spend their time or what they put in their mouths, they forget the people who shop and the people who vote are the same people.

If we can trust people to vote – a difficult and demanding choice with profound consequences – we can trust people to know what to eat, to drink, to buy, what video games to play, and whether or not to smoke.

Voodoo economics and the nanny state[52]

The Senate Nanny State Inquiry has not only revealed that everyone has a pet grievance when it comes to laws regulating behaviour for our own good, but that public health is the home of voodoo economics.

This takes two forms. First, it argues that those who harm themselves as a result of poor choices cause the rest of us to pay more through the healthcare system. Second, it calculates the cost of poor choices in a manner far removed from legitimate economics.

Studies asserting that smoking and drinking impose multibillion-dollar costs on society, for example, well in excess of the revenue they bring to the Treasury, are a good example. The Public Health lobby generates these lopsided figures by counting lost productivity and early mortality as costs to the taxpayer. In reality the costs are private, incurred by the drinker or smoker and sometimes his employer.

But Public Health's rubbery numbers don't stop there. They also include the emotional costs of being offended by a drunk, money spent on alcohol or cigarettes (counted as a cost to the family), and even pain and suffering from hangovers.

While this is sometimes amusing, in economic terms it is ridiculous. If we count a drinker's spending on alcohol as a cost to the family – and by extension to the taxpayer – what of a non-drinker's spending on golf clubs? Or a sports car or boat?

All of these alleged costs are bundled into a category called 'social costs,' then attributed to the taxpayer to justify increases in excise along with coercive laws directed at drinkers, smokers, and many others.

Even if the 'social cost' claims were true, they are a consequence of a health care policy that socialises health care costs. The problem here is that once we start telling people how to live based on their potential to increase health costs to others, the slope gets slippery pretty quickly. Do we want to make it a crime to eat potato chips, fail to exercise or wear high heels?

With a more intelligent approach to healthcare, this argument would not even be raised. For this we could do worse than emulate Singapore, which has the lowest-cost health system among developed countries and yet ranks highly on all health indicators.

Singapore's health spending was US$2,426 per capita in 2014, equivalent to 4.5% of GDP. The global average is 9%. Among OECD countries, health spending ranges from 7% of GDP in Israel to 17.2% (US$ 8,895 per capita) in the United States. Australia is close to the global average, at 9.1% (US$6,140 per capita).

A key principle of Singapore's healthcare is that no medical service is provided free of charge, regardless of the level of subsidy, even within the public system. This reduces over-utilisation of healthcare services, a common problem in fully subsidised universal health insurance systems.

Under Singapore's Medisave program, each employee contributes 8–10.5% of monthly salary (depending on age) to an individual medical savings account, with a matching employer contribution. A personal Medisave account may be used to pay for hospital expenses and expensive outpatient treatments such as chemotherapy, renal dialysis and HIV drugs, incurred by the account holder and immediate family members.

This logic should be familiar to Australians – it's how our superannuation system works. Adopting the Singaporean system would not reinvent the wheel.

To protect against the risk of catastrophic illness which could wipe out their medical savings, Medisave account holders under 80 years of age may use their funds to buy MediShield insurance. This covers hospital expenses and selected higher-cost outpatient treatments. Other primary care costs (e.g. consultations and tests) are typically covered by top-up private insurance, which is very competitive.

The third pillar of Singapore's innovative system is Medifund, which provides means-tested health care for the poor (roughly 10% of the population). The Government established the fund in 1993 and makes additional contributions during years of overall budget surplus. Medifund ensures that no Singaporean is denied good basic care because of inability to pay.

The difference is that Singapore's health care system gives maximum responsibility and choice to patients, who are mostly spending their own money rather than that of other people. However, it also makes sure nobody faces catastrophic medical bills, and that the poor have enough money to buy medical care.

Voodoo economics have no place in public policy. With sensible policies, personal choice and individual responsibility can co-exist, without the Nanny State barging in and telling us all how to live.

Uber and the nanny state[53]

The nanny state is alive and well and it's not just locking you out of your favourite late-night watering hole. It's also stifling new business models.

As a legislator, my most important task when approaching any area of public policy is to ask myself, 'what is the proper role of Government?'

When it comes to the sharing economy – a new and different form of opportunity and wealth creation – the simple answer is 'nothing.' Government should get out of the way.

Both sides of politics are generating a lot of hot air about their 'struggle' to understand the right policy settings for the sharing economy. These debates demonstrate a lack of understanding at the political level about how to encourage job growth and wealth creation.

While technology is driving much of the sharing economy, its new markets and business models would not be so popular if existing services were not so wound up in red tape.

Consumers are clamouring for new services like Uber, Lyft, and Airbnb because the state has stuck its beak into traditional transport and accommodation services, trying to right wrongs that don't exist, distorting market forces and delivering mediocre outcomes that consumers do not find acceptable.

We are punishing people who seek to invest and create jobs because politicians think they can somehow make markets work better.

The latest example of this overreach is the decision by the Australian Taxation Office to treat Uber drivers differently from other contractors or small business operators.

In Australia, if you run a small business and don't bring in $75,000 per year in revenue, you don't have to register for GST even when you are not paid directly by the customer. Making microbusinesses pay GST would run counter to a basic principle of tax administration – it generates little revenue compared to the costs imposed on the microbusinesses and the ATO.

However, the ATO has decided that this sensible arrangement should not be allowed to stand in the case of Uber drivers. Uber has had the gall to provide 15,000 Australians with an opportunity to earn an income when it suits them.

Rather than recognising a new, different model requiring fresh ways of thinking, the ATO – in the words of the Deputy Commissioner James O'Halloran – decided to 'level the playing field.' It has told Uber that its drivers must pay GST from the first dollar they earn.

The ATO is motivated by a desire to help taxi drivers in those States and Territories where regulations ramp up the cost of taxi trips, and because taxi operators pay GST from their first dollar. The ATO considers Uber to be equivalent to a 'taxi travel' provider, and not like truck drivers, bike couriers, food delivery drivers and Airbnb hosts, who don't have to collect GST until they reach $75,000 per year in turnover, and who are often paid in exactly the same way as Uber drivers.

For some reason, Uber drivers are different.

And yet, unlike a taxi, it's not possible to hail an Uber, and there is no 'grey economy' danger, something that has long troubled the taxi industry. Nobody can pay an Uber driver in cash.

For those who think treating taxi drivers and Uber drivers differently amounts to inequality of treatment, the solution is not to treat Uber drivers differently from other microbusinesses, but to ask whether taxi drivers are being treated unfairly. The underlying problem is the government's addiction to taxes and regulation.

Uber has stood its ground and is pursuing the matter through the courts, but this raises a serious issue. Not everyone is Uber, the world's most highly capitalised start-up. Uber has the funds to take the fight to the roadblocks and regulators when they get in the way.

If Uber – with its global presence and investor backing – has to fight tooth and nail to survive against a backdrop of regulatory interference, what chance do home-grown entrepreneurs have? Allowing public sector agencies and regulators to stifle the growth of new business models will kill any chance Australia has of lifting itself out of its current economic malaise.

It's time for government to get its hands off Australian innovation, and encourage disruption, not punish and deter. Until that happens, our economy and country are set for decades of slow growth that none of us can afford.

Bicycle helmets[54]

During the Nanny State Inquiry during the last parliament, which I chaired, mandatory bicycle helmet laws were nominated by many submitters as a primary example of nanny state paternalism.

They argued that individuals should be free to manage the risks involved in a bike ride, and that the ability of the individual to do so is constrained because their assessment of such risk is overridden by the state.

They questioned why Australia can't trust its citizens to assess their circumstances and make that choice for themselves.

They said things like, if we need the law to protect us from ourselves, then what does that say about ourselves? The helmet law is an insult to our civil liberty.

It was argued that the state can only justify interference in the conduct of individual citizens when it is clear that doing so will prevent a greater harm to others.

It was argued that helmet laws don't meet this test because an individual's head poses no plausible threat to the safety and well-being of others.

Indeed, it was suggested that helmet laws are a textbook example of where the State overreaches itself in imposing norms of behaviour where the matter should be left to the individual.

Other related arguments included the view that the individual and societal benefits of cycling (and cycling more frequently) outweigh the risks of not wearing a helmet and, therefore, the health and social costs. In this regard, the view was put that mandatory helmet laws have had a negative impact on cycling participation rates in Australia as they deter people from cycling.

It was suggested that mandatory helmets were responsible for the low participation rates in Australia's two public bike share schemes, which have the lowest usage rates in the world.

It was argued that helmet laws involve unnecessary use of law enforcement resources, and misuse of police power. One witness described being arrested and strip searched for failing to pay fines arising from not wearing a helmet.

Even claims that helmet laws have achieved any meaningful reduction in the rate of brain or head injury were questioned.

Australia was the first country to enact mandatory helmet laws, which became nationwide in 1992. New Zealand and the United Arab Emirates followed, and a number of countries enforce a helmet requirement for children, but that's it. The rest of the world has not adopted Australia's approach.

The requirement for use of helmets is included in the Australian Road Rules, a national model legislation which is adopted by the individual states and territories.

However, a number of submitters noted that the states and territories introduced mandatory helmet laws in order to comply with a Commonwealth ten-point road safety program which included bicycle helmets, and thereby secure Commonwealth funding under the black spot road program. That is, they were either bribed or blackmailed.

There have been reviews of mandatory helmet laws.

In November 2013, the Queensland Parliament Transport, Housing and Local Government Committee recommended a 24-month trial which exempts cyclists aged 16 years and over from helmet laws when riding in parks, on footpaths and shared cycle paths and on roads with a speed limit of 60 km/hr or less.

The Queensland Government did not support the recommendation, insisting that the 'weight of evidence confirms the importance of wearing a bicycle helmet while riding.'

In 2010, the NSW Parliament's Joint Standing Committee on Road Safety noted that the majority of submissions and bulk of evidence received by it support the current mandatory use of helmets for bicycle riders.

This weight and bulk of evidence, so convincing to the Queensland government and NSW Road Safety Committee, but unconvincing to the rest of the world, was equally unconvincing during the inquiry.

As I said, whether helmets actually reduce injuries is contested. Some witnesses suggested they merely change the nature of the injuries sustained.

The point was made that if helmet legislation had been effective in preventing head injuries, there would be a fall in head injury incidents but no other injuries. Yet, the committee was informed that a 1996 study in NSW and Victoria found that the decline in cycling was at least as substantial as the decline in head injuries.

One witness put to the committee that a person cycling two hours per week for 50 years would cycle for a total of 5,200 hours and, over that time, only have a 1% risk of hospital admission for serious head injury.

And yet, it was suggested that even if one traumatic brain injury was avoided, it's worth it. A reduction of civil liberty was said to be preferable to the long-term effect of a head and brain injury on a victim's family, carers and society.

This is the nub of the issue.

Such an assertion is based on an assumption of socialised medicine. In other words, the cost of health care is socialised, via Medicare and other taxpayer funding.

This is a slippery slope. If we are to minimise the burden of health care on each other, then all of us must ensure we avoid risks, and insist others do the same. Every glass of wine, every cigar, every potato chip, every piece of chocolate is potentially increasing the cost of the health system to our fellow Australians. Where does it end?

A better option is to consider health as a private matter, and not the business of the government. This merely requires each of us to have health insurance, with public funding limited to paying for insurance for the genuinely poor.

In the end, the committee recommended a review of the mandatory helmet laws. I would go much further than that.

I believe a cost benefit study would show the impact of helmet laws to be negative, given the low prevalence of cyclist head injury (notwithstanding the seriousness of individual TBI cases) and the negative effects of the policy.

I also maintain, in the absence of compelling evidence demonstrating a substantial social benefit, that there should be a bias in favour of individual choice and responsibility. It is especially not the role of government to protect individuals against the consequences of their own choices when the risks are small, foreseeable and borne personally.

I would remove the obligation from all cyclists to wear helmets, while making clear to parents that their responsibility to their children should include serious consideration of wearing one.

Lockouts[55]

We should all be disgusted about what is happening in Kings Cross these days. I'm not talking about drunken louts. Being shocked by people behaving badly in Kings Cross is like being shocked at Range Rovers in Mosman or sheep near Boorowa.

What I find disgusting is the empty streets and closure of iconic nightspots like Hugo's in Kings Cross and the Exchange Hotel in Darlinghurst.

For more than a century, this area has been Australia's red light district – traditionally the place where both Sydneysiders and visiting sailors could make rash decisions. It is not – and never has been – a place to take your kids on a Saturday night.

Moreover, the fact that this place exists means that people intent on letting off steam will not encounter your kids. Countless thousands of people have visited Kings Cross over the years without harming anybody else, or inflicting anything on themselves more serious than an empty wallet and a hangover. Every major city around the world has a naughty area which acts like safety valve.

Kings Cross has also attracted plenty of rogues, but this has meant that our police know exactly where to find them. By putting the naughtiness in one spot, we are better able to manage it.

The lockout laws, which require pubs to refuse to admit new customers from 1.30 am, and come with a raft of other rules aimed at preventing anyone from having fun, are public policy gone mad.

Already a third of the licensed venues in the area have closed and the rest are hanging on by a thread, hoping that someone in the NSW Government will see sense. And it's not just the pubs, nightclubs and dens of iniquity that are suffering. Restaurants, corner stores and newsagents are also shutting their doors.

Imposing lockout laws on King's Cross is like banning trucks from Port Kembla. And if you think there is something better about conventional jobs compared to jobs in the Cross, you should take a closer look at the office workers' faces in Martin Place on a Monday morning.

In the meantime, some of the politicians who want to tell you how to live can barely manage their own lives. Many had their rites of passage at the Cross but now want to deny others the same opportunity. Others just seem worried that somebody might be having a good time.

Far more disgusting than what goes on at Kings Cross is people being thrown out of work by nanny-statists and politicians seeking to impose their hypocritical standards on us all. But there is something even bigger at stake than that: if the lockout laws effectively close down the Cross, there will be nowhere in Sydney, and perhaps not in Australia, where it's OK to be naughty. Part of the fabric of our city will be lost, and the fun police will have finally won the day.

Enhancing Online Safety for Children Bill 2014[56]

I rise to oppose passage of the Enhancing Online Safety for Children Bill 2014.

I do so because this bill, like so much of the legislation supported by the major parties in this place, mistakes the State for Civil society.

In this instance, the mistake is borne of a desire to 'protect the children,' a cry that is too often turned into an excuse to restrict everyone's liberties.

The Bill implements a commitment to deal with electronic posts that bully an Australian child. It creates a new bureaucracy costing $11 million per year, introduces civil penalties of up to $17,000 for social media sites that don't promptly remove material as directed, and facilitates injunctions on bullies. The injunctions will mandate a requirement to apologise.

The $11 million I mentioned will pay for the establishment of a Children's e-Safety Commissioner as an independent statutory office within the Australian Communications and Media Authority. He or she will administer a complaints system for cyber-bullying material targeted at an Australian child. He will have the power to issue a notice to a large social media service requiring it to remove 'cyber-bullying material' as defined in the Bill.

He has other functions, too – he will promote online safety for children, have power to evaluate and accredit educational programmes, make grants, and advise the Minister for Communications.

Very simply, the Bill is unnecessary.

Under Commonwealth criminal law, penalties of up to $30,600 can already be imposed for posting menacing, harassing or offensive material on a carriage service. There have been 308 successful prosecutions under this law since 2005.

Existing laws simply need to be enforced more expeditiously.

The proposed anti-bullying law could prompt the likes of Facebook and Twitter to remove posts indiscriminately, as soon as there is a complaint, to ensure that they avoid the new penalties. That may have a serious impact on legitimate social media commentary.

The alternative involves waiting to see if the regulator gives a direction to remove the post and then removing it within 48 hours of the direction.

It's worth mentioning that, if a direction comes at 4pm on a Friday, the post must be removed by 4pm on a Sunday. How smart is that?

The Bill defines bullying material as 'material sent via email, messaging, chat functions or social media that is intended to have an effect on an Australian child and that would be likely to seriously threaten, intimidate, harass or humiliate the child.' This covers a private conversation between a group of friends about another child.

The Bill facilitates injunctions requiring bullies to apologise to the bullied. It strikes me as reasonably obvious that the Government should not force apologies. Mandated apologies are insincere.

Moreover, one only has to watch the parade of public figures who – forced by a variety of organisations, both public and private, to apologise – engage in backside-covering 'not pologies' that do nothing to assuage the victim's hurt feelings and serve only to make everyone involved look like complete twits.

The Bill also authorises the regulator to divulge information to principals, teachers, parents, Ministers, public servants, and police. The potential for retaliatory bullying, also known as authoritarian intervention, is enormous.

I am not fond of QANGOS and Agencies. I generally support throwing the lot on a bonfire, partly because they cost the taxpayer money, and partly because they are borne of a belief that we need experts to tell us how to live.

However, occasionally they are worthwhile. The Office of the Australian Information Commissioner – which helps ensure transparent government and access to Freedom of Information – is a worthwhile Agency.

This proposed e-Safety Commissioner is not.

Significantly, the OAIC and the e-Safety Commissioner cost the same amount of money. Yet the government wants to scrap the former and give us a statutory net-nanny, in some sort of perverse, irrational exchange.

First, learn to govern. Then you may earn the right to tell people how to raise their children.

Restoring Territory Rights (Assisted Suicide Legislation) Bill 2015[57]

Mr President, I rise to support passage of the Restoring Territory Rights (Assisted Suicide Legislation) Bill 2015, a private senator's bill I introduced late last year.

In 1997, Kevin Andrews succeeded in pushing a private member's bill through Federal Parliament. It overturned the first legislation permitting assisted suicide in Australia, enacted in the Northern Territory.

Since then, not only does assisting someone to commit suicide remain a serious crime in all States, it is also a crime in the Territories. Three states have life imprisonment as the maximum penalty, while in others the maximum penalty varies from 5 to 25 years.

This is extraordinarily cruel. The denial of the right to die at a time of our choosing can result in a lingering, painful death. It is also at odds with the fact that we have both a fundamental and legal right to choose whether we wish to continue living.

It's important to state this clearly, because people often forget suicide was once illegal, and failed attempts frequently led to prosecution.

In Medieval England, suicides were denied a Christian burial. Instead, they were carried to a crossroads in the dead of night and dumped in a pit, a wooden stake hammered through the body to pin it in place. There were no clergy or mourners, and no prayers were offered.

But punishment did not end with death. The deceased's family was stripped of their belongings, which were handed to the Crown.

This remained the case until 1822. Michael MacDonald and Terence Murphy, in Sleepless souls: Suicide in Early Modern England, wrote 'The suicide of an adult male could reduce his survivors to pauperism.'

This did not change because of a significant campaign for a change in suicide legislation. Instead, there was a gradual realisation that the laws of the day were at odds with society's view, and that care, not prosecution, was needed.

Dr David Wright, co-author of the book *Histories of Suicide: International Perspectives on Self-Destruction in the Modern World*, says that 'from the middle of the eighteenth Century to the mid-twentieth Century there was growing tolerance and a softening of public attitudes towards suicide, which was a reflection of, among other things, the secularisation of society and the emergence of the medical profession.'

This freedom is now mostly well accepted. While suicide is often an occasion for sadness, there is also a recognition that people do not belong to their families or to the government.

An individual may have good reasons to take his or her own life. But even if they don't, it is still their own decision to make.

But there is a catch. The law says we are only permitted to die by our own hand, without assistance. Indeed, in Victoria, NSW, SA and the ACT, reasonable force can still be used to stop a person from committing suicide. And if we are too weak or incapacitated to end our lives ourselves, we are condemned to suffer until nature takes its course. It is a serious offence for anyone to either help us die, at our instruction, or even to tell us how to do it for ourselves.

One of the consequences of this is that it can compel people to end their lives sooner than they would like. Understandably, people prefer to avoid the risk that they will become incapable of committing suicide themselves, doomed to live out the remainder of their lives in pain and helplessness.

Most fair-minded people accept that painlessly ending animal suffering is an act of compassion. As a veterinarian, I have often had the decision to put an animal to sleep, because animals are not people and cannot give consent. However, for us humans, even when we give consent and beg for help, the law prohibits the same compassion.

There is no better marker of individual freedom than the ability to decide what to do with our own body.

If the law prevents us from making free choices about it, then we are not really free at all; our bodies are not our own, but under the control of someone else who tells us what we cannot do with it. In reality, this is the State.

And yet, bodily autonomy is well-recognised in other areas – nothing prevents us from getting tattoos, dying our hair purple, or sporting multiple studs and pierces. We are just not allowed the ultimate autonomy.

Legalisation of assisted suicide is long overdue in Australia. Opinion polls show more than 80% of Australians are in favour, across all political parties. It is high time governments accepted that on this deeply personal matter, their intrusion is not warranted.

Now, I turn to the inevitable objections.

Despite what some people think, this is not about bumping off granny to inherit the house. Assisted suicide is simply helping someone to do something that they would do for themselves, if they were not so ill or feeble.

The absolutely essential element is genuine, active consent. This is emphatically not merely implied consent or acquiescence. Ending someone's life when they haven't given consent is murder. Nobody wants that.

Moreover, this is not about living wills or withdrawing medical assistance. Those are different issues.

Equally, those contemplating suicide should be made aware of the availability of palliative care to make their last days less agonising, and have treatment options in the case of mental illness. Indeed, the decision to die, with or without assistance, should be rational and well informed in all cases, including an awareness of the attitudes of loved ones left behind.

And of course, consent must be verified. I don't believe medical practitioners are any better qualified than anyone else to confirm this, but obviously the decision must be genuine. It is essential to ensure the choice is made without coercion or pressure.

In the short term at least, the easiest approach to facilitate the path to legalising assisted suicide would be repeal of the Euthanasia Laws Act 1997 – the 'Andrews Bill' I referred to earlier. It removed the power of each of the Territories to legalise assisted suicide, with a specific focus on repeal of the Northern Territory's *Rights of the Terminally Ill Act 1995*.

While it is too late to simply reinstate the Northern Territory act, repeal of the Andrews Bill would send a signal to states and territories that their legislatures may now turn their attention to this issue. As a bonus, it would support federalism in law making. For too long, the Commonwealth has waded into areas that are properly the business of the states.

Allowing the states and territories control over their own affairs – which is the point of federalism – also allows innovation in law-making. During hearings for the Senate Nanny State Inquiry – of which I am chair – I learnt that the Northern Territory does not require cyclists to wear bicycle helmets on cycle paths or footpaths.

As a result, the Northern Territory has high cycling participation rates. And despite having the worst road accident injury rate in Australia, when it comes to cyclists, the Northern Territory's serious injury rate is the same as the national average and better than several states where helmet use remains mandatory.

In other words, small jurisdictions can be innovative, and this should be recognised by the Commonwealth. Indeed, I suspect – in response to passage of this Bill – that the Territories will come up with better assisted suicide legislation than the Northern Territory's original Rights of the Terminally Ill Act 1995.

Whatever we might think of the decisions others make about their lives, it is their decision, not ours. The law should respect their right to make their own choices. Whether as legislators or private citizens, our approval is neither necessary nor relevant.

And the permission of the government should not be required, just as it is no longer required with respect to suicide.

Passage of my Bill will set the Territories free.

I commend it to the Senate.

Thank you for smoking[58]

I'd like to address my comments to the roughly 18% of the Australian population that engages in a despised activity.

Ladies and gentlemen, thank you for smoking.

Australian smokers contribute significantly to the pile of money that – as I noted in this place recently – other people then spend.

As you well know there are many such big spenders in this parliament, as are many of the people who malign you.

They don't like your habit, but in my view they have an even filthier habit: spending your money – and other people's money – on things that are often even sillier than spending too much on cigarettes and booze.

Your generosity to the nation's treasury is truly staggering. The government collects around $8 billion in tobacco excise each year. That's a lot of cash.

Last year, smokers imposed $318.4 million in net costs on Australia's healthcare system. Depending on rainfall, smokers also cost the taxpayer about $150 million a year in bushfire control.

If you do even basic arithmetic, these figures disclose that you wonderful, generous smokers pay 17 times as much as you cost.

Of course, I'm aware that the justification for making you pay so much for your smoking is borne of a desire to help you quit and to improve your health. However, every now and again the mask slips.

Tony Abbott – in one of those 'unguarded moments' while in Opposition – made the following comment in relation to the then Government's tax hikes:

> It would only be raising $5 billion or so if people are to continue to smoke, so let's not listen to this palaver about health. This is all about revenue, it's all about tax, it's all about a government that can't control its spending – that's why it hits you in the hip pocket.

Those who would tell us how to live, back this flagrant theft, not because they're prone to agree with Tony Abbott, but because they are troubled by the worrying thought that someone, somewhere, may be having a good time.

Those havers of good times, smokers of Australia, are you.

This is why, having banished cigarette advertising from everything from television to cinema to motorsport and even the internet, and ended the commercial cultivation of tobacco in Australia, the health mandarins have moved on to banning smoking in prisons and insane asylums.

That's right, people in cages who have lost most or all of their rights are denied even this small thing. Yes, prison is meant to be punishment. But the widespread tendency to see prisons as comfortable budget hotels bespeaks a fundamental failure to grasp just what jail means. Rehabilitation means not committing further crime, not being trained to live according to somebody else's values.

The same people worry and worry about Aboriginal and Torres Strait Islander smoking rates, with about half of Australia's indigenous population being daily smokers. Aborigines on income management, like prisoners, are also denied this small consolation. Racial paternalism lives on.

Because the revenues versus costs figure is so lopsided, those who would tell you how to live have tried to add 'social costs' to the healthcare costs I discussed earlier. 'Social costs' take in things like smokers' spending on tobacco, and the lost productivity represented by smokers' earlier mortality. These, allegedly, represent income forgone.

By that logic, deciding to work part time to increase your leisure time is a social cost, as is going on holiday.

Arguments like that suggest to me the anti-smoking lobby is running out of ideas.

But when powerful, well-funded lobby groups run out of ideas and arguments, unfortunately they don't fold up their lobbying tents and head home. They keep lobbying, and we've now reached the point where, thanks to their efforts, the government is about to kill the goose that lays the golden egg, handing all the lovely tax money it extorts from you over to organised crime.

Australia is set to have the most expensive ciggies in the world once Abbott's extraordinary 12.5% a year tobacco tax hikes – taken over from Labor – kick in. Already, in 2012, the WHO found that a pack of cigarettes cost US$14.35 in Australia. Only Norway had higher prices, at US$14.49.

Following the unprecedented 25% tobacco excise increase in April 2010, Treasury's post implementation review observed that:

> The availability of illicit tobacco products (products on which taxes have been avoided) undermines the effectiveness of taxation in many countries in reducing affordability to prevent uptake and promote quitting, particularly among low-income groups.

This should come as no surprise. Here's a little basic maths: if you spend $5,000 a year on tobacco, it's a bigger proportion of your income if you earn $30,000 per annum than if you earn $100,000 per annum. In the trade, that's what's known as a 'regressive tax.'

And if – along with South Park's Mr Mackey – we can agree that 'drugs are bad, mmmkay,' it's probably also fair to say that 'regressive taxes are bad, mmmkay.'

Calling regressive taxes 'sin taxes' doesn't hide the scale of the problem. Smokers are typically poor, which makes this vast tax take all the more perverse. It means, for example, that social planners who want to redistribute money from the rich to the poor need to increase both welfare payments and income tax rates to achieve their goals.

When the 25% excise increase was imposed, the Australian Customs and Border Protection Service noticed an increase in seizures of illicit tobacco. In 2013, it rose to 183 tonnes, representing forgone customs duties of $150 million. Remember, that's the annual cost of putting out bushfires due to cigarettes. And it's also entirely to be expected: tobacco can't even be commercially grown in Australia.

Smokers of Australia, despite your generosity, I need to apologise on behalf of the short-sighted pickers of your pockets in this place. Maybe they haven't studied any history, because if they did, they would learn that the regime controlling cigarettes is no longer one of 'legalise, regulate, and tax.'

Instead, it now resembles two other regimes, regimes that were and are catastrophic failures. I'm thinking here of Prohibition and the War on Drugs.

In a world where cannabis is in the process of legalisation – because illegality simply doesn't work – and where Prohibition enriched Al Capone but beggared the US government, I think people like me need to do better by you, the smokers of Australia.

I am put in mind of a constituent's comment, made to me last week. He pointed out that he valued the e-cigarettes now available because they meant he didn't smoke during the day, and also meant he didn't inflict his smoke or smell on others.

However, he said he was still going to sit on his balcony of an evening, drink a glass of wine, and smoke a cigarette.

He was going to continue to do this because he enjoys smoking.

And that, Mr President, is his choice.

Cigarette plain packaging[59]

For every problem the government tries to solve, it often creates at least one more with no guarantee of fixing the initial problem. That appears to be the case with the former government's laws mandating the plain packaging of tobacco.

In April 2010 when Kevin Rudd first announced the plan, there was some scepticism as to whether it would work. Then Opposition Leader Tony Abbott said: 'Now, the Coalition in principle supports all reasonable measures to get smoking rates down. My anxiety with this is that it might end up being counter-productive in practice.'

Coalition deputy Warren Truss said his 'chief criticism is that for all the cost and the inconvenience it will not deliver any result,' concluding that 'Australia's bulldust barometers are well tuned, and they have been red hot on this government for a while.'

Particularly alarming was the absence of any evidence to support the proposition. Then shadow Attorney-General, George Brandis, in a debate with Penny Wong on ABC radio, put it best when he said: 'And what Penny is pleased to describe as evidence is not evidence at all. It's a supposition. It may or may not be right. But it's not an evidence-based supposition.'

This scepticism appears to have been well founded. After nearly 18 months of operation, plain packaging is not having the effect its advocates intended. Last month, Fairfax newspapers reported official industry data showing that 'deliveries of tobacco to retailers in Australia rose slightly last year for the first time in at least five years, even after the introduction of plain packaging aimed at deterring smokers.' The news piece also reported that 'in 2013, the first full year of plain packaging, tobacco companies sold the equivalent of 21.074 billion cigarettes in Australia … that marks a 0.3% cent increase from 2012.'

But while it failed to reduce smoking rates, plain packaging has led Australia into a legal minefield. Major trading partner Indonesia, along with Ukraine, Cuba, Dominican Republic and Honduras have taken action through the World Trade Organisation to challenge Australia's plain packaging legislation, with a further 35 countries possibly joining the dispute as third parties. They argue it creates an unnecessary barrier to trade in violation of our treaty obligations.

In a second case, Philip Morris Asia is suing the Australian Government under the terms of the Australia – Hong Kong Bilateral Investment Treaty, which provides protections for international investments in Australia including in intellectual property.

These two international cases, which will be decided in the next two to three years, could prove financially disastrous. An adverse result could find Australian taxpayers on the receiving end of a compensation claim worth billions of dollars. Former Fairfax business commentator, Tim Colebatch, said the WTO case 'is shaping up to become the biggest trade dispute Australia has ever faced as a defendant.'

There is another issue too. A recent KPMG study found that since the introduction of plain packaging, the black market in illicit tobacco in Australia has boomed, growing by 19% in 2013, and is now costing the government up to $1.1 billion in forgone annual tax revenue. The report also shows a 35% growth in illicit tobacco consumption since the 25% excise increase in April 2010. Australia already has the highest cigarette prices in the region, a whopping 75% higher than Singapore, so it's not hard to imagine what the forthcoming series of four annual 12.5% excise increases will do to the illicit market.

On 24 October 2013 the Australian Federal Police, Customs, Victoria Police and the Australian Crime Commission announced the arrest of ten people for alleged illegal tobacco importation with around 71 tonnes and 80 million cigarette sticks seized and an estimated total defrauded taxation revenue of more than $67 million. And just two months ago, Victorian Police announced the second major bust in less than six months of crime gangs involved in illegal tobacco operations including the seizure of 35,000 tobacco plants.

For the government, the proliferation of illegal tobacco in the community is a very significant concern. It is not only lost taxation revenue, but a totally unregulated market with no rules or laws about who it sells to, including minors.

The prospect that plain packaging will put further strain on a budget already in the red, whilst fostering a new black market, should be a salutary lesson that governments can't fix every problem. It is also a reminder that governments that inherit bad policy should have the courage to stick to their original convictions and review legislation that clearly isn't working.

Smoking and prisons[60]

Many people won't have much sympathy for the Victorian prisoners who started a riot after being banned from smoking, and I can accept that sentiment up to a point. My sympathy for prisoners does not run deep and I have even less for rioters.

I believe people should be free to do what they like, but once they harm others, they need to be held to account and potentially locked up.

However, this is not about being sympathetic to prisoners – it's about remembering what jails are for. Corrections Victoria's number one aim – and that of most correctional organisations – is to reduce re-offending. This is a commendable aim, because everyone deserves a second chance. Nobody wins when we lock someone up and throw away the key.

Rehabilitation means putting prisoners on a path towards not committing further crime. It does not mean training inmates to live according to somebody else's values.

For prisoners, smoking has long been a small pleasure among the few that are permitted. Even Ned Kelly would have been allowed a smoke more than a century ago, on the sensible grounds that he would not be harming anyone else. The problem is, health bureaucrats have recently decided that prisoners, and people in mental health facilities, should be denied a smoke.

This signals to prisoners that rule-makers are less concerned about rehabilitation than telling them how to live. It blurs the line between living within the law, and living according to someone else's standards. It will no doubt make some prisoners think that if following the rules means denying themselves things they enjoy, they may as well not follow any rules. This breeds resentment, and riots are a predictable manifestation of serious resentment.

And since prisoners can obtain all forms of illicit drugs inside, we can only wish the authorities luck when it comes to preventing tobacco smuggling, or worse, inmates making their own more dangerous alternatives. Prohibition has never worked, and criminalising things we don't need to criminalise just creates more criminals.

Like all bullies, health mandarins are picking on prisoners and mental health patients because they see them as easy targets. But make no mistake the nanny staters are coming for all of us. Outside prison gates, smokers are shoved into ever more isolated areas and forced to stand outside in the cold and rain. Some may not even smoke in their own apartments if a neighbour disapproves. Thousands of people have been bailed up at train and bus stops in NSW over the past few years and fined $300 for lighting up.

Ultimately, some people won't be happy until the whole of society resembles a vast prison, where all of us are regulated 'for our own good.'

Electronic cigarettes[61]

It seems everything is illegal in Australia unless a bureaucrat gives permission. What's worse, you have to go to the trouble and expense of asking the bureaucrat for permission, because if bureaucrats were proactive they would run the risk of serving the public.

A good example is the case of e-cigarettes. These little inhalers can deliver a warm puff of nicotine, without the carcinogenic tar and industrial solvents of cigarette smoke. Alternatively, they can deliver a puff of anything else you could wish for, such as the flavour of mint, chocolate or whiskey.

In Australia, it is illegal to sell e-cigarettes to deliver nicotine. Not because a bureaucrat has made a decision to ban them, but because no-one has yet asked the right bureaucrat for permission.

What Australia is missing is an Oliver Twist – a poor wretched soul who draws the short straw and has to ask the bureaucrats at the Therapeutic Goods Administration (TGA): 'Please, sir, I want some more.'

If anyone gets around to asking the TGA for permission, they will have to jump through the right bureaucratic hoops. They will need to put their hand on their heart and say that the only purpose of an e-cigarette is as an aid to giving up smoking. They will have to swear that no-one would ever use them for enjoyment. And the onus will be on them to prove (at considerable expense) that e-cigarettes are effective quitting devices.

The ban-by-default of e-cigarettes containing nicotine suits zealous public health advocates just fine. They argue that something should be banned until it is clearly demonstrated to be harmless, since we are all incapable of deciding for ourselves. Such reasoning would have banned every human innovation before it could become popular, from the wheel to the internet. We would truly be in the dark ages.

They ignore their international counterparts such as the Royal College of Physicians, which concluded that e-cigarettes offer massive potential to improve public health by providing smokers with a much safer alternative to tobacco. They ignore how e-cigarettes are freely available in the EU and the United States. And they ignore Australia's history of level-headed harm minimisation, such as our pioneering of the option of methadone treatment for hard-core heroin addicts.

It is hard to avoid the conclusion that their primary goal is to achieve a puritanical victory against nicotine rather than to save lives. It's not really about the smokers, it's about them. Like Marie Antoinette, they say to the smokers who could benefit from e-cigarettes: 'Let them go cold turkey.'

In the meantime, Vince Van Heerden, a Perth businessman, lies convicted of the crime of selling e-cigarettes without nicotine. When the WA Health Department took Vince to the Magistrates Court, the case was thrown out because the magistrate found that, while it is illegal to sell something resembling a cigarette, the e-cigarette in question looks more like a pen. Unfortunately the WA Health Department appealed to the Supreme Court, arguing that smoking heralds the apocalypse and anything that could possibly remind anyone of a cigarette must therefore be banned. The Supreme Court was convinced, and Vince Van Heerden was convicted.

But the weirdness doesn't stop there. While it is illegal to sell e-cigarettes in Australia, it is perfectly legal to import up to three months' supply of e-cigarettes, with or without nicotine. So our Government intentionally lets foreign online businesses do the exact thing that they ban Australian businesses from doing. It's reminiscent of the line: 'No sex please, we're British.'

We are left with the most bizarre of situations. It is perfectly legal to sell cigarettes, which deliver death through combustion (along with billions of dollars of excise revenue to the Government). And it is perfectly legal for foreign businesses to sell us e-cigarettes with or without nicotine. But it is illegal to sell e-cigarettes with nicotine in Australia, because no-one has asked the TGA to deem them to be quitting devices. And it is illegal, at least in some Australian States, to sell e-cigarettes to deliver non-nicotine flavours, because – horror of horrors – someone might see someone put something to their mouth. It's like a ban on dancing because it can lead to fornication.

The Government bans by default, then places each Australian in the position of Oliver Twist, where we have to plead with authorities for permission to pursue a humble existence. Dickens, the great champion of justice and common sense, would be turning in his grave.

Narcotic Drugs Amendment Bill 2016[62]

I rise to support passage of the Narcotic Drugs Amendment Bill 2016.

I do so in the knowledge I must not let the perfect be the enemy of the good. As most people in this Chamber know, legalising cannabis is Liberal Democrats' policy. And yes, that includes recreational use. This Bill is good, but far from perfect.

It amends the *Narcotic Drugs Act 1967* to establish a national licensing scheme to allow the cultivation of cannabis for medicinal and scientific purposes. It will allow such cultivation to operate in accordance with Australia's obligations under the three UN Drug Control Conventions.

Those Conventions – the bastard children of US Prohibition and the War on Drugs – mean that Australia is placed in the position where its new regime for the regulation of medicinal cannabis is onerous.

It involves an elaborate licensing regime: one form of licence authorises the cultivation of cannabis for manufacture into medicinal cannabis products; a second authorises research into the cannabis plant that is to be used for medicinal purposes.

It also takes in a strict 'fit and proper person' test. This test will be applied to the applicant farmer or researcher as well as his relevant business associates. It involves consideration of a range of matters, including criminal history, connections, associates and family, financial status, business history, and capacity to comply with licensing requirements.

Licence holders will also be expected to remain 'fit and proper persons,' too. The regime is explicitly designed to ensure the exclusion of criminal elements, who may be tempted – we are told – to use the licence scheme as cover for illegal activities.

In short, if you want to grow or research medicinal cannabis under the new legislation, you effectively let the government set up CCTV in your bedroom.

I recognise why the Bill before us today is comprised almost wholly of red tape. Legalising cannabis for recreational use at the Federal level would constitute a denunciation of the UN Drug Control Conventions and almost certainly have a serious impact on Australia's legal opium poppy industry. Our opium poppy growers in Tasmania – who produce about half the world's legal medical opioids – depend on Australia complying with the UN Drug Control Conventions or they risk their multi-million dollar international markets. Opium poppy growers already work under a licensing regime that mirrors the one this Bill sets up for medicinal cannabis.

That said, it is becoming clear that legalising recreational cannabis at the state level in a Federal system invites a lot of bleating and chest-beating from UN bodies like the International Narcotics Control Board, but not much else. 'The drug control treaties must be implemented by States parties, including States with federal structures,' the INCB thundered after Colorado legalised recreational cannabis.

Last time I looked, cannabis was still legal in Colorado (and Oregon, Alaska, Washington, and Washington DC). And the sky had not fallen.

Australia's fight for legalising recreational cannabis use, it would seem, must largely be prosecuted at the state level. This serves as a reminder that a great deal of international law is nonsense, and does not deserve our automatic respect.

Legalising recreational cannabis use would deprive organised crime, whether Middle Eastern crime gangs, Asian triads, bikie gangs or relatives of Darth Vader, of a major source of income, and relieve police of the cost of finding and destroying illicit crops. Of the $1.5 billion spent annually on drug law enforcement, 70% is attributable to cannabis. That's an expense we do not need.

Then there's the opportunity for increased tax revenue, something of interest to the big spenders on both sides of this Chamber. If its consumption is legal, it can be taxed. I asked the PBO how much money the government could raise if it legalised and then applied the GST to cannabis. The answer? $300 million – and that's just in GST revenue. I didn't ask them about other forms of revenue-raising, because I find high taxes obnoxious.

Finally, it is not a legitimate use of government power to prohibit adults from doing something that does not harm others. It is irrelevant that it may not be wise to use a plant for recreational purposes. I neither endorse nor recommend recreational use. The point is simply that governments do not have the moral authority to ban something based either on disapproval or a desire to protect people from their own choices.

It is also basic reality that most people have tried it at some point. That includes President Obama and me. When the law says one thing, and people do another, a free society changes the law.

Mr President, medical cannabis is only half the answer. This Bill is a step in the right direction, but only a step. It is high time we stopped using international law to justify interfering in adult choices. Government opinions are only relevant to those who are incapable of deciding things for themselves.

Medical marijuana[63]

Few still believe the old myth that smoking marijuana leads to a spiral of drug dependence and dissipation. Some claim prolonged use can adversely affect the mental health of certain individuals, and it certainly has the potential to make driving dangerous, but compared to alcohol it is a drug of peace and tranquillity.

That being the case, it is difficult to understand why marijuana remains prohibited. It is especially bizarre that its medical properties cannot be utilised.

These properties have been known for a long time. Chinese Emperor Shen-nung wrote of the medicinal properties of the cannabis plant in the twenty-eighth century BC. The ancient Egyptians used medical cannabis extensively 4,000 years ago, and the diuretic, antiemetic, antiepileptic, anti-inflammatory, analgesic and antipyretic effects of cannabis were well known in medieval medicine.

In the early twentieth century, before it was banned, numerous tonics and tinctures containing cannabis extract were available. More recently, studies have confirmed the effectiveness of the active ingredients for treating conditions such as glaucoma, migraine and arthritis, providing relief from chronic pain associated with degenerative diseases and spinal injuries, and alleviating the unpleasant side effects of common treatments for cancer and HIV/AIDS.

Its relative safety, long recognised in folk wisdom, has also been borne out by research. When taken as an oral tincture, cannabis-based therapies are not only safe for children but beneficial in treating the frequency and severity of seizures associated with childhood epilepsy.

Despite its continuing prohibition, attitudes are changing. The 2007 National Drug Strategy Household Survey reported that 70% of respondents were in favour of legalising marijuana for medicinal purposes while 75% were in favour of further clinical trials. In 2013 the NSW Legislative Council's inquiry into the use of cannabis for medical purposes concluded there was sufficiently robust evidence to support its use as a treatment option for certain conditions.

The rest of the world is changing faster though. Medical marijuana is already legal in Austria, Canada, Finland, Germany, Israel, Italy, the Netherlands, Portugal and Spain, and under state laws in more than 20 US states. In two of those, Colorado and Washington, recreational use is also legal.

The quest for additional taxation revenue is one of the reasons for this. Colorado, for example, expects to generate US$133 million in taxes annually. Both medical and recreational sales are subject to a 2.9% sales tax, while recreational sales are also subject to a 10% sales tax and 15% excise. The vast majority of the revenue is expected to come from recreational marijuana.

There are many reasons why marijuana should be legal, especially for medical reasons. It is unconscionable to deny people an effective, safe solution for chronic pain, for example. There is no doubt it helps some conditions when nothing else works. It would also be cheaper than most current therapeutics.

The cultivation of cannabis on a commercial scale, along with the preparation and dispensing of medical marijuana, has the potential to generate significant employment. The largest cannabis dispensary in Oakland, California (a third the size of Perth) has over 104,000 customers and employs 120 people.

There is also scope to expand our burgeoning biomedical sciences sector, with particular regard to creating innovative delivery systems such as cannabinoids in lozenge, vapour and tincture form.

Legal availability would deprive organised crime, including some bikie gangs, of a major source of income and relieve police of the cost of finding and destroying illicit crops. Of the $1.5 billion spent annually on drug law enforcement, 70% is attributable to marijuana. State and federal budgets would benefit from reassigning police to catching criminals who harm and defraud other people, and many otherwise innocent people would be spared a criminal conviction.

Legalisation of recreational use would also acknowledge the reality that most people have tried it, legal or not, at some point in their life, me and President Obama among them.

I do not recommend the use of marijuana except for medical purposes, but ultimately whether it is used for medical or recreational purposes should be a matter for adults to decide for themselves. Whether others approve, or would choose it themselves, is not relevant. It is especially not the business of the government.

As the father of liberalism, John Stuart Mill, put it, 'But it is not legitimate, for government to involve itself in things that a person voluntarily does to him or herself, or that people choose to do to each other by mutual consent, when nobody else is harmed.'

Mill was not thinking of marijuana when he wrote that, but he could have been.

SAME-SEX MARRIAGE

Freedom to Marry Bill 2014[64]

I rise to speak about the issue of same-sex marriage, on which I will introduce a Bill in this place tomorrow.

There have been several attempts to pass marriage equality into law, and all of them have failed. I hope, as did the sponsors of those bills, that my Bill succeeds, but I do so for different reasons.

I feel it is important to outline my reasons, if only so those who doubt the value of marriage equality may see that there are a number of arguments in its favour, many of which they may not have previously heard. Those arguments fall under three heads: liberty, conscience, and state power.

I turn first to liberty.

To most people, marriage equality means the right to get married irrespective of gender or sexual preference. But it is much more than that; it is the right to live your life as you choose, and not have the government impose a particular view on you.

Many heterosexual people choose not to marry. My wife of 30 years and I are among them. Fairly obviously, we do not believe we need a marriage certificate issued by the government to confirm that we are married. It is our choice.

No doubt many gay, lesbian, bisexual, trans, and intersex people (known as LGBTI for short) will choose likewise.

However, when the law says that LGBTI people cannot marry, in an important sense it is diminishing their liberty; a major choice is closed off.

The state is interfering, intervening, telling certain people that they can do what they want, except when they can't (while everyone else, of course, can). Indeed, it is worth noting that under current Australian law, intersex people cannot marry anyone at all.

My political tradition, classical liberalism, has always drawn a strong distinction between the public and the private spheres. Indeed, that distinction can be traced back to the Ancient Greeks.

Unfortunately, many people are aware of classical liberals only when we talk about economics. It is not well known, for example, that Milton Friedman – probably the twentieth century's most influential economist – supported marriage equality.

But a great libertarian economist's support for marriage equality should come as no surprise. It was economists like Friedman, Hayek, and Mises who produced ground-breaking research showing that private individuals tend to make better choices for themselves than do experts engaged to decide on their behalf.

Why, then, do we confine marriage choice to some people, and deny it to others?

Support for marriage equality does not require, or indeed imply, approval of any particular marriage or marriage outcome. Nor does it open the door to bigamy, polyamory or any other dire outcomes that some people predict will be the eventual consequence.

It's not as if they will sneak up on us either; for these to be legal, further changes in the law would be required, which would require widespread public debate.

I support marriage equality because I think people ought to have the freedom to choose their own life path. That is, they have liberty: as John Stuart Mill said, 'over his own body and mind, the individual is sovereign.'

All my Bill does is prevent the government from stopping two people from getting married on the grounds that they are not a man and a woman. It does nothing more, and requires nothing more than tolerance.

To my libertarian constituency, it barely qualifies as progress. To them, a better option would be to remove the government from marriage entirely, by repealing the *Marriage Act* and leaving it to the law of contract, as in civil law countries. I don't disagree, and my own situation reflects that. But that is not as simple to achieve as it sounds.

The fact is, the community places a certain significance on the institution of marriage. It accepts that individuals can live together in all kinds of relationships, irrespective of gender and numbers, but marriage is different. We need to respect that.

I turn next to conscience.

One of the most difficult public conversations across the developed world over the last 250 years has concerned the role of religion in both law and public life. This arose at the same time as the enlightenment idea that laws ought to be secular. To that end, I have built into my Bill protection for claims of conscience. As does the existing law, this Bill ensures ministers of religion do not have to solemnise marriages of which they disapprove.

For the avoidance of doubt, I should make it clear that I consider the view of many religions, that there is not only something wrong with marriage equality but also with LGBTI people, to be an error.

I also maintain it is fair to say that religions have become accustomed, over many years, to creating and then manoeuvring the levers of power. When a secular state rules that a given lever no longer matters (as occurred with blasphemy), the anguish for many sincere religious people is real. So it is also when the power to grasp a lever – in this case, that of marriage definition – is lost.

That is why my Bill protects conscience: I believe that those who seek rights – in this case, LGBTI folk – must not remake the world so that error has no rights. Think where that has led in the past.

To that end, I have also ensured that the Bill protects claims of conscience for civil celebrants in the private sector. I realise that the number of private sector authorised celebrants opposed to marriage equality is likely to be small. Nonetheless, a prudent lawyer drafts prospectively, in this case with aware-ness that there may come a time when non-religious people make moral claims that ought to be taken as seriously as the moral claims made by religious people.

I should note that during the drafting of this bill, constit-uents tried to persuade me that authorised celebrants in the private sector are state actors by virtue of being licensed. If that were true, then by the same logic any professional or tradesman who needs a licence to practise from the state is in the state's employ: lawyers, builders, dentists. Present this argument to your solicitor or orthodontist and see how far you get.

However, that there are officers of the state in all this is a truism, so I turn at last to state power.

As I pointed out in my first speech in this place, the state is a wonderful servant but a terrible master. In an important sense, the state stands for all of us, and that quality of repre-sentativeness means that if it undertakes to provide a service, it must do so in a facially neutral fashion. The state must not discriminate, and if it does so, that is an abuse of power.

This is brought home when one realises that some autho-rised celebrants are not only officers of a state or territory, but also employees of the courts. Their functions – of whatever sort – are therefore linked to the core liberal principle of equality before the law.

My approach is to ensure that all those who come before such celebrants can be married.

Indeed, my approach to the question of marriage equality enhances liberty, protects conscience, and restrains state power. I hope it succeeds, because there are also many other important issues that warrant the same approach.

You don't have to be a leftie to support gay rights[65]

The Liberal Democrats are a party of small government and civil liberties. We aim to keep bureaucrats and busybodies out of both the bedroom and the boardroom. Our position demonstrates that you don't need to be a political 'progressive' to support same-sex marriage and LGBTI rights.

While we have very progressive policies on social issues, we do not share the high-taxing economic agenda of the major parties. Classical liberals – or libertarians – can be described as 'pro-choice on everything.'

For example, our budget policy proposes a significant reduction in middle-class welfare. Payments like Family Tax Benefit and childcare subsidies, aimed at families with children, are poorly means-tested. Single people and childless couples – who account for a large percentage of the LGBTI community – bear the burden of this generosity promoted by the major parties.

We have also consistently opposed a plebiscite on same-sex marriage. I introduced my Freedom to Marry Bill in 2014 with a view to getting it voted on by parliament. I find the idea of putting other people's rights to a popular vote disturbing and unfair. Imagine if freedom of speech for 10% of the population – black people, say – were to be voted on by the other 90%? You'd never hear the end of it. As a politician, part of my job is voting on things.

I am also the only politician to have voted in favour of same-sex marriage in this parliament, every vote, every time.

Even during the drawn-out debate on Senate voting reform, I always voted not only in favour of same-sex marriage, but to bring it forward for debate or a vote.

When it comes to LGBTI people and employment prospects, the Liberal Democrats have fought against 'Casino Mike's' lockout laws. The Senate Nanny State Inquiry which I chaired recommended they be scrapped. I know what they've done to Oxford Street and major queer-friendly venues. I also know the tourism and hospitality sector employs a lot of LGBTI people: I'd like them to keep their jobs.

The political left routinely takes LGBTI folk for granted. Certain parties have long assumed the queer vote was theirs for the taking and have given many people the impression you have to be a socialist to support queer rights. That's not the case. You can be pro-choice on everything, and vote Liberal Democrats.

TERRORISM

Australian Citizenship Amendment (Allegiance to Australia) Bill 2015[66]

I rise to oppose passage of Australian Citizenship Amendment (Allegiance to Australia) Bill 2015.

This is the fifth major piece of national security legislation from this government. I have opposed them all, not because I discount the importance of national security, but because in every case they have taken from the rights and freedoms of Australians.

And as the famous saying goes, those who trade essential liberty for a little temporary safety end up with neither.

The core problem with this Bill is that it allows the executive to exercise judicial power when the minister revokes an individual's citizenship. That is a violation of the doctrine of separation of powers. It also applies retrospectively. Thus, I plan to move two amendments that would make the Bill better.

This Bill came into existence at 5.34 last evening, when the government, in cahoots with Labor, added 14 pages to the previous version of its own Bill. Now, those of us who have never seen it before – crossbench and Greens senators – are required to vote on it. This is profoundly undemocratic; between us we represent just under a third of the Australian electorate. It is also a blatant repudiation of the senate's role as a house of review.

I think it's useful to remind the senate of just what has gone before in this national security area. All prior national security legislation was also passed with unseemly haste, including some significant aspects that were passed without the opportunity for senators to quiz the minister about the legislation in a committee stage. And there is still no crossbench or Greens representation on the parliamentary committee which reviewed each Bill.

The first tranche of national security legislation – National Security Legislation Amendment Bill (No. 1) 2014 – passed with Labor's support on September 25 last year.

What may have been a drafting error in one of the sections dealing with Special Intelligence Operations opened a loophole that sanctioned torture. In short, ASIO officers participating in a Special Intelligence Operation – something defined by ASIO itself, without external review – were to receive immunity from prosecution for all offences save the most serious ones.

It became clear that the intention was to protect officers from prosecution in the event that they joined a proscribed terrorist organisation, or had to commit an offence to prove their bona fides.

However, no-one – including the Parliamentary Joint Committee on Intelligence and Security and the Shadow-Attorney-General – realised the same provision provided cover for acts that amount to torture – the sort of torture that doesn't leave marks.

At that point I deployed the 'nuclear option,' and threatened to refuse to cooperate with the government in any but the most limited way. It was sufficient to ensure the Bill was amended, although I was treated to a great deal of condescension in the process.

As passed, the Bill introduced a significant number of nasties, among them expansion of the Control Order and Preventative Detention Order regimes, and section 35P, which allows imprisonment for ten years for intentional or reckless disclosure of an ASIO Special Intelligence Operation. Section 35P also provides no public interest defence. Regrettably, the press only took an interest once it was enacted.

I also opposed the Bill in part because the Attorney-General failed to show how ASIO's existing powers were insufficient for them to do their jobs. They already had extensive powers.

The second tranche of national security legislation was the so-called 'Foreign Fighters' Bill, which passed the senate on October 29 last year. It, too, attacked freedom of speech and the press.

The Bill introduced a penalty of two years' imprisonment for unauthorised disclosure of a delayed notification search warrant. Once again, there is no public interest defence. The provision seems calculated to remove the AFP from any and all journalistic scrutiny.

The Bill also introduced an offence of 'advocating terrorism,' punishable by a term of five years. It goes far beyond 'incitement to violence' at common law. The new offence requires only that the speaker is 'reckless' as to whether what is said causes terrorism. Incitement, at common law, has always required the element of intent.

The new offence also takes in the 'promotion' of violence – a term broad enough to capture a general statement endorsing revolutionary violence in a third country. This is again different from incitement, which has always required that words ought to operate directly on the intended audience.

Minister Brandis complained that the problem with incitement is that it's difficult to prove. This seems to be rather the point. It's meant to be difficult to prove because if it were easy to prove the authorities would be able to lock people up for things they say pretty much willy-nilly.

Also worthy of note is that organisations can be 'proscribed,' or listed as terrorist organisations, on the basis of 'advocating terrorism.' Once again the definition of 'advocacy' employed is considerably broader than that captured by 'incitement' at common law.

The consequences of listing are severe, and there is a real danger that community associations run by amateurs may finish up being listed based on only a few members' views.

The third tranche of national security legislation, the Counter-Terrorism Legislation Amendment Bill (No 1) 2014, expanded the Control Orders and Preventative Detention Orders regime, a regime that had already been expanded in the first tranche of legislation.

These regimes are obnoxious because they are contrary to the basic principle that people should not be deprived of their liberty without a finding of guilt. Both impose significant constraints on an individual's liberty – including imprisonment in the case of Preventative Detention Orders – for the purpose of preventing terrorist acts.

Alarmingly, the Preventative Detention Order regime requires surveillance of the entirety of an individual's telecommunications activities – including, as Nick Hanna discovered when he represented one of the men arrested in the September 2014 counter-terrorism raids in Sydney – discussions between a solicitor and his client.

The fourth tranche of legislation was the Telecommunications (Interception and Access) Amendment (Data Retention) Bill 2014. It's the one mandating that ISPs retain everyone's metadata for two years.

In my view, it's the most illiberal of all five pieces of national security legislation.

It applies to everyone indiscriminately, treating us all as presumptive criminals. Everyone has something to hide, and something to fear, from mandatory data retention. It's one thing to require monitoring of certain individuals where there is reasonable cause. But the idea that the government needs to store everyone's metadata without cause, including my 85-year-old mother's, should not be countenanced.

Data retention will do nothing to save us from terrorists. Paedophiles are already canny enough to use the dark net and avoid it. Instead, data retention places the entire population under surveillance, no matter who they are or how blameless their lives.

So, I come to the Bill before the Senate today.

It provides for two ways for citizenship to be revoked: by 'conduct' and by 'conviction.'

In the 1948 Citizenship Act, there was only one 'conduct'-based ground for revocation – service in the armed forces of a country at war with Australia. This Bill adds more, including service in and to terrorist organisations, travel overseas to fight with terrorist organisations, and financial aid and assistance to terrorist organisations, of which the Kurdistan Workers Party is listed as one.

'Conduct' based revocation is considered to be 'automatic,' but is still brought about by executive government with no need for judicial involvement. This by-passing of the judiciary was not a concern when a person's conduct was as clear cut as donning an enemy's uniform and engaging in battle directly against the Australian Defence Force. But under this bill, a bureaucrat will make fine distinctions about what you were doing and who you were doing it with, and won't need to bother about what your intentions were.

The 1948 Act did not provide for revocation of citizenship based on conviction. This Act provides for citizenship to be revoked once a conviction has been secured for a number of offences. Such revocation of citizenship is nevertheless an executive act, done by the Minister. It is not done by a court.

The Bill nonetheless seeks to make revocation of citizenship 'self-executing.' The minister is deemed not to be the decision-maker. His role is reduced to that of administrative functionary. He merely 'issues a notice' after citizenship has been renounced by the person to whom the notice is issued. The notice, we are assured, 'does not have any judicial effect.'

I'm a businessman, not a constitutional lawyer. Maybe this verbal sleight of hand will win the day in the High Court. I don't know. But tinkering with the inner workings of the doctrine of separation of powers is not something that should be pushed through with such haste. I note that I received a copy of the Attorney-General's letters to Shadow Attorney-General Dreyfus outlining the Solicitor-General's advice at 7.28pm last night. The Solicitor-General's advice itself has still not been made public.

In addition to a minister exercising power that should properly be exercised by a court, this Bill assumes there will always be a war on terror. It will therefore remain law forever unless amended now or repealed one day in the future. Just as with the prior four bills, that is not desirable.

To that end the amendments I will move at the committee stage will apply a sunset clause of ten years to the Bill.

Sunset clauses allow draconian laws – unless a future parliament decides otherwise – to automatically expire at a set date. They aren't an ideal solution. As others have said, if laws were well-drafted in the first place, sunset clauses wouldn't be necessary.

I propose sunsetting the Bill because I refuse to accept the suggestion that there will always be a war on terror. We will not always be at war in Eurasia.

The Bill also provides for the retrospective application of the criminal law. Although this retrospectivity is limited and only applies to a small number of persons who will attract little public sympathy, it is contrary to the rule of law and to fundamental principles of the common law. Australians considering their conduct now should be able to weigh up the consequences based on the law as it stands now. The fact that I need to point out such a basic tenet is of great concern.

Retrospective action is not necessary, as the government already has a suite of powers to ensure that people who have served their sentences for terrorist offences are monitored.

As such, I will move amendments to ensure that no part of the legislation applies retrospectively. We can do better than destroy our liberties in the name of securing ourselves against an illiberal enemy.

Finally, I wish to say a few words on citizenship as a concept.

I don't happen to believe our fundamental rights flow from citizenship – of Australia or any other country. I think our rights flow from being human, and are inherent.

However – for better or for worse – we live in a world where legal rights often are contingent on citizenship. If citizenship is to be revoked, it should be revoked by a court in all but the most straightforward circumstances, such as when a person lines up against the Australian Defence Force in battle.

Inevitably, this Bill creates two tiers of citizen – people who can have their Australian citizenship revoked, and people who can't. The answer 'well, some people have another one' doesn't really cut it. People have dual citizenships thanks to immigration, not because they bought their other citizenship in a shop.

Terrorism can be beaten without us losing our rights as free people. Just as I opposed the previous national security legislation on those grounds, I also oppose this Bill.

Why our intelligence agencies need to smarten up[67]

An Australian Bureau of Statistics recent report on causes of death says that nearly 60 Australians died in 2011 after falling out of bed, 26 died falling off a chair, and four after bumping into another person.

I mention this, not to put you off your morning coffee, but to suggest that we ought to keep the risks that surround us in perspective.

Our national security is important to us, the threats are real, and the acts carried out by terrorists with jihad on their mind are truly despicable. But our reactions to threats should be kept in proportion.

Numerous studies have shown that the world is experiencing an historical period of relative peace. The main difference these days is that graphic horrors are streamed into our lounge rooms and home offices.

Following the events of September 11, 2001, the world went into meltdown. Aeroplanes were grounded, grandmothers made to take their shoes off at airports, and all of us forced to keep deodorants out of our luggage.

This is despite the fact that academics estimate the chance that any one of us will die from a terrorism related event is 1 in 12.5 million in a given year – which is in the realm of the likelihood of dying from a lightning strike.

However, unlike the risks of lightning strike or falling out of bed, we spend a lot of money combating terrorism. Australia's intelligence agencies have grown like the One Direction Fan Club, with ASIO enjoying nearly triple the growth in spending we allocated to either health or welfare from 2000 to 2010.

With ASIO and our other security organisations bursting at the seams with staff and public money, you might think they would be sufficiently resourced to leave us alone and get on with their jobs. But you would be sadly mistaken.

Their recent efforts to have laws changed to allow them to track our activities on the internet suggest they are either incompetent or don't have enough to do. When they feel it is necessary to impinge on the freedom of 23 million Australians for the sake of a handful of people who, in any case, are posting pictures of themselves on Facebook, you would have to wonder if the sleuths they are recruiting are super enough.

Even in minimalist form, data retention will require the storage of a huge amount of useless information, with an equally huge potential for misuse and needless invasions of our privacy. More to the point, this information may also end up making investigations more complicated.

If finding a bad guy can be equated to finding a needle in a haystack, then data retention will simply make the haystack much bigger. Like all policing, national security work needs to be targeted. It can be done successfully with tools already available, including warrants to investigate and retain the data of those for whom there are reasonable suspicions.

And just to add insult to injury, ASIO is also seeking legislation that gives them protection from criticism.

As they have on previous occasions, our security organisations are overreaching. Their business is to allow us to enjoy our freedom. They should be reminded that they are servants of the public, not our masters.

Dear Mr Shorten, I'd like a word[68]

Leading the Opposition, in case you haven't noticed, is your job. So could you do it, please? I'm not the Opposition Leader, despite the fact that the media keep pretending I am.

Don't get me wrong: I admired the way you faced down the Australian Christian Lobby on marriage equality, but in your position, once is not enough. If you don't stand up for civil liberties, we will soon have no liberties left to defend.

At the moment I'm the only consistent defender of civil liberties in the current parliament. On 35P and journalists going to jail, 18C and people choosing to be offended, or super-secret search warrants that cannot be mentioned – I am the only one to have raised objections each time. Of course, there are people in all parties who agree with me, but they're either unwilling to speak up or selective about their concerns. I've also had minimal support from the Coalition media commentariat, who don't seem to understand that their 'team' will not always be in power. I'm left to do it, and I'm sick of it.

Your desire to avoid being seen as 'soft' on terror has led to a situation where you're competing with Tony Abbott to see who has the hairiest chest, and since we've all seen Tony in his budgie smugglers, this is a competition you are destined to lose.

It's time to drop the bipartisanship, particularly on the data retention proposals. These have nothing to do with national security and everything to do with allowing every busy-body who works for the government to snoop on ordinary citizens.

I'd like you to tell the Australian people that until the European Court of Justice struck down the EU's 2006 Data Retention Directive earlier this year, the equivalent legislation in the UK to Australia's Data Retention Bill was used to chase people for things like minor welfare fraud, littering, and dog fouling. Yes, I know that standing in dog poo isn't fun, but spying on perpetrators isn't going to help defeat Islamists either.

Data retention will not bother the technically competent and those who hide in the recesses of the dark net. It will catch the journalist who finds the odd leak and the parliamentarian who wanders into a brothel with his iPhone switched on. Thanks to the wonders of GPS, the Chinese will know every Australian politician's geographic foibles for the previous two years.

And I'm sure the ATO and the ACCC will love data retention as much as their counterparts did in the UK. In fact, I'm fairly sure it will be used to spy on petrol stations in the ongoing 'bowser wars.'

Your bipartisanship on national security is also galling because it is stopping the Senate from functioning as Australia's

'House of Review.' During my first week as a senator, in early July, you may recall inviting me to meet with you and Penny Wong, where you stressed the importance of allowing the Senate to do its job and not curtailing debate.

This 'bipartisanship' meant that last Wednesday, a number of useful amendments to the risible, illiberal Foreign Fighters Bill were voted down without a single word of debate. This happened because on Tuesday, Labor agreed to the Government's guillotine motion.

Only now, after passage of that Bill into law, have you written to Tony Abbott asking him to 'please reconsider' both tranches of the national security legislation. Only in the hurly-burly of the chamber in the midst of a sitting week did you let your Shadow Attorney-General produce some decent quality amendments.

I doubt that any amount of legislator's remorse will be of much help to the people who discover they have been criminalised.

I urge you to lead the alternative government, the government-in-waiting. Labor once had a fine tradition of defending civil liberties. What happened to that? Just because the Coalition is struggling in the polls at the moment doesn't mean victory in the next election will drop into your lap like a ripe plum off a branch.

I know the scene at the end of Stanley Kubrick's Spartacus – where lots of people stand up and claim to be Spartacus – is one of the great cinematic moments, but that's not how Australian politics works. You are the Leader of the Opposition. You need to stand up and be counted.

The Foreign Fighters Bill[69]

I rise to speak against the Counter-Terrorism Legislation Amendment (Foreign Fighters) Bill 2014. I do so because I don't believe the Bill is urgent or even necessary, and also because it contains measures that, like the previous National Security legislation, erode our rights and freedoms.

It is somehow fitting that this Chamber is close to empty because it reminds us of Edmund Burke's observation that bad things happen when good people do nothing.

Last week, the Government snapped to attention in response to video threats made by a 17-year-old jihadist from Bankstown. I then attracted some attention when I used some mildly unparliamentary language to describe him. Mr President, I stand by that description. And for that and other reasons, I don't believe there is any reason to give security agencies additional powers to prevent those like him from causing harm.

We have heard constant claims that we are now operating in a 'changed security environment' where 'Australia is under threat.' Because Da'ish is enjoying success in Iraq and Syria, and a sympathiser has perpetrated an atrocity in Canada, the argument goes, we should all be hiding under the doona and giving ASIO and the AFP additional powers to protect us.

I say that's not so. This Bill has nothing to do with defeating Da'ish in Syria or Iraq. And it will not keep us safer here in Australia.

The Attorney-General says that that the number of Australians presently involved in the conflict in Iraq and Syria is unparalleled. According to his figures, 160 Australians are currently supporting or fighting with extremist groups.

And yet, 66 Australians fought in the Spanish Civil War. As a percentage of the Australian population in 1936, more Australians thought helping Communists or Fascists was a good thing than are currently supporting jihadists.

Young men with a thirst for action and too much time on their hands have long joined gangs and become entangled with organised crime. These days, at least for a few, it seems violent religion provides an equivalent outlet.

Then there is the basic reality that the government already has substantial powers on the books to deal with any terrorist threat. Apart from the fact – as Bret Walker SC often points out – that violence and conspiracy to commit violence have always been crimes, Australia's security agencies have extensive surveillance capacities. They can, for example, obtain Data Preservation Orders that ensure metadata is retained and an individual's activities on the internet examined. They can obtain warrants to intercept phone calls. People can be held and compelled to answer questions. Preventative Detention Orders and Control Orders – without any crime having been committed – stop people leaving their homes if it is suspected that they may commit a crime in the future. Passports can be cancelled.

Some of these powers are so over the top they're already incompatible with a liberal democracy. No case has been made for the need to add to them.

In Australia, lightning kills five to ten people every year. This does not mean our security agencies should have the right to enter our houses to check on us or imprison those who would walk around during storms.

People have pointed out that Da'ish makes sophisticated use of social media and videos, deliberately aimed at the young. Wouldn't it be better, I've been asked, if watching those videos were made illegal? Wouldn't it be good if we could legislate Hizb ut-Tahrir out of existence?

I've formed the view that the new offence of 'advocating terrorism' – which can be committed by both individuals and organisations – is present in this Bill purely to get at Hizb ut-Tahrir and any others like it. It does this in two ways.

First, it defines 'advocacy' so as to include the 'promotion' of terrorism. This is broad enough to take in a general statement endorsing revolutionary violence with no particular audience in mind. Second, the offence is drafted in such a way that it requires only that the individual or organisation be reckless as to whether the words in question will cause another person to engage in terrorism.

At common law, incitement has always required the element of intent, whereas 'promotion' goes beyond the requirement – also present in incitement – that words ought to act directly on their intended audience.

Last week, I looked at Hizb ut-Tahrir Australia's website. Of course ASIO probably already know what we do on our parliamentary computers, but I'm letting senators know because it was actually an enlightening exercise. Hizb ut-Tahrir, like Da'ish, supports a global Islamic Caliphate. It seeks the imposition of Sharia, including the 'Hudud' ordinances. These take in nasties such as stoning people to death for apostasy and adultery. It's difficult to avoid the imputation that, given a choice, Hizb ut-Tahrir would prefer Da'ish to the Commonwealth of Australia.

The issue, of course, is that making Hizb ut-Tahrir illegal won't stop Da'ish's videos being made or distributed or watched. In fact, they're likely to acquire a sort of weird cachet from their very illegality: lots of youngsters, when adults in authority tell them not to do something, immediately go out and do the opposite. This phenomenon is not confined to Muslims.

What proscription and listing as a terrorist organisation will achieve when it comes to Hizb ut-Tahrir is to drive the organisation underground.

Mr President, I like the fact that I can read Hizb ut-Tahrir's website. I like the fact that one of their obnoxious spokesmen turned up on Lateline and revealed to all and sundry just how uncomfortable he is around independent, educated women. I also like the fact that their public presence exposes them to ongoing scrutiny and forces them to speak, not fight – sunlight is indeed the best disinfectant. It may be possible to legislate bodies like Hizb ut-Tahrir out of existence, but not the sentiments it represents.

Thanks to the alleged urgency and necessity of this bill, the Parliamentary Joint Committee on Intelligence and Security was forced to come up with something approaching a review in a fortnight. Labor, of course, is being its usual supine self on national security, although – to be fair – the recommendations made by the committee are all sound. There's only one problem. They're like putting a band-aid on cancer.

Yes, it would be nice to have words like 'encourage,' 'promote,' and 'advocate' defined with clarity (or at all). It would also be good if the Foreign Minister can't simply declare entire countries off limits. I agree the idea of 'subverting society' needs work. It clearly hasn't occurred to the Attorney-General that some countries and societies actually make good candidates for subverting: Zimbabwe, for example, or North Korea. I'm happy to say I support the overthrow of Kim Jong-un and Robert Mugabe and I wouldn't mind if there was a bit of advocating terrorism to achieve that. What does that make me?

Even better are the proposals to reel in the lengthy sunset clauses for PDOs and Control Orders: instead of 2025 or 2026, they'll stay on the books for a mere two years after the next federal election. So about four years then, give or take. Mind you, that's still a long time for bad law to hang around.

Then there's the recommendation – when it comes to unauthorised disclosure of delayed notification search warrants – to take the public interest into account. However, as with the previous national security legislation, this safeguard will only go into the explanatory memorandum, not the Bill itself. I may have slept through some of my lectures in law school but I remember enough to know that a court only takes the explanatory memorandum into account when the words of the statute are unclear. And the words in this Bill are perfectly clear.

These kinds of laws will effectively turn our security agencies into various versions of secret police.

Last week, News Corp's Lachlan Murdoch criticised the attack on freedom of speech that sailed through this place with the support of both major parties in relation to special intelligence operations: laws that could see journalists jailed up to ten years if they disclose information about them. This Bill seeks to prevent so-called 'delayed notification warrants' from being disclosed. Mr President, we are talking about a warrant.

One assumes that Lachlan Murdoch will one day be at News Corp's helm. The way things are going, there will be nothing for his journalists to report aside from the colour of Kim Kardashian's knickers.

Even with the acceptance of all the Parliamentary Joint Committee on Intelligence and Security's recommendations, we are still left with a Bill that enables the Foreign Minister to declare large swathes of territory no go areas, allows the AFP to conduct searches without telling anyone about it for up to 12 months, places further constraints on the ability of Australians to speak freely, engages in extra-territorial overreach, and tells journalists they must go to the Inspector-General of Intelligence and Security if they come across misconduct rather than reporting to the wider public in the normal way.

Mr Abbott tells us that the 'delicate balance' between freedom and security will have to shift 'for some time to come' in light of the heightened terror risk. What he fails to realise in enacting laws like this one and the National Security legislation, is he is curtailing the very liberties that distinguish free countries like Australia. Australia has the rule of law, procedural fairness, the presumption of innocence, free speech and a free media. It is simply not acceptable to give those good things away – surrendering freedom for safety – in response to windy threats from the Ginger Jihadi of Bankstown. We can do better than that.

Giving away freedom for security is like giving your possessions to a thief so you will not be robbed.

At the risk of repeating a worn phrase, it would be tempting to call Mr Abbott and Mr Shorten the girly men of personal freedom, but I don't know of any girls who would be intimidated by threats from a spotty youth on YouTube.

Mr President, young men with limited skills and an aggressive cast of mind have always been attracted to violence, and have often committed crimes. That those crimes are now sometimes committed in the name of Islam does not make them different from crimes committed in the name of Communism or Fascism, or even just due to testosterone. There is nothing unprecedented or urgent or super-risky about any of this. The internet has changed many things about the modern world – often for the better – but Communists and Fascists alike were able to convince Australians to fight in Spain in 1936 without it.

When I came to write this speech, there were lots of words and phrases I could have used at the outset to describe the Foreign Fighters Bill. I could have called it 'Orwellian' in its desire to put the Australian people under surveillance. When discussing Hizb ut-Tahrir, I could have pointed out that the best response to speech is more speech. I could also have suggested that the government was in the process of tearing up Magna Carta and depositing the bits in Lake Burley Griffin.

I didn't use that language at the outset precisely because it has become stereotyped.

However, that doesn't make it any less true.

Look at what you are doing to Australia's democratic heritage. And then, in the name of all that is decent, do better.

Seven reasons to hate the Foreign Fighters Bill[70]

Both the government and opposition have realised you cannot be a hero unless you first make people believe there is a crisis.

With that in mind, we are now dealing with poorly thought out legislation – known as the Foreign Fighters Bill – that will supposedly protect us from terrorists. The problem is, it will also throw out many of our basic rights.

In no particular order, here are seven reasons you should be seriously concerned:

7. It is rushed

Legal experts tell me the legislation has all the signs of a rush job, including typographical errors. Everyone needs to take a deep breath. The real risk of terrorism must be addressed, but I promise there will not be any Muslims hiding under your bed any day this week or the next. It is far more important to get this legislation right than to rush it through.

While Tony Abbott and Bill Shorten were busy trying to prove whose chest is the hairiest on security, legislation giving additional powers to ASIO blew through the Senate last month like a southerly change.

It seems that only now are people waking up to the fact that some appallingly draconian law has been passed, and is here to stay. So it is with the proposed Foreign Fighters law: times may change but bad legislation will remain.

6. Delayed notification 'warrants'

Having your warrant notification delayed sounds like it could be a minor inconvenience. But in fact, what we are talking about is a law allowing the cops to break and enter your property and tell you about it later.

What's more, they may also enter your home in order to enter the property of a neighbour.

If this legislation is passed, what will be the difference between a burglar and the Federal Police? Not much, except that the feds will be obliged to send you a letter within six months telling you about it… unless, of course, they get an extension.

5. Secrecy provisions

The secrecy rules attaching to delayed notification warrants mean anyone – journalists, bloggers, Facebookers, town gossips – could be jailed for two years for merely telling others about the AFP's nocturnal activities, and in their defence could not argue the disclosure was in the public interest. This is a provision the East German secret police would have loved.

4. Promoting violence

The legislation proposes a new offence of 'advocating terrorism,' punishable by imprisonment of up to five years. People can already be arrested for incitement of violence, but this broadens the definition to include the promotion of violence. An organisation with only a few members 'promoting' violence – whatever the Federal Police decides that means – can then be listed as a terrorist organisation. Other members of such organisations – who do not even share these views – can be exposed to serious criminal offences. To take this to extremes: if a handful of NRMA members expressed enough hatred of cyclists or Volvo drivers, everybody in the NRMA could find themselves in a listed terrorist organisation.

3. Declared areas

In another provision reminiscent of laws beloved by authoritarian states, the Minister for Foreign Affairs will be allowed to declare certain areas off limits. If you travel there you will need to demonstrate you went to that place solely for a legitimate purpose, or risk imprisonment for ten years. The government has offered advice about where people could travel for a long time, but this takes it to a whole new level and sets a worrying precedent: next thing, the government will be telling you where you're allowed to take your annual leave.

2. Failure to explain why we need it

Australia's security organisations already have extensive powers available to them. Other than vague rhetoric about threats of terrorism, the Government has simply failed to explain why they need more power.

1. Assumption of good will

No matter how long and hard you look into the big brown eyes of George Brandis, it is not possible to imagine you are looking at a malevolent dictator. Indeed, you may also think that, on the whole, the people in our security organisations are good Australians like you and me.

But if you think that, you'd be falling into a trap.

History demonstrates that people of any colour or stripe can and do behave like animals. Many people who are drawn to security organisations have a fondness for power and its various applications, which may explain why some of the worst human rights abuses are carried out by people working for government agencies. When these actions are given the legislative sanctuary, people have nowhere to hide.

Senator Brandis might be a fair-minded bloke, but the security laws he is sponsoring may well be remembered as one of the most shocking assaults on civil liberties in Australia's history.

National security legislation[71]

It was the night of 25 September 2014, and Senator George Brandis was taking Australia into a reign of terror. There were only a handful of witnesses, even though there were seats for hundreds and cameras covering every angle.

He was shepherding into law a Bill that gives our spies and their friends a licence to injure, to embed malware into anyone's computer, to break into the houses of people suspected of nothing, and to arm and train rebel groups to overthrow governments in foreign countries.

A Bill to jail anyone who reports on past corruption and misconduct in our spy agency. A Bill so fuelled by paranoia that it seeks to jail spies who dare to use a photocopier without an explanation.

Three exasperated Senators stood in opposition to the Bill at one end of the tennis-court-sized chamber. A trio not used to standing together – Senator Xenophon, Senator Ludlam, and me. A trio armed with too few votes, and whose weapons of reason were useless in the absence of open ears and minds.

At the other end of the chamber were the closed ears and minds of Senator Brandis and his Labor counterpart in the Senate, Senator Jacinta Collins.

The chamber was otherwise almost empty, save for a few clerks and staffers.

The PUP Senators had just left the chamber, after successfully amending the Bill to add their personal touch of draconia. They proposed a tenfold increase in the penalty for disclosing the identity of a spy. The government and opposition, not wanting to seem soft, backed the PUP thought bubble despite expert groups and security agencies seeing such a change as unwarranted.

The PUP senators then joined Coalition and Labor backbenchers for dinner in the Parliament's dining room. The backbenchers needn't hear the arguments against the Bill. They would vote for the Bill because their leaders told them to do so. It could have been to reintroduce the death penalty; their vote would still be yes.

The media were missing from the galleries – despite this being one of the most important moments for press freedom in Australia's history – because the Attorney-General had sprung a surprise sitting on everyone and the journalists had gone home.

So the unlikely trio of Leyonhjelm, Xenophon, and Ludlam soldiered on in the near empty chamber. Each attempted the mildest of amendments to inch Australia back from Brandis's Brave New World.

We attempted to limit our spies to hacking 20 computers per warrant. To limit hacking to whatever was necessary to carry out an authorised operation. To remove the offence of disclosing intelligence information in instances where no-one is endangered and no operation is prejudiced. To remove the offence in instances where disclosure is in the public interest, such as disclosures of ASIO corruption and misconduct. To require judges to consider the public interest when sentencing someone for disclosing intelligence information. To ensure the law only stays on the books until 2025.

We even attempted to amend what seems like a clear drafting error: that the Attorney-General commits an offence when he discloses general information about past intelligence operations.

In spite of an earlier commitment to consider our amendments, the Attorney-General summarily dismissed them all.

So attention then turned to Labor's position.

The Labor spokesperson, Senator Collins, listened carefully to our amendments and responded that they were 'minimalist' and 'may indeed warrant further consideration.' She then went on to say that Labor would not be supporting any of the cross-benchers' amendments.

It was a jaw-dropping, George Costanza-inspired, do-the-opposite moment. Had anyone been in the Chamber, there would have been gasps of disbelief. Senator Collins went on to explain that Labor would vote the Government's Bill into law, but would consider fixing up the law at a later stage.

Now while I am new in this job, I can count. Labor can't fix up the law once it has been passed in the Senate. They don't have the numbers in the House of Representatives.

The Bill is now the law. And finally, too late, no less a Labor figure than Anthony Albanese refers to it as draconian.

September 25 was a bad day for freedom in Australia.

Torture[72]

In December 1974, at the height of The Troubles in Northern Ireland, four people were arrested for bombing the Guildford Pub. Four people died in that bombing, 65 were injured, and Britons were left feeling unsafe not only in their beds, but most other places as well.

Those arrested came to be known, collectively, as The Guildford Four. That they did not fit the typical profile of IRA terrorists was of no moment: there was enormous public pressure to secure both arrests and convictions when it came to the Provisional IRA. Indeed, two of them were living in a squat, one had what in normal circumstances would be a cast-iron alibi – she was at a rock concert – and another just happened to be visiting his aunt in London. They were Irish, and that was all that mattered: the arrests gave form and substance to the old joke about 'innocent until proven Irish.'

Under legislation just passed, the police could hold people without charge for a week, rather than the usual 48 hours, and did not have to act on 'reasonable suspicion.' At the same time, use of suspect interrogation techniques – ranging from intimidation (threats to family members and mock executions) and the infliction of pain (typically, ear-twisting) – had become routine not only in the Royal Ulster Constabulary, but had spread to forces with better reputations, including the Met.

Under torture – torture that left no marks, and caused no injury – everyone confessed, either to bomb-planting or making explosives. All four served sentences of between 15 and 16, except for Patrick Conlon, who died in prison. And the only reason the Guildford Bombers were released was because it became clear that the confessions – all of them false – had been obtained under torture. The police had also fabricated evidence when torture proved ineffective at extracting sufficient detail: people in pain tend to produce stories lacking the colour and movement that persuades courts and juries.

In 1989, long after this gross miscarriage of justice, the convictions were quashed. Those still incarcerated were released. In 2005, PM Tony Blair finally apologised, saying 'I am very sorry that they were subject to such an ordeal and injustice... they deserve to be completely and publicly exonerated.'

Fast forward to September 2014 and Australia. Attorney-General George Brandis's National Security Legislation Amendment Bill will grant immunity from civil and criminal liability to participants in special intelligence operations. ASIO agents, and anyone else listed as a participant, will not be able to kill, inflict serious injury, or commit a sexual offence. But nothing will prevent them, Australians all, from doing what was done to the Guildford Four. Worse, Brandis's Bill proposes to gag journalists and bloggers if they tell anyone, with a ten-year jail term if they do.

Every time the state wants to curtail liberty in the name of security, it seems people like me have to stand up and shout how badly this can go wrong. Many Australians – like many Brits during The Troubles – seem to operate under the comforting illusion that we in liberal democracies are all decent people and can undermine our institutions with nary a thought as to the long-term consequences. We seem to think our natural good intentions will prevent us from coming to resemble those against whom we fight.

In fact, there is no such thing as natural good intentions. The reason we don't butcher each other in the name of some crackpot religious ideology – and make no mistake, these Islamists are barbarians – is not because we are special examples of the human, intrinsically better than Islamic State or Hamas or the Provisional IRA. Rather, we are better because our institutions and civic culture are better, things that had to be built up over centuries, even millennia. As early as the third century AD, the Roman jurist Ulpian observed that not only did torture produce false confessions, but even when it 'worked,' it was institutionally corrupting.

It is also relevant to note that ASIO and the AFP have apparently just busted up a terror cell without the benefit of laws permitting extra breaches of our civil liberties to help them do their jobs.

If we are in the business of defending liberal democracy, then we must fight freedom's cause in freedom's way. I do not wish to see 'innocent until proven Muslim' in my country. And Australia's air is too pure for torture.

Everyone has something to hide if universal data retention becomes law in Australia[73]

Last week, Attorney-General George Brandis described data retention as 'absolutely crucial in identifying terrorist networks and protecting the public.' On that basis, he argued for passage of the government's data retention legislation.

This assertion is simply false. The government has all the power it needs.

French police and intelligence agencies had access to targeted real-time metadata to track suspected terrorists in the lead up to the Charlie Hebdo attacks. In addition, the terrorists in question were already on EU, UK, and US no-fly lists and had been banned from purchasing firearms.

Similarly, in Australia, Man Haron Monis was already well and truly on ASIO's radar, and Australia's security agencies have extensive surveillance capacities. They can, for example, obtain data preservation orders that ensure metadata is retained and suspect activities on the internet examined. They can obtain warrants to intercept phone calls.

And yet, data retention didn't help the police – or the public – one bit.

To his credit, French Prime Minister Manuel Valls admitted 'a clear failing in security and intelligence.' It's become clear from the fall out – as the Charlie Hebdo attacks are pored over by France's security experts – that part of the problem is too much data. Finding a needle in a haystack is not made any easier by adding more hay to the stack.

For Brandis's benefit, I'm going to outline what his proposed mandatory data retention regime will achieve for everyone, not just individuals of interest.

Late last year, I undertook a controlled experiment: with assistance from Mark White of the *Sydney Morning Herald*, I had a technical firm record my metadata for a month to see what it revealed.

Before entering parliament I ran an agribusiness services company, Baron Strategic Services. Data monitoring equipment was installed in BSS's office and connected to the router. Because it only collected data relating to office traffic, there was no smartphone-derived geographical information.

The results were revealing. Without knowing any more than the name, metadata showed the sector in which BSS operates in less than a day. It was possible to work out which bank it uses and a complete record of its purchases and those of the staff – everything from furniture to renovations to compulsory third party insurance.

Metadata also revealed how often and for how long staff used social media like Facebook, where they planned to go on holiday, what one wanted to buy for Christmas, and when an employee knocked off early.

As an employer, I've never been interested in monitoring employees in this way. I've always taken a dim view of people who time their employees' loo and cigarette breaks. That said, if the boss gets too invasive, an employee at least has a fighting chance of telling that person or company where to get off.

Trying to tell the government – which is far more powerful than any employer, union, or professional association – where to get off is a whole other kettle of fish.

Despite my desire to keep politics and business separate, metadata also revealed my membership of the Inner West Hunters' Club and the subjects I and other members discussed in group emails, including gun law reform. I wasn't the only person identifiable either – everyone who corresponded with me had their identities revealed.

It was possible to establish who was publicly in favour of gun law reform, and who was in favour of it privately but unwilling to say anything about the issue in public for, say, employment reasons. The possibilities for blackmail are obvious. That the data will probably be stored offshore – mainly in China where it is cheap – makes the risk of hacking a real concern.

Had the analysis included my smartphone, with its site data, it would have been easy to jump to conclusions based on my location.

What would a telephone call or Google search placed in front of a brothel, gay bar or abortion clinic reveal? Imagine the caller were not me – with my classical liberal views – but a conservative Christian politician. What mischief could be had at his or her expense?

Everyone has something to hide, and something to fear, if universal data retention becomes law. It is one thing to require monitoring of certain individuals, but the idea that the government needs to store my mother's metadata is ridiculous and should not be countenanced.

Data retention will do nothing to save us from terrorists. It places the entire population under surveillance, no matter who they are or how blameless their lives. And thanks to its sheer volume, it will make terrorism harder, not easier, to stop.

FREE SPEECH

Offence is taken, not given[74]

Nobody forces us to fall in love or to feel happy or sad. Why then do we blame others when we take offence? If we are responsible for our feelings in some cases, surely we are responsible in all cases.

In the Australian vernacular, being called a bastard can be intended as a serious insult, a minor criticism or a term of endearment, yet someone may find the term offensive irrespective of the intent of the person making the comment.

The same is true when it comes to comments about political beliefs, sexual orientation, appearance, gender identity, age, religious values or innumerable other factors that some claim gives rise to offence. Nobody can say with certainty how a comment might be received.

In tort and criminal law a person can be liable for all consequences resulting from activities that lead to injury to another person, even if the victim suffers unexpectedly high damage due to a pre-existing vulnerability. Known as the egg shell rule, it means liability may be severe if a person suffers injury as a result of assault or negligence and has a skull as delicate as the shell of an egg.

This relates only to physical injury though, and there is no such rule regarding verbal matters. Nonetheless, there is a growing tendency to attribute blame for the consequences of offence at the feet of those who utter the words irrespective of the circumstances of the person claiming to be offended.

When a UK nurse received a prank call from a Sydney radio station pretending to be the Queen, the immediate response focused on its entertainment value. Yet when the nurse committed suicide, the announcers who made the call were immediately blamed even though the nurse had the psychological equivalent of an egg shell skull, having made two prior suicide attempts.

The *Racial Discrimination Act* makes it unlawful to 'offend, insult, humiliate or intimidate' someone because of 'race, colour or national or ethnic origin,' and yet whether anyone is indeed offended, insulted, humiliated or intimidated is up to the receiver of the message. Given an inability to know in advance how the recipient might choose to feel, the only option is to avoid saying anything much at all.

This can have significant consequences for the way we speak. In America, and increasingly now here, it has become customary to wish everyone happy holidays rather than merry Christmas out of concern that non-Christians may feel offended.

Filmmakers, cartoonists, artists and authors are reluctant to tackle certain subjects, such as the life of Mohammed, because individuals or groups claim to be offended, sometimes even responding with violence.

Like anger, frustration and loneliness, feeling offended is an emotion. But while they can be powerful, emotions are within our control. Apart from clinical depression perhaps, none is involuntary.

Even when a comment is intended to be hurtful, or there is indifference as to whether hurt is caused, how we respond depends on the core beliefs we have accumulated over a lifetime. Sometimes these are so odd that the most benign comment can arouse offence.

Because there is no cause and effect, the right of free speech does not require the right to offend. That does not mean we should ignore cultural norms like good manners and consideration for the feelings of others, but we do not need the law to tell us that the wrong response to the question 'does my bum look big in this?' can lead to problems.

The very notion that someone else can govern the way we feel diminishes our independence and self-ownership. If nobody can force us to think in a particular way, nobody can compel us to feel offended.

No matter how bigoted, ill-informed or obnoxious, our reaction to someone else's words is always up to us. Unless words are coercive, by threatening, tricking or forcing us to do something against our will, we are responsible for how they are received. If we feel offended, we have the option of choosing another feeling.

I hate to break it to you, but we are not all Charlie[75]

The reason is simple: Charlie Hebdo was consistent in its support for freedom of speech. Its editors were not just targeted by Islamists: they'd been hauled through the French courts (where they won) and were figures of hate to both the French extreme right and conservative Catholics.

Charlie Hebdo had been out on a limb for years, true to the freewheeling anti-clericalism that owes its origins to the protests of 1968. Charb, its editor, refused to buckle.

The rest of us – with the partial exception of the US – have buckled. There are widespread restrictions on speech, in France and elsewhere. Australia has 18C, among many others.

Hate speech laws are frequently based on the supposition that hate speech has the same effect as the common law offence of incitement. Incitement requires a demonstrable effect on the intended audience. Burning a cross on a black family's front lawn, for example, amounts to incitement to commit acts of violence against that family.

It's also important to remember hate speech laws are akin to the definition of 'advocating terrorism' in the national security legislation. Because – as George Brandis told me last year – incitement is difficult to prove, governments look for other ways to restrict speech. 'Advocating terrorism' in the Foreign Fighters legislation removes the requirement for demonstrable impact.

At the heart of criminalising hate speech is an empirical claim: that what an individual consumes in the media has a direct effect on his or her subsequent behaviour. That is, words will lead directly to deeds.

But because this is untrue – playing Grand Theft Auto and watching porn hasn't led to an epidemic of car thefts and sexual assault – justifications for laws like 18C and hate speech laws now turn on the notion that offence harms 'dignity' and 'inclusion.' Obviously, 'dignity' and 'inclusion' can't be measured, while crime rates can.

Support for 'dignity' and 'inclusion' produces weird arguments – white people are not supposed to satirise minorities, for example. Sometimes, legislation is used – bluntly – to define what is funny.

Allowing what is 'hateful' or 'offensive' to be defined subjectively, as 18C does – and not according to the law's usual objective standard (the 'reasonable person') – means 'offence' is in the eye of the beholder. It enables people who are vexatious litigants and professional victims to complain about comments the rest of us would laugh off.

Tim Wilson, Australia's Freedom Commissioner, has already argued that 18C ensures an Australian Charlie Hebdo would be litigated to death. Despite the fact that 18C refers only to race, Tony Abbott's justification for backing down on repeal was to preserve 'national unity' with Australia's Muslim community. This conflates religion with race in the crudest possible way.

This conflation is what leads to the coining of nonsense terms like 'Islamophobia.' 'Homophobia' actually means something, because being homosexual is an inherent characteristic, not a choice. Islam is an idea, and it is perfectly reasonable to be afraid of an idea.

18C is far from the only potential constraint. The equivalent Victorian legislation explicitly takes in religion as well as race. A smart lawyer would bring suit in Victoria, because Charlie Hebdo would probably be caught there.

The confusion of religion for race is so pervasive – even in the United States, where people ought to know better – that French people across the political spectrum have been forced to point out – while France does indeed have hate speech laws – they are used to protect characteristics that people cannot change, like being black or gay.

'We do not conflate religion and race. We are the country of Voltaire and Diderot: religion is fair game,' French left radical Olivier Tonneau wrote in response to repeated claims that attacking Muhammad or Islam was racist.

Apart from being unsupported by anything approaching evidence, hate speech laws have serious unintended consequences. Recently, UK polling firm YouGov surveyed British attitudes to Muslims, and discovered that Britons see Islam negatively, but are unwilling to say so.

In other words, governments and law enforcement have to rely on anonymised polls conducted by private firms to find out what people really think.

It's not maintainable to have partial freedom of speech. The fact that most Western countries now do makes what little freedom we still have harder to defend. Muslims who respect arguments for free speech can't help but notice our inconsistencies. Anyone who thinks they don't notice is guilty of treating people who profess a certain faith like children.

We won't be Charlie until we have purged 18C, its state-based equivalents, and the illiberal national security legislation from the nation's statute books.

18C pigeonholing[76]

There's a caricature for opponents of section 18C of the *Racial Discrimination Act*. They're supposed to be racists who are just itching to offend Muslims, Asians and Aborigines.

I support the repeal of section 18C so I have been conscripted into this caricature. The thing is, I opposed conscription in the 1970s, and I oppose conscription now.

So that voters don't fall for the caricature, let me be clear. The Liberal Democrats have no objections to Muslim Australians.

I voted against every one of the recent draconian national security bills, which gave government and law enforcement bodies increased power to harass Australians, including Muslims, without due process or scrutiny.

I oppose Australia's counterproductive military involvement in the Middle East and central Asia, which has been ratcheted up without parliamentary scrutiny.

I oppose restricting immigration on the basis of religion. We must properly screen individuals, not groups, based on their character, criminality and commitment to liberal democratic values. Indeed, there is a strong case for making citizenship conditional on these qualities.

I believe food companies should be free to purchase halal certification, as long as it's in a free market and not funded by taxpayers.

And I believe Muslim women should be free to wear clothes that cover their face if they wish (although I strongly prefer to see the faces of my fellow Australians, because it's important for building mutual empathy). But we all have a right to criticise such women for their obvious refusal to integrate and assimilate.

To those who want to hurl insults at Muslims, let me be clear. I am not one of you. I do not share your views.

That said, I believe you should be free to hurl your insults, but only so that others can then deliver withering rebuttals for all to hear and learn from.

I believe you should be free to hurl your insults, so that others don't need to reconsider what they say when they want to make more considered contributions to debates on Islam.

And I believe you should be free to hurl your insults, because then there would be no need for the speech police, and abolishing this office would then mean we could all get a tax cut.

As I have said before, there's a caricature for opponents of section 18C. They're supposed to be racists just itching to offend Asians. The Liberal Democrats don't fit this lazy caricature. We welcome Asians and their impact on Australia.

My Bill to repeal s. 18C [77]

I speak in support of my Bill to repeal section 18C of the *Racial Discrimination Act*.

I am also a co-sponsor of the bill, initiated by Senator Bernardi, to remove insult and offend from 18C. My Bill would also remove the other two prohibitions, humiliate and intimidate, leaving nothing remaining.

This extra step is important. The articles by Andrew Bolt discussing affirmative action policies were ruled unlawful not just because they were considered to insult and offend. They were also considered to humiliate. And we should remember that state and territory laws already prohibit intimidation, so there is no need for a federal prohibition on race-based intimidation.

In the debate about the origin of our rights, I am on the side of John Locke, not Thomas Hobbes. I believe we are born with rights, and don't derive them from governments.

Governments can protect our rights, and that is their proper role. When governments attempt to limit or remove a right such as free speech, the onus is on them to provide sufficient justification.

It is not legitimate to ask, why do you need it, on the ground that you don't have it unless you can justify it. You have it, whether you use it or not. The same as you have rights such as a right to life, association, justice, and equality before the law.

In the case of section 18C of the Racial Discrimination Act, the government has provided no good reason for it. It is misdirected law, ineffective and illegitimate. It inhibits free speech without achieving any offsetting benefits. It should go.

In an ideal world, none of us would entertain racist thoughts. But some of us do, and some also make racist statements that echo those thoughts.

What 18C seeks to do is discourage racist speech, in the hope that it will somehow change racist thoughts.

It won't. In fact, it makes it more likely. Racists are prone to conspiratorial thoughts. Suppressing their speech is like suppressing flatulence – it might not make itself known in the same way, but it is still there and will surely erupt somewhere.

Far better to allow racist speech and to attack it with more speech. There is no shortage of people willing and able to do this – racists are vastly outnumbered by non-racists. And it is incredibly easy to refute racist speech, which essentially relies on the idea that all people of a certain race think and act the same way. It is collectivist nonsense, not unlike the idea that all gay people think and act a certain way, or all women, or all disabled people.

We should remember that Weimar Germany had hate speech laws protecting Jews. Joseph Goebbels, Hitler's propaganda minister, was taken to court because of anti-Semitic remarks, and Julius Streicher, editor of the Nazi publication *Der Stürmer*, was imprisoned twice.

The laws made minor heroes of Goebbels and Streicher. Every time Streicher's magazine was sued (36 times in about a decade), he got media attention. A young Hitler even waited for him outside jail. Even worse, while hate speech cases were prosecuted, the majority of assaults on Jews weren't. A clear abdication of state responsibility. And with what came next, there is no clearer example of the futility and laws like 18C.

18C also purports to protect the feelings of those who hear racist speech.

You can insult, offend, humiliate or intimidate someone about their lack of wealth, education, class, intelligence, morals, strength or beauty, but if you try to do that on the grounds of race, the law leaps to their defence.

What is it about feelings about race that makes them so different, that they warrant the protection of the law?

Are we really such delicate little daffodils that we're fine if we are insulted, humiliated or intimidated when it comes to our children, our choice of partner, our IQ and where we live, but we can't handle offence when it comes to race?

What complete and utter claptrap. Ridiculous and obnoxious. And for those who think 18C is primarily there to save non-white people from insults made by white people, that's also quite racist.

The implication that non-whites particularly need their feelings protected is reprehensible.

In fact, the law should never be used to protect us from hurt feelings of any kind. The law has a legitimate role to save us from physical harm, sticks and stones. But just as we learn in school, if we go running off to the teacher when the rude boy calls us nasty names, and we are told to toughen up and deal with it, so should we not go running off to the law when the same thing occurs to us as adults. It's not only childish, but a misuse of the law.

Some say this is not the time to be removing 18C because it will compromise national unity.

Actually, free speech does not have a timetable. You either believe that we are entitled to say what we think, or you don't. You either believe this is a free country or you don't. You either get the first line of our national anthem, or you don't. There is no such thing as a bad time for free speech.

In fact, I think it's incredibly dangerous that immigrant groups in this country are being told they will face hate and vilification if 18C is repealed.

There is no reason to believe that might be true, but in any case if we are talking about speech, not actions. We should not be encouraging people to believe that views and opinions they don't like, and don't want to hear, should be suppressed by the law.

When immigrants come to Australia, we expect them to adopt our liberal democratic values. That includes support for free speech.

They come to Australia, at least in part, because it is a free country. We expect them to not only enjoy, but also defend, that freedom. We are not going to introduce the death penalty on the basis that they had it in their former home. And neither should we compromise on free speech just because some people are not used to the idea of hearing things they don't like.

Rather than endorse suppression of that speech, they need to learn that, first, there is no obligation to listen and, second, free speech means they also have a right of reply.

Liberal democracies were never meant to be places of unity; that's a feature of fascist and communist regimes and, dare I say it, Islamist regimes.

What characterises a democracy is that propositions are put to the test of public deliberation. People who make 'national unity' arguments in a democracy probably do not understand democracy at all.

We cannot believe in freedom but make exceptions for when someone might have their feelings hurt. I, along with a lot of people I suspect, are sick of hearing about exceptions to freedom.

Questions of Aboriginality and Australian identity are matters of great public importance. They should be debated on the basis of evidence, without fear of being unlawful. Likewise, the Palestinian question is a matter that should also be debated, and assessed on its merits.

I lived in South Africa for a time during the apartheid era and saw racism up close and personal. I hated it. I also have no time for other types of vilification. But we cannot have a situation where important matters are closed off from debate because of the potential for someone to claim they have hurt feelings.

In short, it is not a bad time to repeal section 18C in the name of 'national unity,' rather, it is a good time to repeal section 18C in the name of 'national diversity.'

In any case, there is no evidence that to offend, insult, humiliate or intimidate someone is to incite violence against that person. Indeed, what evidence we have shows the opposite effect, because words often serve to replace violence.

As the law currently stands, instead of issues being debated and ideas criticised, toxic attitudes are driven underground or through the wires of the internet. This implicitly justifies handing over increased powers to Australia's security agencies, so that the speakers of various nasty words can be watched over by the powers that be.

If people were free to speak, there would be less need for such surveillance.

Sir Robert Menzies once declared the whole essence of freedom of speech 'is that it is freedom for others as well as (for) ourselves ... Most of us have no instinct at all to preserve the right of the other fellow to think what he likes about our beliefs and to say what he likes about our opinions... (But) if truth is to emerge, and in the long run be triumphant, the process of free debate – the untrammelled clash of opinion – must go on."

Shutting down speech by claiming you're 'offended' or that something should not be said, or inhibiting speech by criminalising journalism, is an admission of failure to understand the whole concept of free speech. And if you don't understand free speech, you don't understand freedom.

Unfortunately there are quite a few people in that category, who don't understand free speech. I became aware of just how many when the Chaser decided to make fun of me because of my support for the free speech of Wicked Campers, a company which has slogans on its vans that some people find offensive.

The Chaser team waited outside my house in Sydney at 7.30 in the morning with a van painted with slogans based on those of Wicked Campers. They told me not to be a wowser and thought it was very funny that I didn't find it terribly amusing. They also suggested that made me hypocritical in relation to my support for free speech.

A few details are relevant – they didn't identify themselves, which led me to advise a *Daily Telegraph* journalist that I had been the subject of a protest outside my house. I told them to eff off, as I wasn't amused at being accosted outside my home, and one of their slogans was homophobic. It appeared to me they were going to trespass into my front garden, which is why I said I would call the police.

What my critics have overlooked is that at no stage did I say they had no right to say what they did. At no time did I suggest they should be prevented by law from saying it. I didn't think they were terribly smart, and what they did was in poor taste and upset my wife, but that's where it ends. Free speech does not require me to find them amusing, or appreciate what they said, or even to remain and listen to them. All it requires is that I do not invoke the law.

And can I say, to Nina Oyama, Craig Reucassel, Zoe Norton Lodge, Kirsten Drysdale, and the others, it would not require a lot of effort by me to find out where you live, and to set up a sign outside your place which said rude things about you.

If your response was to tell me to eff off, and that's all, then perhaps there might be hope for you and your understanding of the concept of free speech. But I doubt if that's how you would react. I suspect you would act like cry-babies and go running off to nanny government, asking for the nasty man to be shut up. And that's why I say, I don't believe you understand freedom, let alone free speech. And that's a shame.

Freedom of speech is the paramount freedom. Without it, we struggle to exercise our other freedoms. With it, we can fight for those freedoms.

It may be offensive, insulting and make governments and people uncomfortable, but if this is the price to be paid for living in a society where all claims are open to question, then it is a price worth paying.

FIREARMS

A nation of victims [78]

Legally, Australians have a right to self-defence.

What we don't have is the practical ability to exercise that right. Owning any object for the purpose of self-defence, lethal or non-lethal, is a criminal offence. Those trapped within the Lindt café were left helpless, as carrying items for self-defence is not allowed under state law. What's worse, the offender possibly knew it.

Prohibited self-defence items include pepper sprays, mace, clubs and personal tasers. In some states carrying a pocket-knife is illegal and even wearing a bullet-proof vest is banned.

Those agile enough to retreat from an assailant can do so, and it is lawful to use items at hand such as screwdrivers, kitchen knives and beer glasses. But for those who are unable to flee, insufficiently strong, or with no improvised weapon, there is no option but to rely on the police.

The Prime Minister is protected by armed guards at taxpayers' expense, and the wealthy can hire armed security guards, but everyone else relies for their safety on the police. And as the saying goes, when seconds count the police are minutes away.

What this means is that self-defence is not a realistic option for most people, and especially not for the majority of women, elderly and disabled. We have become a nation of defenceless victims.

This is not to criticise the NSW police, who did their best in difficult circumstances. But the police cannot be everywhere and we shouldn't expect them to keep us safe all the time.

Australia's ban on practical self-defence sets it apart from most other countries. Almost none prohibit non-lethal means of self-defence, while many permit ownership of firearms at home.

Australia's prohibition on practical self-defence is recent, emanating from the 1996 changes in firearms laws that followed the Port Arthur massacre. Not only were many types of firearm prohibited, but Australia embraced an international push to prohibit civilian ownership of firearms for self-defence.

This was driven by several factors. One was a desire to avoid America's 'gun culture.' However, this was broadened to include all means of self-defence. There was also a strange version of the precautionary principle – the wrong-headed belief that average citizens would one day be overcome by murderous tendencies.

Then there are perennial claims that resistance is futile and that items of self-defence can be turned against those using them. Any woman who has fought off a would-be rapist – and there are many – knows this to be untrue.

Mythologising about firearms is a feature of Australian public debate. Many seriously believe the solution to any crime involving a gun is more gun laws. And yet the offender in the Lindt café did not have a gun licence and in any case the sawn-off shotgun he was using is illegal.

Perhaps Australians will never embrace the use of guns for self-defence except in special cases (a battered wife dealing with a murderous ex-husband, for example). But they never agreed to or accepted being rendered defenceless. If asked, I believe most would unequivocally demand the right to practical self-defence, at least using non-lethal means.

And it should never have reached this stage. Only an authoritarian society would treat its citizens as victims, with the government masquerading as a guardian angel. Free societies have a strong emphasis on individual self-reliance.

Restrictions on non-lethal means of self-defence should be removed, while methods with potential to cause harm should be available but restricted to trained, responsible adults. It is time to stop pretending the government can protect us from events such as the Lindt café siege.

The truth about Australia's gun control experiment[79]

Australians pride themselves on 'telling it like it is,' but when it comes to gun laws, straight-shooting often takes a back seat to a determined effort at silencing debate.

In 1996, Australia passed some of the most restrictive gun laws in the western world. They included bans on self-loading rifles and self-loading and pump-action shotguns, universal gun registration and a taxpayer-funded gun confiscation program costing over half a billion dollars. The ongoing costs of running the firearms registration systems are unknown but have been estimated at around $28 million per year, or $75,000 per day. That's more than what the average Australian earns in a year.

For that price tag, any accountable democracy should expect to have a decent debate about its efficacy. But in Australia, debate about guns has been all but silenced. Anti-gun zealots, within and outside the halls of parliament, smugly try to convince the rest of the world that Australia's model of firearms management has been a resounding success. 'We saved lives!' they claim. 'We stopped mass shootings!' they say.

To satisfy their conceit, they manipulate statistics to suit themselves and pretend that 'the science is settled.' This is an outright lie. When you look at the real facts, it becomes very obvious that the Australian experiment with gun control is nowhere near as clear-cut as the gun prohibition lobby wants the world to believe.

There is a growing body of peer-reviewed research into the impacts of Australia's 1996 gun laws. Some of it comes from anti-gun groups, some from pro-gun groups, and some from groups which have no personal connections to firearms one way or the other.

Using a range of different statistical methods and time periods, not a single one of these studies – not even the ones conducted by anti-gun affiliated researchers – has found a significant impact of the legislative changes on the pre-existing downward trend in firearm homicide. Firearm homicides were decreasing well before the laws were implemented, and the decline simply continued after the legislative changes.

This decline in Australia is not unique or unusual. At least two other Commonwealth countries (Canada and New Zealand) experienced similar or greater declines in deaths over the same time, even though those countries have far less restrictive gun laws than Australia.

The relationship between Australia's gun laws and suicides is uncertain. Again, deaths were declining well before the legislative changes. Some studies find that the downward trend accelerated after the 1996 gun laws, while others find impacts only among certain age groups. Some research finds little evidence for any change, others show displacement from firearms to other methods (such as hanging).

Anti-gun lobbyists cherry-pick the statistics that suit them and ignore studies that do not fall into line with the story they desperately want to tell. The fairy tale they prefer is that the gun laws have 'saved 200 lives a year,' a claim based on laughably poor statistical modelling which produced estimates so ridiculous that they have been dismissed by Harvard researchers as 'stretching credulity.' The scientific reality is there is no consensus whatsoever about firearm laws and suicide in Australia.

A claim you will often hear is that there have been no mass shootings since 1996, from which anti-gun lobbyists conclude that Australia's gun laws have stopped mass shootings. But this is a half-truth. The full truth is that Australia's close neighbour New Zealand – a country very similar to Australia in history, culture, and economic trends – has experienced an almost identical time period with no mass shooting events despite the ongoing widespread availability of the types of firearms Australia banned.

The absence of mass shootings in New Zealand, despite having semi-automatic firearms, does not seem to be a product of any pre-existing differences between the two countries. Studies taking into account the different numbers of people have found that mass shootings before 1996/1997 occurred at a comparable rate between countries. The inescapable conclusion is that something other than gun laws is likely to be driving the merciful absence of mass shooting events in both countries.

And yet, despite all the scientific evidence to the contrary, the anti-gun lobby continues to promote untruths, unchallenged. Notwithstanding the massive price tag attached to Australia's gun laws, proper debate is still not taking place. Despite the fact that other policies may be far more effective at saving lives, dissenting views about the gun laws are ridiculed and shrilly shouted down. Yes, the rest of the world can indeed learn a lesson from Australia's gun control experiment. But that lesson is really not about gun laws. It is about the dangers of allowing lobbyists, politicians and the media to prevent a rational debate.

The folly of the Adler shotgun ban[80]
Last week the Council of Australian Governments (COAG) decided to make the National Firearms Agreement more stringent by placing lever action shotguns of more than five rounds

into Category D, while lever-action shotguns of up to five rounds will be placed in Category B.

For most of Australia's 800,000 licensed firearm owners, Category D firearms are simply unavailable. Category D is restricted to professional shooters, of which there are only a few hundred in the entire country. Moreover, those holding a Category D licence have access to semi-automatic firearms and no interest in lever actions. This means there will be no demand for lever action shotguns of more than five rounds.

For the rest of us, shotguns are currently in Category A and available to most licensed shooters, while Category B covers centrefire rifles. Once the COAG decision is enacted into state law, lever-action shotguns will join them in Category B.

If you think this is a bit weird, that's because it is.

It all began when the Adler seven-shot shotgun was portrayed as a 'rapid fire' firearm. When then Prime Minister Tony Abbott was looking for a terrorist announcement each week, Justice Minister Michael Keenan came up with the Adler. Just imagine if a terrorist got hold of one, he said.

To ignorant politicians, media and commentators, not even that amount of justification was required. While most wouldn't know a lever action shotgun from a pump-action water pistol, any action short of a complete ban (unless belonging to a government official) equates to taking Australia down the American path. And of course everyone is an expert on America because what happens on television and in the movies is real, right?

If evidence or reason were relevant, it would be immediately apparent that a five-round restriction on the magazines of shotguns, which are only dangerous to about 70 metres, is absurd when 303 rifles from the First World War are available with a ten-round magazine and lethal to more than 500 metres.

Or that other shotguns, including straight pull actions with up to five round magazines, are to remain in Category A. Or that pistols, for those licensed to own them, are allowed with ten-round magazines.

Moreover, lever action firearms are never used in crime. They are old technology, clunky to use and virtually useless if sawn off. A shotgun of the type used in the Olympic Games, when sawn off, is far more attractive to criminals.

In truth, not many sporting shooters are all that interested in lever action shotguns. There is far more interest in lever action rifles – the trusty 30–30 being a favourite for shooting pigs. Some farmers would find them useful though; eliminating a mob of pigs in a paddock of lambing ewes would be far easier with a seven-shot Adler, for example. Pinpoint accuracy, necessary with a rifle, is not as crucial with a shotgun and a mob of pigs can be big enough to require multiple shots.

It will still be possible to convert a five-shot Adler into seven or more, simply by fitting a longer magazine tube under the barrel, but whether that remains legal is unclear. It is also unclear what will happen to the lever action shotguns already in use which have magazines that hold more than five rounds. Unless there is a buyback, all those political terrorists planning to cause mayhem with a lever action shot gun (which is presumably what we are supposed to fear) may still be able to get their hands on them.

What the COAG decision signifies is that creeping regulation of firearm ownership remains a problem, for farmers as well as hunters and sporting shooters. The Firearms Section in the Attorney-General's Department has had an agenda of incremental restrictions on firearms for over a decade, with semi-automatic pistols, pump-action rifles, lever action shotguns and lever action rifles on its list.

Their objective is the ultimate disarming of law-abiding Australians, of preventing them from enjoying their sporting, hunting and collecting activities, towards the end envisaged by

John Howard in 1996 in which only the police, military and security guards have guns.

That's not an outcome we should welcome. And fear, imaginary threats and ignorance are not a basis for sound government.

The economic value of hunting[81]

I rise today to celebrate the contribution Australia's large hunting community to the economy and the environment.

Nobody is prepared to say it – even though I know some here agree – but I am happy to say I celebrate hunting and the freedom to choose to own guns and go hunting.

I will start with a quote from U.S president and Nobel Prize winner, Theodore Roosevelt:

> The encouragement of a proper hunting spirit, a proper love of sport, instead of being incompatible with a love of nature and wild things, offers the best guarantee for their preservation.

Like many minority groups, hunters are often vilified for their activities by those who have never taken the time to understand them or the deep cultural and intergenerational bonds that are a significant part of the hunting ethos.

Instead, those opposed to this traditional activity – one so embedded in the evolutionary DNA of the human race – heap scorn and vitriol on hunters who go quietly about their activities, self-reliant, self-funded, not asking for handouts or grants or approval – only tolerance.

Indigenous peoples hunted to sustain themselves long before white settlement and are given special privileges to hunt some species in the present day for cultural reasons. Why would anyone believe that only Aboriginal people have a cultural attachment to hunting?

Indeed, a friend has introduced each of his five children, three boys and two girls, to hunting and even though all but one are now adults, they recently spent a weekend in the high country hunting and camping together, just as he did with his own father years before.

As for myself, I am proud to have been a shooter and hunter for most of my life – and to show that I am not biased, I also happen to think vegetarians are cool. All I eat are vegetarians – except for the occasional fish.

The naysayers – animal rights activists and gun haters – who have no qualifications other than their moral indignation, and are far fewer in number than the highly regulated and licensed hunters, complain long and loud about hunting, but bring nothing positive to the discussion on how we manage our burgeoning populations of introduced feral pests.

A study published recently in the journal Wildlife Research by Associate Professor Peter Murray from the University of Queensland's School of Agriculture and Food Sciences – titled Expenditure and motivation of Australian recreational hunters – showed Australia's 300,000 hunters spent over $1 billion per annum on their hunting activities.

State governments that actively engage with the hunting community appear to reap the strongest economic benefits.

A report released in June by the Victorian government shows that licensed game hunters spent $417 million in 2013 on their activities, with 60% of that spent in regional areas.

Millions of dollars in taxpayer funds are spent trying to encourage increased visitation to regional Australia while recreational hunting continues to grow and contribute to the regional economy without costing the public purse at all.

The long heritage of hunting, with its strong cultural traditions, its economic contribution, as well as its potential for aiding wildlife management, have largely been ignored, and to our detriment. However, some positive change is occurring.

After more than 15 years of lobbying by hunting organisations, the Victorian government established the statutory Game Management Authority on July 1 to regulate and enhance game hunting in Victoria.

This positive approach to game hunting is likely to substantially increase the expenditure on hunting recorded in 2013. Other states would be well advised to closely monitor the progress of the Victorian initiative so they too can maximise economic potential for their rural and regional communities.

Insofar as improving Australia's poor management of pest animals and threatened native species is concerned, I quote the report lead author Peter Murray: 'Wildlife management in Australia could benefit from greater engagement between wildlife managers and the recreational hunting community.

'The potential exists for this large and active community to become a valuable resource for wildlife managers as many are already hunting feral pests.

'If the public understands there are pest animals eating native animals and destroying native habitat throughout Australia, it makes a lot of sense for hunters to be allowed to assist in the management of those populations at no cost to the government.'

Of the 7,200 recreational hunters surveyed as part of the study, 99% indicated they would be willing to participate in pest-control activities if they had the opportunity to do so.

In a neat corollary to President Roosevelt's statement many decades earlier, Dr Murray stated that in other OECD countries such as the United States, recreational hunters are widely engaged with wildlife managers, and hunting taxes contribute the majority of conservation funding in that country.

Let me emphasise that point.

Taxes on hunting equipment in the U.S constitute the majority of conservation funding. Legislation also dictates that some of the funds must be used to employ trained wildlife specialists.

These hunter-supported actions have contributed to a well-founded belief in the hunting community that hunters are the true conservationists. Hunters support their beliefs with funding and effort. This stands in stark contrast to the carping and lack of productive action by naysayers.

More than two thirds of the report's survey participants supported the idea of paying a levy on hunting merchandise to contribute towards wildlife conservation above and beyond the removal of feral animals.

90% of the hunters who supported a levy were prepared to pay between 5 and 10% for wildlife conservation.

Dr Murray believes that 'should such a levy be introduced in Australia, it could generate significant funding for conservation in this country.'

My own view is that the implications for policymakers from the study are two-fold. First, the Australian recreational hunting community is large, active and willing to spend large amounts of money on hunting.

Secondly, the majority of hunters surveyed by the report are willing to contribute financially to wildlife conservation and actively assist in the removal of pest animals.

In July, the environment minister appointed Australia's first ever Threatened Species Commissioner in an attempt to focus concerted action on the declining numbers of native species. A major contributing factor is feral predators.

However, no policy initiative has been put forward to fully harness the benefits of hundreds of thousands of hunters assisting resource poor land managers while at the same time contributing significantly to the local economy.

This study provides the evidence to the minister that he has the support of the hunting community to help provide at least part of the solution to controlling pest animals, all at no cost to the taxpayer.

Now, I'm going to suggest to the hunting community something somewhat contrary to the Liberal Democrats' guiding principle of 'no tax increases.'

The United States' experience of the long-standing *Pittman-Robertson Act* – it adds a small levy to purchases of hunting merchandise – has been so successful in promoting wildlife conservation, that if the Australian hunting community decided to support such a levy, as hunters have done in the United States, and self-determined the extent of such a levy, the Liberal Democrats would support it.

What I would propose to the environment minister is that he assists state government land managers, perhaps through Caring for Country funding, in becoming more proactive in their engagement with hunting organisations to address the growing problem of pest animals.

Many small-scale programs on a local level have been run for years, controlling pest animals in specific locations to protect species like Brolgas. These programs have usually been initiated by hunters concerned about species survival – even if those species are not game, such as Brolgas.

The opportunity now presents itself for the minister to learn from the success of these efforts, engage with hunters, and reproduce these effects on a much larger scale.

From our record of pest animal management to date, it is self-evident that public land managers need all the help they can get.

In conclusion, I say to Australia's many hunters:

Thank you for hunting.

Thank you for the billion dollars you spent last year.

And most of all, thank you for helping the environment by killing tens of thousands of introduced pests for free – nobody else could or would.

FREEDOM ISSUES

The police are not our masters[82]

A bit over three years ago, in response to a brawl between rival outlaw motorcycle gangs on the Gold Coast, the Queensland government introduced the so-called VLAD law. This gave the police enormous powers to stop, search and detain motorcyclists. Refusing to answer questions attracted a five-year prison term and three motorcyclists riding together could constitute an offence.

The Queensland police were, to put it mildly, zealous in their application of the law. Although most motorcyclists are not members of organised motorcycle gangs, and only a minority of members of OMGs are criminals, uninvolved clubs were raided, motorcyclists were stopped, searched and harassed at random, and some motorcyclists were forced to give up certain occupations. There were numerous examples, including YouTube videos, of appalling police behaviour.

In late 2013 I attended a rally in Brisbane to protest against the VLAD laws. As a senator-elect at the time, I addressed the crowd and made the following remarks:

> The police and the public, at least the motorcycle riding public, are on a collision course and they wonder why no one comes to their aid when they are in trouble. For myself, I am never going to help

someone who thinks it's OK to pull me up, search me and threaten me with jail if I don't answer their questions, merely because I ride my motorcycle in company with a couple of other people. If that's what they think, they can lie on the side of the road and bleed to death.

In 2015 in NSW, in the context of an inquiry into the nanny state, I observed that A-League football fans applied the saying 'ACAB' to the police.

Referring to claims of very heavy-handed treatment of fans, my words were, 'There is a saying amongst them of ACAB, or all "cops are bastards." The cops have earned that label, they have to un-earn it. The police are not our masters, they are our servants, and I think they should remember that.'

Australians excel at outrage. Whether it's about sentencing criminals or the words of public figures, a lot of people hold very strongly held opinions and are determined to vehemently express them.

I am accustomed to outrage in politics. On my personal one to ten scale, the outrage following my NSW comments was only about four. The meter barely registered when I first made my Queensland remarks, but their recent re-publishing by a junior journalist has now pushed that to about eight. Suddenly, a lot more people have decided they are outraged.

Among those most outraged are serving police, former police, and their families. Some of the latter are relatively prominent in the media. Quite a few have been seriously abusive, including threats of violence, while others were keen to ensure I was aware of the heroic and selfless nature of police work. Very obviously, most did not believe the police should be criticised at all, especially by a politician.

Deliberately or not, many of those outraged chose to ignore the conditional nature of my Queensland comments. When I said, 'If that's what they think,' it was obviously not intended to apply to them all. It was also largely rhetorical; what an individual police officer involved in an accident thinks is hardly likely to be known by me or anyone who shares my view. Even if my comment was taken literally, it infers I would assist police other than those who I know to hold such views.

Similarly, many chose to ignore the fact that in NSW I was repeating what fans were saying about the police. Much of the abuse I received was based on the proposition that they were my words. Outrage and accuracy of facts are not comfortable bedfellows.

That said, it hasn't been all one way. I have received lots of messages of support from those who either have no love for the police, or agree with my specific comments. Examples of egregious misconduct by police, for which nobody has been punished, have also been brought to my attention.

What is clear is that many police feel unloved and undervalued, and are lashing out at those who fail to show due deference. Chief among those are the police unions.

The Police Association of Victoria, for example, posted a picture of me on their Facebook page with the caption, 'They [police] can lie on the side of the road and bleed to death.' There was no link to the source, the rest of the statement, or any other attempt to provide context.

Responding to my NSW comments, the Police Association of NSW called for the abolition of the senate and my removal from a parliamentary committee on law enforcement. It also described fans of the Western Sydney Wanderers FC, whose complaints the inquiry had been examining, as 'grubs' and 'thugs.'

To libertarians like me, the police and criminal justice system are among the few areas of government that we would not seek to privatise. Notwithstanding constant lies about 'keeping us safe,' we acknowledge the police have a key role in the protection of life, liberty and property.

However, to perform this role successfully they must have public support. Sir Robert Peel's famous principles of law enforcement, written in 1829 upon the establishment of the London Metropolitan Police, are just as valid today as they were at the time. Key among these is the need for 'public approval of police existence, actions, behaviour and the ability of the police to secure and maintain public respect' and 'the police are the public and the public are the police.'

Fairly obviously, respect and approval can only be won, not demanded. Moreover, bashing people in Queanbeyan police station in NSW, or Ballarat police station in Victoria, does not contribute to that. In my view, neither does the behaviour of the police when enforcing the Queensland VLAD law, or dealing with WSW football fans in NSW. The police responsible for such conduct are not entitled to public support or the support of decent, honest police. Fairly obviously, they don't have my support.

Perhaps the most troubling aspect of the outrage is the implication that unless I speak positively about the police, I should not expect their assistance in the event I am involved in an accident or other misfortune. Indeed, there were suggestions by some that individual police would go further and retaliate against me. Not only is this characteristic of a police state, it reminds me of the days of the Bjelke-Petersen government in Queensland when the police were seriously corrupt, ignored criminal activity and used their power to abuse their critics.

The outrage inevitably moves on to another subject, but the issues raised in this instance remain. The police must earn our respect, on an ongoing basis, and are not entitled to demand it or retaliate against those who question them.

And they must absolutely not protect those who bring policing into disrepute.

Speed limits[83]

Did you cop a speeding ticket these holidays? Many did. Speed limits have the status of holy writ, with everyone expected to obey them. Officially, fines are atonement for sinning.

We are repeatedly told how many people were killed in road accidents over the holiday season, invariably attributed to excess speed. There are gory advertisements warning of lifelong injuries, with big brother enforcement via fixed and hidden cameras, double demerits, average speed cameras, aerial monitoring and highway patrols.

The underlying message never varies – below the speed limit is safe, above the limit is not.

The public thinks otherwise. In the absence of visible enforcement or perceived hazards, voluntary compliance with speed limits is low. A 2009 survey found less than 20% of drivers admit to always driving at or under the speed limit. Another found only 41% thought speeding by up to 10 km/h in a 100 km/h zone was unacceptable, while 38% admitted to speeding by 10–19 km/h and 21% by 20 km/h or more.

Outside narrow suburban streets, exceeding the speed limit is not seen as a problem.

The National Road Safety Strategy seeks to change that. Its aim is to 'reduce poor road user behaviour' through 'behavioural change,' and has a vision that 'no person should be killed or seriously injured on Australia's roads.'

It asserts we need lower speed limits, additional enforcement including in-car speed monitoring, plus increased penalties.

There is a link between speed and the risk of accidents and injuries. The degree of correlation is disputed and there is some evidence that modestly higher speed limits would reduce the accident rate, but higher speeds certainly lead to more serious accidents and ultimately more of them.

The question is, why not drastically lower speed limits? Given the aim of zero deaths and injuries, why not reduce the speed limit to something like 20 km/h so that accidents are either eliminated or only have minor consequences?

The answer, fairly obviously, is that it would be unacceptable to the community. There is an implicit assumption in speed limits that there will be a certain level of deaths and serious injuries as the price paid for convenient travel. The vision of the National Road Safety Strategy is not only unobtainable, but irrational.

That raises an interesting question. When the law says one thing and most people have a different view, which should prevail? And perhaps more to the point, who should set the speed limits?

The people who currently set them are anonymous, unaccountable bureaucrats. Perhaps the most powerful people in Australia, they essentially decide how many people should die on our roads. Governments and ministers come and go, but they and their speed limits are always there.

This is massive bureaucratic overreach. It is the public, not bureaucrats, who ought to determine the trade-off between travel convenience and the road toll. There is even an internationally recognised method of achieving this, known as the eighty-fifth percentile formula. Briefly, it involves the temporary removal of speed limits while speeds are monitored. At the conclusion of the period a limit is reimposed at or slightly above the speed at which 85% of drivers travel.

The method is based on the assumption that the large majority of drivers are reasonable and prudent, do not want to crash, and wish to reach their destination in the shortest possible time.

Evidence shows that those who drive above or substantially below speed limits based on the eighty-fifth percentile are far more likely to cause accidents. Enforcement directed at those drivers thus has a positive impact on road safety while enjoying a high level of driver support.

If the public becomes concerned about any increase in road deaths or injuries, this can be expressed through periodic retesting of the eighty-fifth percentile.

If the government serves the people rather than vice versa, speed limits should have the approval of most drivers. Instead of being treated like sinful children and a source of revenue, motorists should be the ones who decide what the limits are.

Thank you for riding a motorbike[84]

Today I'd like to say, 'Thank you for riding a motorbike.'

In fact, motorcyclists should take a bow.

The more people ride motorbikes, the more the rest of the community benefits. And I am pleased to say that motorcycling is enjoying a sustained surge in popularity.

Older people and women are now more likely to become motorcyclists, and there is a broader range of motorcycles available – from low powered scooters to large touring bikes.

In most Australian states, motorbike registration has out-stripped car registration on a percentage basis in the last five years, growing nationally by 25%. In NSW, motorcycle registrations have enjoyed a 60% increase.

But this growing popularity is largely in spite of state and federal government policies, not because of them.

People ride motorbikes to commute, for touring, and for trail riding.

Motorcycling offers affordable mobility, avoiding traffic snarls, stress relief and the personal freedom of touring. Then there's the pleasure of just riding. Riding a bike anywhere is worth it.

Motorcycling also offers social interaction with others, an enjoyable leisure activity, and the means to share an activity with like-minded friends.

For many, the thrill of participating in or being a spectator to motorcycle racing adds further value to their lifestyle.

A motorbike is more capable of negotiating heavy traffic than other vehicles, with trip times up to a third less than cars.

But why do motorcyclists deserve to be thanked?

Because motorcycling in our cities significantly eases congestion. On the road and also with parking. This is beneficial to other road users.

Motorbikes use less fuel, produce fewer emissions and cause less road wear than other vehicles. Up to five motorbikes can occupy the same parking space as a single car.

Another reason is that motorcycle touring is a boon to our regional economy; the average motorcyclist spends $120 to $140 per night in regional towns, compared to an average $18 spent by 'grey nomads.'

I am among those who deserve to be thanked.

I have been riding motorbikes for 40 years; it is a part of my life and gives me great enjoyment. My current bike is a recently acquired BMW S1000R. A 1,000 cc rocket ship.

Living in Australia's biggest city, I particularly like being able to weave my way through the traffic. And in the process I use less fuel, take up less space on the road, share parking spaces with other bikes, and cause less wear and tear on the roads.

Given all that, you might think that planning for, and encouragement of, motorcycling would be high on the agenda of road planners and traffic authorities. You would be wrong.

Not only are motorcycle riders invisible to many car drivers, they are also invisible to policymakers.

In the 173-page National Road Safety Strategy Review, just two pages are devoted to motorcycling issues.

Even though motorbike use in the Melbourne CBD increased 73% between 2006 and 2014, and there are now over three quarters of a million motorcycles registered nationally, they are ignored in road safety planning.

And when authorities actually pay attention to motorcyclists, they typically begin from the wrong starting point.

Instead of encouraging and enhancing the growing trend towards motorcycling, the policymaker mindset is stuck in prohibition and regulation, in an attempt to curtail and control motorcycling.

Because the consequences of accidents are more serious for motorcyclists, the authorities consider motorcyclists feeble-minded and in need of saving from themselves.

It is well known that doctors and nurses in hospital emergency departments refer to us as 'organ donors.'

They, and others who also never ride a motorcycle, feel entitled to impose restrictions and constraints on motorcycling.

And yet, motorcyclists know the risks that flow from having an accident. We are adults, we have minds of their own, and we accept those risks. Ask any one of us.

A better attitude to motorcycling, with a more constructive approach by policymakers, would translate into broader recognition and acceptance by the public of the benefits to all road users from motorcycling. The do-gooders and nanny staters should back off.

We encourage the use of public transport as an alternative to commuting by car. We should also acknowledge that motorcycling is a viable means of easing traffic congestion. It is not a nuisance.

Road rules and parking provisions should facilitate motorcycling, not inhibit it. The National Road Safety Strategy should do likewise.

The Transport and Infrastructure Council, chaired by the Minister for Infrastructure, is the peak road safety policy forum in the country.

I urge the minister to get motorcycling on the agenda for the sake of all road users in Australia.

And it is high time that police, engineers and road safety experts stopped making life hard for motorcyclists. The three quarters of a million Australians who choose to ride a motor-bike deserve better.

Nanny state lockouts report[85]

In the previous parliament I chaired the Nanny State Inquiry. A final report was not produced because of the election, but some excellent interim reports were issued.

One of the issues that the committee examined was the Sydney lockout laws.

On 7 July 2012, at around 10 pm, 18-year-old Thomas Kelly was fatally assaulted in a 'one-punch' attack in Kings Cross. In response, the NSW Government introduced legislative and policy changes affecting the sale and service of alcohol at licensed venues in Kings Cross and other areas of central Sydney.

Venues in the Kings Cross precinct were subject to special licence conditions. Every night of the week there was a ban on glasses, glass bottles and glass jugs after midnight. For Friday and Saturday late-night trading there was a ban on shots and doubles after midnight, individuals could not buy more than four alcoholic drinks at a time after midnight; and no alcohol could be sold in the hour before closing.

In December 2012, the area affected was expanded to a total of 134 licensed venues. A license freeze was implemented, preventing the establishment of any new higher risk venues or the expansion of existing venues.

One year later, in December 2013, a second tranche of legislation changed licensing conditions for venues in Kings Cross. These included:

- a centralised ID scanning system (rolled out in June 2014), with a requirement for all high-risk venues to operate a linked identification scanner to prevent banned persons from entering licensed premises;

- temporary and long-term banning orders, linked to the ID scanner system, barring individuals from entering venues on the basis of antisocial and violent behaviour;
- a requirement for licensees to record daily alcohol sales and report these quarterly.

These particular measures were constructive. They focused on the individuals who caused trouble and did not treat everyone as equally troublesome. But they never had a chance to work.

On New Year's Eve 2013, before these changes were in effect, 18-year-old Daniel Christie was killed from a one-punch assault. Even though the punch happened at around 9 pm, the NSW government announced even more restrictions for after midnight.

In addition to stricter sentencing, it introduced 1.30 am lockouts and 3.00 am cessation of alcohol service, applying across an expanded entertainment precinct. These provisions came into effect on 24 February 2014.

Clubs, hotels, general bars and on-premises licences, within the Sydney CBD or Kings Cross, are not allowed to let people into their venue after 1.30 am.

People already in a venue before 1.30 am can stay until the close of business. They are able to leave at any time, but if they leave after 1.30 am, they are not able to re-enter during the lockout period, or gain entry to any other venue subject to the lockout.

These venues are not allowed to sell or supply liquor after 3 am.

If it trades after 3 am, the venue can remain open for dining or entertainment, but is not allowed to serve liquor. Liquor sales cannot resume until the commencement of the next trading period.

Other measures included a ban on takeaway alcohol sales after 10.00 pm across NSW and a freeze on new liquor licences and approvals for existing licences across the new Sydney CBD entertainment precinct.

It did not escape anyone's attention that the casinos were exempted from the lockout regime.

A review of the lockout laws was commissioned by the NSW government, undertaken by former High Court Justice, Ian Callinan QC. His report was released two months ago.

He recommended reducing the lockout period by half an hour and allowing home delivery of alcohol up to midnight.

For those who believe in the individual rather than the collective, and who thought Mr Callinan did as well, the report was a serious disappointment.

Easing last drinks restrictions by half an hour will not return Kings Cross to its former glory. Allowing late-night entertainment at the Cross without alcohol will not help much either.

In fact, inviting international visitors to view our budding artists while choosing between soft drinks will make us a laughing stock.

And the hundreds of young people in the hospitality, entertainment and tourism industries who became unemployed will not get their old jobs back.

The ridiculous thing about all this is that the lockout laws would not have prevented the assaults that led to the formulation of the laws in the first place. The assaults occurred relatively early in the evening.

Absolutely none of this makes any sense.

Why can't Sydneysiders be trusted to stay out past 2 am? Is there something in the water that means Melburnians can stay out late but not Sydney people?

Why can Sydneysiders be trusted to visit Melbourne and stay out late, but not vice versa?

Or does all of this have more to do with that madness where governments have come to believe that they must act as our de facto parents?

Perhaps this kind of result is to be expected if you allow people who have forgotten the last time they had a good time to set the rules for a party.

Prominent amongst these people have been the doctor's associations, populated by those who have grown bored of making people feel better, and now just want to tell others how to live their lives.

There are the residents associations, who are concerned about where things happen. Whether it's smoking, drinking, playing music or anything else they disapprove of, it's definitely not something they want in their neighbourhood. This is known as NIMBY, or Not In My Backyard. But it's also known as Now It's My Backyard, which refers to those who move into an area and start complaining.

And of course there are the wowsers and moralists who live in constant fear that somebody, somewhere, might be having a good time.

Including the hypocritical moralists who think it's OK to ban alcohol consumption but are relaxed when it comes to drugs such as ice.

Sydney should be Australia's most vibrant city. It has a glorious history of naughtiness that dates back at least to when the convicts were unloaded onto the shores of Port Jackson in 1788.

As Sydney grew, Kings Cross became the place where sailors on shore leave have let off steam. It has provided rites of passage for thousands of Australians, and been the one place in Sydney where bohemians and artists have felt at home. Somehow they have co-existed with us for decades without harming anyone, and without needing to be told when to go to bed.

There should be a place in Sydney for these people, and so long as they are not harming anyone else, we should leave them alone.

Of course, I welcome any moves to relax current restrictions, but the reported changes will not revive the nightlife of Sydney. It should be revived.

Constitutional recognition[86]

Seven years ago, the Rudd government apologised to the Stolen Generations. As the recently released Closing the Gap report indicates, this achieved nothing for Aboriginal living standards.

The unemployment rate for Aborigines and Torres Strait Islanders is still three times the national average, and Aborigines overall have shocking health outcomes and die at younger ages, especially in rural and remote areas.

You'd think the politics of the empty gesture would have fallen out of fashion by now. But no; if anything, things are getting worse. They now include the ridiculous claim that recognising Aborigines and Torres Strait Islanders in the Constitution will somehow improve their health and welfare.

I've had to sit through speeches in the Senate asserting this, and have read newspaper articles making the same argument. And yet there is not a shred of evidence to support the claim.

The national fondness for political symbolism became evident with full force when I made a speech in the Senate opposing Constitutional recognition. I argued that it would be conjectural, divisive, and contrary to the rule of law.

It was the last point that generated the most vitriol. My argument was that we should all be equal before the law, while Constitutional recognition is a campaign for the specific recognition of a specific people. Apparently a lot of people think otherwise.

Prior to 1967, the Constitution included the power to make laws for 'The people of any race, other than the aboriginal race, in any state, for whom it is deemed necessary to make special laws.' We now recognise this as racism. What made it racist was not just that it had been interpreted negatively, but that it allowed people to be treated differently because of their race.

If the constitution is to be changed, it should be to remove the remaining 'race power,' which allows parliament to make laws for 'The people of any race, for whom it is deemed necessary to make special laws,' and section 25, which allows the exclusion of whole races when drawing up electorates. No constitution should permit governments to make laws that apply to certain races and not others. It is racist, and amounts to a standing invitation to engage in abuse of power.

But I don't kid myself that removing those sections will have any effect on Aboriginal and Torres Strait Islander health or welfare. The Constitution may be an important document, but individuals needing special assistance should be treated equally before the law, whatever their race. And Australia must be colour blind when it comes to reducing poverty and disadvantage.

Indeed, my party, the Liberal Democrats, deliberately has no policy relating specifically to Aborigines. Our policies are simply about people. In that vein, we think the property rights of remote and rural Aborigines should be upgraded to the same as everyone else, allowing them to fully participate in the general economy.

In the book *Recognise What?*, Anthony Dillon writes movingly of those Aboriginal people who have enjoyed success in wider society without constitutional recognition.

'Do not segregate yourself from society,' Mr Dillon advises. 'Treat others with respect and see them as equals; pursue an education (whether it be formal or informal); make valuable contributions to the community in which you live; be a role model for others to emulate; make healthy choices; and adhere to a personal moral code.'

This is good advice. Constitutional recognition will not 'close the gap.' In fact, it is not likely to achieve anything positive at all.

Closing the Gap 2016[87]

When I was a kid in primary school, I shared classrooms with kids from Aboriginal families. By the time I got to high school, they were no longer there. Not one of them went on to high school with me and my peers.

That was over 50 years ago. But little has changed since. Too many kids see no reason to go to school, and neither do their families. Too many suffer from diseases that the rest of us regard as a thing of the past. Too many live-in households where their diet comprises chips and soft drink. And too many never become productive members of society when they grow up.

Considerable blame for this lies with our governments. With the support of people who ought to know better, governments maintain policies that foster dysfunctional Aboriginal communities, attitudes and behaviours.

In doing so, they are holding back improvements in Aboriginal living standards. The gap is not narrowing.

At its heart is a preference for fawning and hand wringing rather than pragmatism, for sounding good rather than doing good, for empty symbolism rather than practical change, and for truthiness rather than truth.

The gap between indigenous and non-indigenous living standards is largely explained by the poor outcomes in rural and remote Aboriginal communities. This is where Aborigines go to school the least, where employment is rare, where we see the most hospitalisation from assaults and substance abuse. And it is where we see the most appalling family violence, child abuse and neglect.

To their credit, many Aborigines are voting with their feet, getting out of these hell-holes. May there be many more.

But the Government holds back this exodus with programs like the Community Development Program. This gives Aborigines more money with fewer conditions compared to the dole, so long as they stay in these dysfunctional communities.

Under the Community Development Program, Aborigines are supposed to do some community service during the week. Decisions about what this involves are devolved to self-appointed Aboriginal leaders, and can entail tasks like mowing the yard of these same Aboriginal leaders. It's neither a real job, nor preparation for a real job.

The Closing the Gap report re-affirmed the squalor of rural and remote Aboriginal communities. But the Government's response is to redouble already failing efforts, repeating the mantra of local empowerment.

As it stands, local empowerment is a big part of the problem. The local Aboriginal leaders who get to act like bosses under the Community Development Program have no expertise or qualifications in preparing people for real employment, have no track record in improving the lot of Aboriginal communities, and in many instances were not chosen by those they lord over. What's more, as the program boosts their status and power, they have a strong incentive to keep it going and preserve their fiefdoms.

The Closing the Gap reports make little effort to scrutinise policies affecting Aborigines. For a semblance of scrutiny you have to go back to 2010, when the accountants in the Department of Finance wrote their Strategic Review of Indigenous Expenditure.

This was only made public thanks to Freedom of Information laws. It uncovered poor governance and leadership in rural and remote Aboriginal communities and called for government intervention to help Aborigines leave unsustainable and dysfunctional communities.

But this message fell on deaf ears. The Government continues to treat Aborigines in rural and remote areas like museum exhibits and perpetuates violence, child abuse and neglect.

Governments regularly use language that casts Aboriginal offenders as victims. The Prime Minister said, 'When young Aboriginal and Torres Strait Islander men see jail as a rite of passage, we have failed to give them a place in our society, in our community, and an alternative pathway where they can thrive.'

I accept that support is sometimes needed to remain within the law. But people can rise above their upbringing and anyone can reject violent behaviour.

It is irresponsible for the Prime Minister to wave away the notion of personal responsibility.

Governments prop up dysfunctional behaviour by having indigenous sentencing courts. These give Aboriginal offenders more options for how their sentence will be determined. But they haven't reduced the high rates of Aboriginal re-offending.

Our governments enable child abuse and neglect through their Aboriginal Child Placement Principles. These require child protection departments to consult with Aboriginal organisations prior to the removal of any Aboriginal child, to arrange alternative care with extended family or another local Aboriginal family if possible, and to ensure that the child maintains a connection to Aboriginal culture. This results in delays and uncertainty regarding the removal of children at risk, does not necessarily mean the child is any better off, and discourages people from reporting abuse and neglect.

The idea that a kid is better off growing up illiterate and unhealthy in an Aboriginal household, rather than literate and healthy in a non-indigenous household, is destructive racism.

Irrespective of whether the stolen generation was a result of racism or paternalism, we should not pretend that it is OK to allow kids, indigenous or not, to remain in situations of neglect and abuse.

Finally, our governments are holding back Aboriginal living standards by propping up dysfunctional attitudes.

Governments maintain affirmative action programs, including targets for government employment of Aborigines in the public service and government procurement from designated Aboriginal businesses. These programs extend to anyone who is accepted by Aboriginal elders as being Aboriginal, even fair-skinned people who have had more opportunities than many of their fellow Australians. Affirmative action programs encourage Aborigines to get ahead through special pleading. And they encourage non-indigenous Australians to view Aborigines as charity cases. Governments tell Aborigines fairy tales, which encourages them to consider themselves special. They say our nation is as old as humanity itself, as if the out-of-Africa thesis were debunked. They say Aborigines were undoubtedly the first Australians, as if they know exactly what happened 40,000 years ago.

These comments are not true, but they are 'truthy,' in that the speaker desperately wants them to be true.

Encouraging Aboriginal exceptionalism with 'truthiness' is a mistake, because it risks making Aborigines think the rules for getting ahead that apply to everyone else, don't apply to them.

Governments also encourage dysfunctional attitudes by lamenting the injustices done to Aborigines, while failing to note that this refers to previous generations. Many non-indigenous Australians have ancestors who suffered terrible injustices too. Hanging on to injustices that weren't done to you is paralysing and shouldn't be encouraged.

Finally, governments routinely tell Aborigines that they are defined by a strong connection to country and culture, so those who don't feel a strong connection to country and culture feel they aren't really Aboriginal.

Aboriginal living standards are not improving as they should.

We honour Aboriginal culture and want to see it preserved, but we should not expect Aboriginal Australians to endure third-world living, health and education standards in the process.

Their culture is not at risk when they own freehold property, when they learn to read and write in English, when they gain a decent education, when they are encouraged to move to where the jobs are, when they get real jobs instead of pretend jobs, and when their kids are removed from abuse and neglect.

When refugees come to Australia, we expect them to join mainstream Australia. Indeed, we go to great lengths to help them achieve that. The gap would close a lot quicker if we took the same approach to our indigenous people.

Political party quotas[88]

On behalf of the Liberal Democrats I must issue an apology. Unlike other political parties, we cannot guarantee that half of our candidates will be women. We understand that many of you like to see a 50/50 male/female split – whether on the ballot for a politician or in the Yellow Pages when looking for a plumber. But, unfortunately, our hands are tied.

It's our members you see. They're so annoyingly principled. They've got it stuck in their heads that individuals have rights that the collective cannot overrule. And to bind the party, they've ratified policies supporting civil liberties and equality before the law, and opposing affirmative action.

So if an individual in our party is the best person to promote the party's principles and policies in Parliament, that individual will get our nomination.

Not only can't I guarantee that 50% of Liberal Democrat candidates will be women, I can't guarantee that a quarter of them will be born overseas, that half of them will be under the median age of 38, or that half will have below-average intelligence. Merit is the only consideration. Race, age, sexual orientation and secret cross-dressing tendencies don't matter either.

In fact, I have a huge admission to make. Our candidates are not at all representative of the general population. Each of them believes that you can run your own life and that you pay too much tax. With views like this, our candidates are freaks.

I can't even guarantee that each Liberal Democrat candidate will be local either. At the last election our party had the temerity to nominate a Queenslander to run in Western Australia, simply because he was an intelligent and hardworking libertarian with experience in the West, a willingness to move back there, and a desire to implement policies that would make West Australians better off.

Our party does not accept that having lived in the same postcode and supported the same footy team for your entire life should be a qualification for political office. Our members believe it is what you think, what you know and what you'll do that matters.

The big parties have it so much easier. As the price of an affirmative action policy they can screw the hard working and talented individuals who would be the best candidates. But since the big parties require their new politicians to just repeat what the frontbenchers are saying, no-one notices that the best candidates haven't been selected anyway.

So back to my apology. If the men in parliament like me are only there because we elbowed out women in our ranks, we should fix the problem ourselves rather than expect the blameless young men of our parties to sacrifice themselves. I therefore propose that Tony Abbott, Bill Shorten and I immediately resign, to be replaced by women. I'll do it once they do, promise.

ENVIRONMENT
AND CONSERVATION

Access to and privatisation of National Parks[89]

On the weekends and in other recreational time, our freedom to enjoy the great outdoors is unnecessarily hampered by the meddling of Commonwealth, state and local governments.

Today, I want to make a bold claim and propose a bold solution on behalf of both the Liberal Democrats and the Outdoor Recreation Party, our sister party in the New South Wales election.

The bold claim is that Australia's national parks are chronically mismanaged by both Commonwealth and state governments.

National parks are not protected from feral animals, weeds, rubbish, bushfires or vandalism. These problems are pervasive. Whole mountainsides are covered by mats of impenetrable weeds, undergrowth often fuels massive bushfires, and the paucity of native wildlife is such that Tim Flannery describes our parks as 'marsupial ghost towns.'

The bold solution of the Outdoor Recreation Party and the Liberal Democrats is two-fold.

First, people should be allowed to use national parks for a much wider range of recreational activities than is currently the case.

Second, most of our national parks should be privatised.

Australia has over 1,000 national parks comprising 28 million hectares, accounting for about 4% of our land area. A further 6% is protected in state forests, nature parks and conservation reserves.

In our national parks, commercial activities such as farming are prohibited – even the humble and environmentally-friendly business of bee-keeping, to produce Australia's delicious and distinctive honey, is substantially restricted. Indeed, all human activity is strictly controlled. Few dare to challenge the assertion that humans are the main environmental threat and should be kept out as much as possible.

Many national park users are disenfranchised and excluded through prohibition and regulation. Even worse, few people in power engage with the numerous groups of knowledgeable and outdoor-oriented people who are willing to help.

Local communities adjacent to parks, along with hunters, fishers, campers, fossickers, trail-bikers, horse-riders, kayakers, four-wheel-drivers, bushwalkers and many more are prepared to volunteer time and effort for better managed and more inclusive national parks. Instead, they are largely ignored.

Long-time former CEO of Parks Victoria Mark Stone used to say that parks could not be managed successfully without the support of local communities and stakeholders. He was right; governments will never have sufficient funds to do all that is required and certainly do not have the expertise or local knowledge necessary to manage parks via central planning.

In the UK, national parks make up a similar share of the land area as in Australia. In England they account for 9.3% of the land area, in Wales 19.9%, and in Scotland 7.2%.

But that is where the similarity ends. Much land within UK national parks is owned by private landowners including farmers, the thousands of people who live in villages and towns within those parks, plus organisations like the National

Trust, the Royal Society for the Protection of Birds, various Wildlife Trusts, the Woodland Trust, English Heritage and Historic Scotland.

The management of UK national parks is also profoundly different. Whereas ours are subject to central command and control – mainly by state governments – each park there has its own National Park Authority. While these authorities sometimes own bits of land, they work with all landowners to protect the landscape.

National Park Authorities are run by boards comprised mainly of locals. They employ staff who work in offices, field-work stations and visitor centres, and have many volunteers who undertake jobs such as leading guided walks, fixing fences, dry stone walling, monitoring historic sites and surveying wildlife.

Every authority is obliged to produce a National Park Management Plan setting out a five-year plan for the park. Local communities, landowners and other organisations are asked for their opinions and help in achieving the plan.

Farming plays a key role in shaping the landscape of UK national parks. Sheep are common in the hillier and more rugged areas, while there is some cropping in lower areas. Quite a few farms in national parks have diversified by opening farm shops to sell their produce direct to visitors, or opening their farms for school trips. They are also given preference in grant applications for environmental projects.

In 2013, I visited a farm in the Lake District National Park in England. It ran sheep and also had a farm shop and café. It wasn't a source of riches, but it supports a farming family adequately well.

The farmer explained that there were areas of the farm where he was subject to a range of constraints on such things as grazing, fencing, pasture renovation and use of fertiliser, and where tree preservation was a higher priority. In other areas he was free to farm as he chose, receiving the same agricultural subsidies as farms outside the park but additional grants for tree planting, maintenance of dry stone walls and other environmental initiatives. Critically, he had to allow access to his land for a number of outdoor pursuits.

He took enormous pride in the fact that he was a custodian of both a productive farm and an environmental legacy for the benefit of future generations, including his own children. He was adamant that both productivity and environmental values had been enhanced under his care.

When something is owned by everyone, it is effectively owned by no-one. That is the problem facing Australia's national parks. Management is centrally controlled, governments can never employ enough public servants to manage them properly, and there is little volunteer involvement. Nobody is personally responsible. This means feral animals and weeds run rampant while bushfires are more serious and difficult to prevent.

Imagine if the UK approach were adopted in Australia. Imagine if significant parts of national parks were privately owned, they were managed by locally run boards in accordance with locally agreed management plans, land was farmed where viable and tourism was encouraged, with some of the money currently used for park management offered as incentives for owners to preserve environmental values.

Would the environment be any worse off than it is under a policy of locking it up and looking at it through binoculars, with just a privileged group of park staff having free access?

Recruiting volunteers on a large scale to address specific problems such as track clearing, pest animal and weed control, or species monitoring, could save taxpayers millions and deliver vastly superior environmental outcomes.

As it stands, biodiversity and environmental values in Australia's national parks are in decline. Using the skills and enthusiasm of volunteers in local communities and park users to address basic management tasks would be one way to arrest this decline. As Professor Flannery went on to say, 'the truth is that things are now so dire that we cannot afford to persist with business as usual: a change of direction is essential.'

Farmers would have a strong incentive to control feral pests such as goats, pigs, foxes, rabbits, and cats. Their presence in the parks would also help keep tracks open and detect problems. The proceeds from selling the park, with environmental caveats, could be used to upgrade visitor facilities and fund research.

The very idea of this offends some people, not least the public sector unions that represent national park employees. But it is not radical. As the UK shows, it is perfectly feasible. Australia is a big country with plenty that is unique. We are not so unique that we cannot learn from others.

National parks are for people as well as nature. We should never forget that.

Keeping native animals as pets[90]

Australians are good at many things – but conserving native fauna is not one of them.

In the last 200 years, 11% of our native mammals have become extinct, one of the worst conservation records in the world. There are species of kangaroos, wallabies, bilbies and potoroos, and of course the Tasmanian Tiger, that are no longer with us.

According to the Proceedings of the National Academy of Sciences, a further 36% of our remaining mammals have reason to be nervous about their prospects for survival.

Some argue we should simply throw more taxpayers' money into preservation. But that amounts to doing the same thing over again and expecting a different result.

The Commonwealth national parks agency, Parks Australia, spends nearly $90 million a year to look after just six terrestrial national parks. In terms of resources available per property, it must be one of the world's richest national park organisations.

And yet Australia's last mammalian extinction is believed to have occurred on Christmas Island, one of the areas they manage. In 2009, attempts to capture a once common small bat known as the Christmas Island Pipistrelle failed.

Writing about this in the *Sydney Morning Herald* in 2012, Professor Tim Flannery recalled asking the then Environment Minister, Peter Garrett, for assistance to save this species from extinction only to be told that nothing needed to be done, on the grounds it would survive if we looked after its environment.

Now it appears that the Christmas Island Pipistrelle is a casualty of this fallacy, and its extinction may yet be remembered as the longest lasting legacy of Mr Garrett's career in politics. This is ironic considering that as lead singer of Midnight Oil, Mr Garrett once released an album called *Species Deceases*.

A study of Kakadu National Park, another park overseen by our very well-resourced commonwealth national parks agency, found there has been a 71% decline in the number of native animals over recent decades. It found that almost half its area has no native mammals at all.

In other words, National Parks do not guarantee species survival. Because they and the animals in them belong to everyone, they also belong to no-one. They have no value.

There is thus no incentive for anyone to keep them safe from predators, whether that is dogs, cats or foxes. Yes, they can be protected by building enclosures to keep these animals out, but the only source of funds for this is taxpayers. Private investment is uncommon.

And yet, the long-term survival of at least some Australian animals is assured because they are kept as household pets in other countries. Sugar gliders, certain species of wallabies, and blue tongue lizards are among them.

This is because people take care of animals that belong to them.

As it stands, Australians may own a pet that can, and may in fact, kill scores of native animals. They may also own a few varieties of snakes and native birds, such as budgies, galahs or cockatoos. Dingoes and a few native animals may be kept in some states on a strictly non-commercial basis.

But the vast majority of our beautiful native mammals may not be kept as pets. And very few people can keep them if they want to.

Allowing native animals to be kept as pets will ensure their survival. Just as cats and dogs are in no danger of dying out, the same will be true if native animals are privately owned. It means they have value.

Some who oppose native animals as pets cite welfare concerns, saying they may not be well cared for. By that logic, we would have no pets. The experience overseas is that Australian animals such as sugar gliders and blue tongue lizards live much longer in captivity than they do in the wild.

In reality, most of those who oppose keeping native animals as pets are fundamentally opposed to private property. It's not about the animals, but about ideology.

There is no disputing that some native animals may make unsuitable pets, at least in certain situations. Many are nocturnal, for example, which might require us to adjust our own sleeping habits to enjoy them.

And obviously there is no suggestion of taking animals from the wild. Like cats and dogs, and also like budgies, galahs and cockatoos, they need to be bred as pets.

But allowing for those considerations, widespread ownership of native animals as pets is something that should be promoted.

Sugar gliders could be owned by Australians, as well as foreigners. Certain kinds of wallabies make great pets. The quoll may replace domestic cats. The bilby is often nominated as a great candidate for domestication. In the right circumstances, possums, Tasmanian devils, wombats, native rats, antechinus and bandicoots would also be great pets.

My party, the Liberal Democrats, and our sister party in New South Wales, the Outdoor Recreation Party, believe Australians should be free to keep native animals as pets.

And the sooner we are free to do so, the sooner the future of our native animals will be assured.

Big wind: the new deniers[91]

The Senate Select Committee inquiry final report on wind turbines is a wake-up call for the wind industry. My actions to establish the inquiry have been vindicated by the exposure of the remarkable failure of state governments to properly regulate the industry.

No longer is it credible for Big Wind to hide behind specious denials that sound from wind turbines does not cause adverse health impacts to anybody, at any time, or at any distance. Nor can it claim to be either a good neighbour or a good corporate citizen.

The denials of the industry have been overwhelmed by the evidence of expert acousticians, doctors, and residents. And regulators conceded the monitoring of noise emissions from wind farms had failed community expectations and reasonable standards.

For well over a decade, Big Wind and its cheerleaders have steadfastly refused to accept that large industrial turbines taller than Sydney Harbour Bridge, with a blade sweep area greater than 12 house blocks, could generate sufficient sound energy to disturb nearby residents.

This is despite the industry's own consultants expressing concern about noise emissions and the effects on nearby residents as far back as 2004. This callous indifference is reminiscent of tobacco industry tactics of years past denying a link to lung cancer in the face of growing evidence.

Before anyone accuses me of being anti-renewables, let me assure them I accept renewables have a place in the mix of energy sources to drive a twenty-first century economy. Solar, hydro and biomass already do this without making anyone sick or driving them out of their homes. With appropriate planning processes and independent monitoring of noise emissions, I accept wind energy can contribute as well.

But here is the nub of the problem. In their rush to secure large investments in rural areas and be seen to be 'doing something' about renewable energy, state governments relaxed planning procedures. They also exempted the wind industry from the same level of scrutiny applied to other industries.

In some states there is no requirement to even measure infrasound, let alone limit what is emitted. The rationale for setbacks between turbines and residences, which ranges from 1-2 km, has absolutely no basis in evidence.

The lack of noise monitoring by regulators was an alarming feature of evidence in every state. Regulations to gain planning approval and community acceptance exist, but the states do not ensure compliance with the regulations, choosing instead to allow the industry to self-monitor.

The evidence the inquiry heard about the ineptitude of state planning regimes in regulating wind farms painted a picture of continuing incompetence and indifference to statutory obligations that would have made Sir Humphrey Applebee blush.

At the hearings it was difficult to comprehend the level of incompetence or arrogance when hearing of the Gullen Range wind farm debacle where 69 of the 73 turbines were built in the wrong locations contrary to planning approvals. Some turbines were hundreds of metres closer to residences than allowed. It was only after repeated complaints by residents that regulators took any interest in the project they were supposedly regulating.

The primary body overseeing health and medical research in Australia, the National Health and Medical Research Council came under severe criticism from health professionals and affected residents alike. Ministers, health departments and the medical profession rely upon the NHMRC to provide advice about possible adverse health impacts from wind turbine operations. For almost a decade the NHMRC has equivocated with its advice providing ambiguous, conflicting and confusing public statements before deciding earlier this year to provide hopelessly inadequate funding of half a million dollars a year for research into this long-running multi-billion-dollar issue.

The inquiry report noted that 'senior public health figures have also recognised that the quality of research of the NHMRC's systemic review was sub-optimal.' Other respected medical professionals gave evidence of the NHMRC that 'they have given meagre advice to the public, none to the health profession and ineffective and uneducated advice to the government.'

The Australian Medical Association's 'slavish repetition of the findings of the NHMRC reviews' was described in the inquiry report as 'irresponsible and harmful' with the committee concerned by the lack of rigour behind the AMA's public statements on noise emissions from wind turbines.

It is hardly surprising that residents living in the vicinity of wind farms feel disenfranchised and ignored when wind farm operators, the health profession, ministers and state governments all say 'move along, nothing to see here' in response to repeated complaints of planning abuse and adverse health impacts.

It is self-evident that state governments have failed comprehensively to ensure that the wind industry is regulated as other industries are and this has been recognised by previous inquiries.

It is abundantly clear from the evidence of regulators, the community, local councils and wind farm operators that the status quo is untenable.

The inquiry recommendations to government are not the end of the industry if adopted, but simply provides a framework to improve the very poor regulatory governance of the wind industry and help it retain its social licence to operate.

Greenhouse[92]

Once again, the Government has been getting its knickers in a knot over climate change. And once again, despite three politically shrewd options to choose from, it is choosing a dumb fourth option.

The first of the shrewd options is to withdraw from the Paris agreement and abandon the pledge to force Australian emissions in 2030 to be 26 to 28% lower than emissions in 2005. In the process, the government could announce that it would commit to reduce emissions as part of an enforceable international agreement based on equal effort, but that the Paris agreement is neither enforceable nor based on equal effort.

This option would enable the government to abolish the renewable energy target, the emissions reduction fund (i.e. 'direct action'), the renewable energy agency, the clean energy finance corporation and the clean energy innovation fund. It would save taxpayers at least $150 million over the next three years alone, and would also cut electricity bills. What's more, there would be no need to introduce a carbon price.

The second option is to stick with the Paris agreement but better align our planned emission reductions with the pledges of the world's big emitters. India, China, Iran, Saudi Arabia and Indonesia each pledge to more than double their emissions from 2005 to 2030. Russia and Brazil each pledge to increase their emissions by a third. Mexico also pledges increased emissions, while South Korea and South Africa each pledge that their emissions in 2030 will be much the same as in 2005. Japan pledges to reduce its emissions, but to a lesser extent than Australia. The only pledges that exceed Australia's planned effort come from Obama's US, Trudeau's Canada, and the EU of Hollande and Merkel.

Option two is based on the idea that each country should make a comparable effort to reduce emissions, because all will suffer from rising global temperatures. (Indeed, it would be reasonable to expect those countries that might suffer less from rising temperatures, like Russia, to go to less effort to reduce emissions.)

Arguments that poor countries should be spared from the costs of reducing emissions are just flimsy arguments for foreign aid. The industrial revolution that brought great wealth to the West has also lifted much of the rest of the world out of poverty. So if the industrial revolution is causing climate change, then the responsibility to respond rests with every nation in the world.

Option two would require the retention of some of the current policies to reduce emissions, but at least it would avoid the need for the introduction of a carbon price.

Unfortunately Prime Minister Turnbull and the average voter probably couldn't face up to the realpolitik underpinning options one or two. The warm and fuzzy feelings surrounding Australian emission reductions are just too addictive.

But there remains an option that, while more harmful to Australians than options one or two, is still politically shrewd. Under option three, a carbon tax would be used to fund high-end income tax cuts, while all other programs that reduce emissions would be abolished. In addition, nuclear power would be legalised.

Devoting all the proceeds of a carbon tax to fund cuts to top personal tax rates and the company tax rate would make Australia more competitive, boost investment, reverse the brain drain and create jobs. Moreover, as an emissions-free source of base load power, nuclear power has no equal. The only ones who would not like it are those who hate the rich, and those who choose to ignore France's nuclear success.

Abolition of bureaucratic programs like the renewable energy target would make it impossible to establish new projects, like wind farms and solar arrays, unless they were competitive without subsidies from other forms of generation.

But despite the Government having three politically shrewd options, Prime Minister Turnbull seems to be fixated on option four – do nothing. He's keeping us signed up to the unenforceable Paris agreement, sticking to an emissions reduction target that is out of step with the world's big emitters, and tying himself to costly policies like the renewable energy target that the Greens love but Coalition supporters hate.

If only he were more agile and innovative.

Murray-Darling basin[93]

As the first European to view the plains of the Riverina in 1817, John Oxley despaired of 'a country which for bareness and desolation has no equal.'

A century later he would have said the same. During the Federation Drought, in 1914, the Murray River ran dry. A century later it would have run dry again during the Millennium Drought but for the release of water from dams.

In 2010, on the other hand, the Murray–Darling Basin received record breaking rain, filling dams to capacity and causing widespread flooding. Dorothea Mackellar's famous description of 'a land of droughts and flooding rains' was never more true.

These were obviously natural events, and yet many saw the Millennium Drought as reason to panic. There arose a bizarre perception that this time it was different, and that it might never rain properly again. The result was the Murray–Darling Basin Plan.

This plan is a blueprint for returning a large volume of water to the environment, through a combination of reduced supply to agriculture and fewer losses during movement and storage.

A Senate Select Committee, which I chaired, has been investigating the impacts of the Basin Plan. Its report was tabled in parliament last week.

The committee received numerous submissions and held eight public hearings in each of the basin states. While there was no serious opposition to better use of water for the environment, there were numerous concerns about the way the plan is being implemented.

The most common concerns came from rural communities suffering a decline in irrigated agriculture. While most affected farmers voluntarily sold their water rights to the government, there has been nothing voluntary about the decline of businesses that provide goods and services to those farmers, the businesses of those handling and marketing the commodities, or the consequences of people moving out of the area.

Senators Bob Day, John Madigan and I produced 31 recommendations, which government senators signed onto. Labor also supported many, leaving only the Greens and their kindred spirit Nick Xenophon with major disagreements.

Among the committee's recommendations is for the *Water Act* to be amended to make clear that economic, social and environmental needs and outcomes ought to have equal standing. We do not want to drain the Murray and we cannot return the environment to what it was prior to European settlement, but we also do not want to send businesses broke, destroy jobs or ruin people's lives.

The committee recommended the Productivity Commission undertake a long overdue cost-benefit analysis of the Basin Plan, including analysis of the value of forgone production and food processing due to reduced irrigation water. The dairy industry in northern Victoria has lost so much irrigation water that production has not returned to levels preceding the Millennium Drought, notwithstanding growing global demand for dairy products.

Another recommendation is for a study into whether the Ramsar listing of the SA Lower Lakes should be estuarine rather than fresh water, and whether the barrages near the mouth of the Murray, which prevent the Lower Lakes from returning to an estuary, should be modified or removed. The committee heard evidence that much of the fresh water sent down the river to the Lower Lakes simply evaporates and could be replaced by sea water. Contrary to previous claims, we also heard a weir or lock near Wellington was feasible, which would protect the supply of fresh water to Adelaide and South Australian irrigators and landowners.

Other recommendations relate to the need to secure Broken Hill's water supply, to have the Commonwealth assume liability for damage to private property when it is flooded without owners' consent, and to hold a judicial inquiry into maladministration and possible corruption in the Victorian Government's Goulburn Murray Water Connections Project.

Finally, the committee recommended an end to further buybacks of water. Large untargeted water buybacks during the drought, before the Plan was adopted, were opportunistic, non-strategic and are a continuing heavy burden on some communities. Communities and farming simply cannot have so much of their water taken away and then be left to fend for themselves.

Since Oxley's time we have created best practice agricultural production and built an irrigation system the envy of the world, supported by vibrant entrepreneurial communities. It does not serve anyone to cripple that through a panic-based reimagining of reality.

Nuclear power[94]

Barack Obama's former energy adviser, Steven Chu, recently referred to Australia's stance on nuclear power as terribly strange. It's not surprising. If any country in the world should embrace nuclear power, it is Australia. We have millions of tonnes of uranium, a government capable of responsibly regulating the industry over the long term, and a stable landmass in which we could safely store nuclear waste.

But instead we have banned both the processing of uranium into nuclear fuel and nuclear power plants. It is akin to Saudi Arabia banning oil refineries and cars.

Nuclear has proven to be far safer than just about any other form of power generation.

Almost certainly, at least one person working on a solar installation in Australia fell to their death from a roof this year. This will go unrecorded as being related to solar energy, either in the media or in any records concerning mortality in power generation. What's more, the accident will be repeated dozens of times in many places around the world.

By comparison, it is likely that there were few if any deaths related to nuclear industries anywhere in the world. Deaths due to accidents in mining uranium, processing it into nuclear fuel, and turning it into power, are rare.

By way of confirmation, no-one at Fukushima was exposed to enough radiation to get so much as a runny nose.

Similarly, environmental problems associated with nuclear power are greatly exaggerated. It is true that Fukushima will be costly to clean up, but renewable energy like solar and wind farms routinely occupy huge swathes of land for relatively small returns. You need to have drunk a particularly strong ideological kool-aid to believe a technology that covers the landscape in metal is good for the environment.

The volume of nuclear waste produced by nuclear power is smaller than most people are led to believe, it can be safely stored, and it is likely to become re-usable as technology develops. In contrast, producing solar panels generates significant amounts of waste, including heavy metals of the kind that are a major environmental and public health problem in China.

Nuclear power is also better for the global environment. It is puzzling to encounter greenies professing to be alarmed about carbon dioxide emissions, yet are opposed to one of the few genuine solutions. It seems some people are less afraid of climate change than having to admit they're wrong about nuclear power.

Many environmentalists have worked out that the scare campaigns about nuclear power's safety and environmental impact lack credibility. That's why, when politicians from the Greens speak about nuclear energy these days, they're likely to spend most of their time talking about the economics of nuclear power.

However, taking advice from the Greens about economics is like getting tips from ISIS on human rights.

Studies suggest nuclear power may be more expensive than coal fired generation in this country, but nuclear continues to demonstrate its viability in other countries and, with the construction of dozens of new reactors across Asia, is likely to become more competitive.

If it is true that nuclear power is not and never will be economically viable, the Greens should have no problem repealing laws prohibiting nuclear power plants. This costs nothing.

I'm not arguing taxpayers' money should be thrown at nuclear power. The best path to cheaper electricity and the return of Australia's competitive advantage in energy production is to stop throwing taxpayers' money at any power generation.

Even if Australia does not adopt nuclear power, we have enormous opportunities to add value to our mining by processing uranium. We also have enormous opportunities to store nuclear waste, which faces no ban. As Bob Hawke once pointed out, the storage of nuclear waste has the potential to be a multi-billion-dollar earner for Australia.

Some environmentalists – like George Monbiot and Mark Lynas – have looked at the facts and ended their opposition to nuclear power. But the ideological warriors struggle on. They claim nuclear power is on the way out, cherry picking examples from a few countries but ignoring the fact that more than 60 reactors are being constructed right now, including 20 in China.

Whether nuclear power becomes viable in this country, there are enormous opportunities in the nuclear fuel cycle that we are leaving to our developing neighbours. Apart from anything else, this means Australia will increasingly find it hard to have any influence on policies for nuclear safeguards.

All we are saying, is give nuclear a chance.

POLITICAL ISSUES

On the job[95]

After I was elected, during a trip to Canberra, I stood at the Australian War Memorial and looked down Anzac Parade. Parliament House dwarfed its predecessor, stretching its concrete arms across red paving stones and turf, encircling the smaller building. People, black dots picked out against a red and white field, scurried to-and-fro. This was a sitting week, and there were 5,000 people in its 4,500 rooms.

And I was to be one of them.

We do not produce anything. We make legislation, tell others to make legislation, or tell someone else to do something entirely unrelated. Some of us spend your money telling you what a great job we're doing or what a bad job the people down the corridor are doing.

This week has been particularly unedifying. The public appears disenchanted with their political representatives; party members seem dissatisfied with their leaders. The electoral cycle keeps turning but few MPs or voters look to the wider horizon: What do we want from our politicians? What is important in government?

I stood for parliament in the hope of making a difference.

One of the strangest insults regularly levelled at me is that, as a classical liberal, I am ideologically driven. Who knew that having a consistent, principled belief system – and representing a large chunk of the population in the process – would be viewed as grounds for criticism?

I also thought I knew about politics. I followed issues closely, read widely, ran as a candidate, and for several years had daily conversations with John Tingle when he was in the NSW Legislative Council. I was such a political tragic I even read Hansard.

And because classical liberalism is an important part of the Western political tradition – it's what led Whitlam to oppose conscription, Fraser to oppose apartheid, Hawke to support uranium mining and microeconomic reform – I thought at least other politicians and members of the Canberra press gallery would be aware that classical liberals don't exist just to make Labor see sense on economics and Liberals see sense on civil liberties.

I anticipated having to explain my political views to the electorate. I see that as part of my job and I take it seriously. I also expected people – from both left and right – to disagree with me.

But I did not expect to be criticised for being consistent.

'How can you support both marriage equality and firearm ownership?' they ask.

Or, 'How can you be in favour of both drug decriminalisation and lower taxes, or assisted suicide and welfare cuts?'

Or 'How can you support removing feral pests from our national parks and yet say nothing about climate change?'

Or even, 'How come you're opposed to data retention and national security overreach, and yet support the repeal of 18C?'

These were some of the questions fired my way during my first six months on the job. Sometimes the issues were combined differently, although the incredulous pairing of freedom to marry and freedom to carry has been common.

I have lost count how many times I've had to explain that classical liberalism is a philosophy concerned with the individual's relationship to the state. In a nutshell, it means 'the only purpose for which power can be rightfully ever exercised over any member of a civilized community, against his will, is to prevent harm to others.'

Yet even when keeping John Stuart Mill's famous quotation in mind, it's important to remind people that it's not possible to make the world perfectly safe. Attempts to do so often result in gross denial of personal freedom and responsibility. A world free of risk is also impossible: should we – because human beings persist in having accidents with them – ban cars, motorbikes, and bicycles? And let's not start on alcohol or assisted suicide.

Some people base their arguments for restrictive gun laws on firearms accidents, particularly those involving kids. This all seems plausible until one realises that other things – widely considered safe – are far more lethal to children than firearms. Backyard swimming pools, for instance. Should we ban those, too, while we're busily banning everything else?

When I raised the issue of self-defence following the Lindt Café siege, there were instant declarations of support for our restrictive gun laws. There was no understanding of whether it is prudent to rely on feel good laws or questioning of whether those laws can be enforced. There was also no regard for law-abiding gun owners, and no evidence presented. It was simply a chorus of 'I don't want to be armed, so I don't think anyone else should be able to choose to be armed.'

Just because you don't like the idea of two women getting married or the bloke down the street having a well-stocked gun cabinet doesn't mean you should seize the levers of power and stop either or both from happening.

Just because you don't like cigarettes or marijuana doesn't mean you get to stop other people lighting up, either through de facto or actual prohibition. And of course, just because you find someone's words hateful or offensive doesn't mean the rest of the country has to agree with you, or give you grounds for insisting that someone be dragged through the courts.

After six months in the job I've come to realise that I am effectively starting from zero when it comes to getting people to join the dots. People intuitively support 'liberty for me but not for thee,' with some going so far as to argue that anything they like should be paid for by the taxpayer, while anything they dislike should be banned or regulated to death.

The challenge is increased by the sheer administrative burden of the role. Being a senator is the most demanding job I've ever done, far worse than being a veterinarian or owning an agribusiness consultancy. I always thought anyone who could spend a sizeable amount of time with his arm two thirds of the way up a cow's behind could handle anything life threw across his path. Not necessarily.

Some people assume that politicians permanently live in Canberra, while others presume that politicians only work when they're in Canberra. Both assumptions are wrong. I actually have an electoral office in Sydney that the government spent $350,000 refitting. The decision to spend that much money was taken without consulting me – I could have saved the taxpayer $150,000 had I been trusted to do it myself.

This is part of a broader failure to trust people to make their own decisions.

There is a fair amount of empirical evidence to show that individuals make better decisions than experts engaged on their behalf, especially when it comes to spending their own money. That's why taxing people and then returning money to them in the form of welfare or subsidies amounts to taking $100 in crisp twenties, burning one, and handing $80 back to the taxpayer. It's wasteful, and pretends that government is capable of knowing every individual's preferences in advance. It's far better to take less tax and let people spend their money as they see fit.

The administrative burden is evident from the phone calls, emails and letters I receive. Emails arrive in the thousands – sometimes tens of thousands – seeking to influence my vote. Many offer a free character assessment while they're at it, although there are occasional compliments and some praise, too.

Sometimes I write back – even to the abusive ones – and I've had correspondents express shock when they discover there's a real person on the other end. I have also refused to let my election change my basic personality. If people give me an earful of colourful language, I may respond in kind, especially if they've already called the office and abused my staff. That's what led to the incident where I told an abusive constituent to go and do something anatomically impossible.

I have to admit I didn't appreciate the extent to which both major parties lack consistent policy positions – it's mainly feel-good populism combined with an arcane proceduralism that works to the advantage of those who know the system. It also benefits those in the community who fight tooth and nail to keep things as they are.

All the banning and regulating indulged in by the state means that government has finished up invading every nook and cranny of our lives, with the inevitable corollary that it has waxed fat at our expense. Government spending now amounts to more than a third of Australia's GDP, and despite its rhetoric, the Abbott government has done little to remedy this.

Because I thought more people knew about classical liberalism, I went into the job expecting my troubles to be more mundane. People wouldn't be able to pronounce my name, for example. But in fact my hassles are mostly a result of the fact that few of my colleagues and even fewer in the media have any experience of a parliamentarian who publicly subscribes to a consistent philosophical position. As I keep explaining, and as many keep struggling to understand: if it's not harming anyone else, it's not the government's business, whether they approve or not.

So – moving forward, to use a well-worn phrase – now I know what to expect, what do I hope to achieve, given that I'm still only one vote?

I hope always to take that vote seriously and use it wisely. I may fail in this, but not through want of trying. I certainly make a real effort to understand legislation and the many amendments that are proposed, and to think issues through.

I want Australians to reconsider whether handing their money over to the government is better than keeping it themselves. I want people to understand that disapproving of something does not justify prohibition or regulation. I want people to appreciate the connection between the liberties they care about and the liberties that other people care about. I hope to provoke a national conversation about Australia's tendency to be oppressive in some areas, and liberal or indifferent in others.

Consistent with my classical liberal beliefs, I also refuse to be captive to special interests. That is, I'll support things because I think they're right, not because people lobbied me one way or the other, or, heaven forbid, because they donated to the Liberal Democrats.

And I mean it when I say I'll never vote for a reduction in liberty or an increase in taxes.

Seven days in Hell[96]

Last Thursday in the Senate, in a moment of tiredness, I admitted I'd had an interesting life before becoming a senator. After my election, I said, it's been all downhill.

Running an agribusiness consulting company, helping farmers with everything from sheep-dip to fertiliser to vaccines, plus patching up sick animals: these may not seem particularly thrilling, but they're at least useful. At the end of most days, I could say 'I achieved something.' In politics, I can go a whole week and wonder what happened.

Like last week.

Tuesday

When I arrived in Canberra on Monday I knew the week would be a circus due to the Senate voting reform Bill. What I didn't expect was that we we'd still be considering it after lunch on Friday. We sat for 39 hours, the longest continuous sitting in Senate history.

First came the government's 'time management' motion, requiring us to sit until the electoral reform bill, plus ten others, had been considered. Ricky Muir immediately sought to move a motion replacing electoral reform with the government's Australian Building and Construction Commission Bill as the week's key Bill. Despite arguing this Bill was critical to its legislative agenda, the government – with the Greens' support – gagged debate and voted down Ricky's motion. This was the first of Ricky's many forays into the week's politics and policy, proving he is far more competent than some of the nameless backbenchers in the major parties. He'd make a great Labor member for the seat of Gippsland.

As for the Coalition voting against its own ABCC Bill, at the time this seemed bizarre. Reinstating the ABCC is long-standing Government policy, was an election promise, and the Liberal Party has been dreaming about it ever since the Gillard Government abolished it. This week's announcement that the Senate will be recalled to consider the Bill now explains why it voted as it did.

I then moved a motion adding a same-sex marriage Bill to the list of bills to be voted on that week. In the chamber, I managed to finish a short speech while being yelled at from all sides. It was like orating in the middle of a tornado.

I chose the Greens' Bill rather than my own to give the Greens an opportunity to achieve same-sex marriage with their own Bill – some Greens didn't like my Freedom to Marry Bill – with feedback via indirect channels suggesting Nick McKim, Sarah Hanson-Young, and Robert Simms were interested.

Doing his best to feign outrage, Richard Di Natale said his party always supports marriage equality – just not today. He posed six questions to Penny Wong, but then the Greens joined the government and Nick Xenophon to vote down my motion, preventing her from giving a speech in reply and ensuring she won't be getting married any time soon.

This was extraordinary. If my motion had succeeded and the Senate had considered the same-sex marriage issue, I believe it would have passed. It would also have presented the Prime Minister with an opportunity to be 'agile' and pursue same-sex marriage through the House of Representatives, instead of through a costly and acrimonious plebiscite.

The Greens successfully moved to take over Labor's 'private senators time' on Thursday, so the Greens' same-sex marriage Bill could be debated instead. This meant it was only considered for a little over an hour, and could only come to a vote if debate were gagged and Senators prevented from expressing their views. I knew this; Labor knew this; the Greens knew this. That explains why, when the Greens did try to gag debate to bring the Bill to a vote on Thursday, only the Greens, Ricky Muir, and I were in favour.

While I have a firm policy of never voting for a reduction in liberty (and thus always voting in favour of same-sex marriage), it was obvious there would be a lot of senators wanting a say. It was idiotic for the Greens to believe they could force a vote after such a short debate.

The Senate sat until just after midnight.

Wednesday

On Wednesday, during a brief pause in debate on electoral reform, I gave a speech on Australia's deteriorating financial position and alarming similarities to Greece. During question time I asked the Minister for Finance, representing the Treasurer, whether Australia would ever see a budget surplus again. He gave an answer to a different question.

Debate resumed later in the day, pausing for new Liberal senator James Paterson's excellent first speech. I do hope he sees the light and joins the Liberal Democrats.

Debate on electoral reform continued into the night.

Thursday (all day and all night) and Friday (all day)

On Thursday morning I tried again to move an amendment to the Government's time management motion to allow full consideration of the Greens' Bill on same-sex marriage. Once again the Government gagged debate, with Greens' support.

Debate resumed on electoral reform later in the day in the knowledge it would continue until the Bill had been decided. Labor was hoping to force the Government, with Greens' support, to gag debate. And yet, despite voting to gag debate on their own bill, the Greens told the Government they would not support using the gag on this Bill. With Rambo-like resolve, Mathias Cormann vowed to stay as long as it took. There was also something Rambo-like in his unswerving determination not to answer the question as to whether how-to-vote cards promoting 'Just Vote 1' would be legal.

A filibuster is a test of endurance, and most parliaments have them from time to time. They involve debate for a prolonged period in an attempt to frustrate the Government, use up all available time, or weaken the other side. Labor knew that unless someone moved the gag, debate would eventually have to stop. However, they were also determined to ensure this did not occur early Friday morning so the government couldn't simply announce on the morning news, 'we won.'

Thus began a night of interminable speeches, many profoundly boring but with occasional moments of hilarity. While few senators were in the Chamber, most of us watched from our offices. Some slept on couches, on the floor, or in chairs. Several times during the night we were called to vote when Labor moved debate be suspended. The Government was having none of it.

I slept for perhaps ten minutes, interrupted by division bells. I was in the Chamber when Stephen Conroy named the front parties established to assist Lee Rhiannon's election to the NSW parliament in 1999. I heard Sam Dastyari's description of Richard Di Natale's fashion shoot with GQ Magazine, where he labelled him 'the Black Wiggle.' I heard Glenn Sterle talking about his colonoscopy and, tired as I was, I laughed when Doug Cameron quoted Monty Python's 'I fart in your general direction.' I didn't laugh at walking photo opportunity Nick Xenophon turning up in embarrassing, vomit-suit pyjamas for what became #SenateSleepover.

By mid-morning it was clear the gag would not be moved. Labor allowed matters to progress to committee stage, when amendments are debated. I moved a number of amendments which would have improved the bill, to no avail. Labor and several other crossbench senators did the same. The only amendments that passed were those from the government and Greens.

One of Labor's amendments was to incorporate the Greens' political donations policy into the Bill. Its rejection showed both donations reform and same-sex marriage are less important to the Greens than getting rid of their minor party competitors.

In fact, until they voted against donation reform (and people realised how cynical they are), I was accused – repeatedly and with defamatory crudeness – of 'pulling a stunt,' of being 'put up to it by Labor.' The NSW Greens – on their official Facebook page – asserted I was opposed to same-sex marriage. False and malicious attacks are apparently acceptable when Greens' hypocrisy is exposed.

As it happens, I wasn't a party to the decision to filibuster although I was happy that it put the dirty deal between the government and the Greens in the spotlight. Nobody has ever argued that Senate voting reform was not needed, but the government's changes will merely replace one set of problems with another. Entrenching the Greens is one of them.

So now we have Malcolm Turnbull citing Senate voting reform as a 'significant Government achievement.' Forgotten are bracket creep, our spending problem, and the 'economic narrative.' It's all about 'clearing out the crossbench,' as if somehow giving the Greens and Xenophon the balance of power will make the senate more compliant.

And if there is a lesson for the week, it was to show how Labor is the only major party that understands the art of persuasion. It can do something neither the Greens nor Coalition can: negotiate. Whatever the merits of its policies, it is inconceivable that Labor in government would have set out to replace the crossbench with its political enemies due to an inability to bargain.

As I said, all downhill.

Living the dream[97]
Ladies and gentlemen. Fellow libertarians.

When Senator Sam Dastyari and I pass each other in the corridor at parliament house, we occasionally mutter 'living the dream.'

That's because being a senator is a dream job. And for the 15 to 20 weeks that we spend in parliament house each year, it's like one of those dreams from which you wake up screaming.

Let me describe a few of the best bits.

In Canberra, there's the hours. The days are never less than 12, often 14 or 15. It's not uncommon to miss meals. Mind you, on those odd days when I can get some sleep, I sleep like a baby. By which I mean I wake up every few hours screaming.

There's the lobbying. I hear special pleading, people with their noses in the trough, protectionists, regulatory junkies. And that's just the government and opposition. Everyone wants to influence my vote. It's a dream to tell them they're dreaming.

There's the free character assessments. I get hundreds of these by email, letter and telephone. And social media is just about the most anti-social place imaginable. Who knew you could be both a legend and an arsehole at the same time? The dream is, I sometimes get to respond with a bit of Anglo-Saxon English.

There are more events to attend than there are hours in the day. It's a dream having such choice.

It's a dream being interviewed by the media, multiple times every single day. After a night doing Lateline and a morning doing AM, and a constant fear of being tripped up for not knowing the price of eggs or the name of the Head of ISIS, the 24-hour news cycle can leave you feeling like a sock caught in a washing machine.

And it is a dream to review bills, amendments and motions that nobody is ever likely to hear about, before we even get to the serious legislation and whether it is worth trying to move amendments.

But that's before I get to the perks. They're a real dream.

For example, I am regularly criticised for benefiting from the parliamentary pension. You know – the one scrapped ten years ago, in 2004. It's a dream telling people they're a decade behind the times.

There's the free trips. We don't have to pay for our own flights to and from Canberra or those tightly wrapped pieces of cheese they hand out. I bet you dream of that.

In Canberra there's the exclusive dining (chips and hamburgers in the staff canteen) and lavish entertainment (usually while standing up and often interrupted by the division bells). I dream of decent food.

I could go on.

When I mention some of the dream aspects of the job, I am sometimes asked, why do you do it? It's quite remarkable how many people believe they would make a brilliant senator, which of course I'm not.

But I intend to continue living the dream. Because I think I am starting to make a difference. And if it's necessary to live the dream, then that's what I will do.

I presume many of you will have heard or read my first speech. I know somebody has, because it has now been viewed tens of thousands of times on YouTube.

The most common response I heard following my speech was:

That was fantastic. So inspiring, And I agreed with everything except for a couple of points.

And of course, in later conversations, two tends to become two dozen. Consistent libertarians are a rare breed.

Just how rare became obvious when I introduced a private senator's bill last year to reduce eligibility for Family Tax Benefit Part A. It would have saved a few hundred million. I just wanted to prove at least one of the crossbench wasn't totally feral.

A couple of weeks after I introduced the Bill I used private senator's time to debate it. And a few days prior to the debate I had a chat with the Minister for Finance, Mathias Cormann. He conceded my Bill made sense but that the government couldn't support it. I knew Labor and the Greens would be against it too, so I then asked if he could help me bring it to a vote. He agreed to do that.

So the Bill was debated, brought to a vote and a division was called.

Now, in order to call a division you require two voices. I arranged for my friend Bob Day to be the second voice, but when the senators took their places with the ayes to the right and the noes to the left, he went with the noes. Family First is just as keen on spending other people's money as the Liberals are.

In the end I was the only senator to vote for the Bill. Literally everyone else voted against a modest reduction in middle-class welfare. Here is the picture to prove it.

I am told it will be written up in Odgers, the book on Senate procedure, because it was the first time there was a division with just one vote in favour.

What this confirms is that spending other people's money is a national addiction. I am pretty much unique in consistently voting against it. Other senators sometimes tell me they agree with my small government approach, but they always have exceptions.

The obvious conclusion is, we need more Liberal Democrats in parliament. Not just the senate but also the upper houses of state parliaments.

But it is not all bad news. Being close to the decisions of government does have its moments. I have achieved a few things.

And since I am now officially a politician, and have an audience, I'm going to list them here. Sorry about that.

In my first week in July, I blocked the reversal of a tax cut bundled in with the carbon tax repeal bills. The total value was $1.55 billion and as a result all of you who pay tax are better off by an average $80 a year.

I encourage you to remember this in years to come when you see me cleaning your windscreen at the traffic lights, in an effort to compensate for my lack of parliamentary pension.

With my background in agriculture, I took an interest in agricultural levies and how they are supposedly set by the farmers themselves. My agitation led to the establishment of a Senate inquiry, which confirmed that the voting system is a sham that makes student union elections look like the epitome of democracy. It will be fixed.

There was an inquiry into illicit firearms, established by the Greens. The Greens were planning a séance. They would set up the Ouija board, ask the spirits whether guns were bad, and all the participants would put their fingers on a token and push it towards 'yes.' I crashed the party. With a stiff middle finger I slid the token to 'no' – with help from the Coalition and a quaint concept called evidence. The Greens accused me of determining the outcome. I was flattered.

I established a select committee into wind turbines, looking at their governance and economic merit. The motion was hotly contested and only passed by one vote. The committee has the potential to provoke much needed change in the renewable energy sector. If we could get the self-serving supporters of the Renewable Energy Target to vent their hot air at one side of a turbine, and to be vacuous on the other side, then we might finally find a turbine that spins for more than a third of the time.

I spent a lot of time fighting the national security legislation. I moved lots of amendments, and spoke and wrote about the threat to liberty, especially free speech. I failed on every count except one – which was to force the Attorney-General to agree not to allow ASIO to undertake torture. It should never even have arisen, but at least I won that. Unfortunately I was unable to prevent torture by the Attorney-General, who subjected me and a handful of other Senators to his speeches, which deprived us of anything that made sense.

Putting up with the Attorney-General proves that I am an absolute believer in free speech. On that issue, I co-sponsored Bob Day's Bill to amend section 18C of the *Racial Discrimination Act*. It won't succeed, but it puts pressure on the government. But only the Greens joined me in opposing the anti-free speech provisions in the national security legislation. And they oppose amending 18C. Some people who claim to support free speech are pickier than a fat kid at a salad bar.

A real success was to win security of tenure for the shooters at Malabar rifle range in Sydney. There are 60,000 recreational shooters in Sydney, and this range is central to the future of shooting in NSW. I was delighted to gain the promise of a permanent lease, with no obligation to move until a replacement location is provided. The original plan was to ensure it didn't cost taxpayers any money, but then the government decided not to sell Malabar so it will now cost up to $20 million. Tough.

For my support on the Bill to reintroduce Temporary Protection Visas, I got a Productivity Commission inquiry into our policy of using a tariff rather than a quota to select immigrants. That inquiry has just kicked off and I would encourage you to make a submission in support of it.

I co-sponsored a Greens Bill to allow medical marijuana. That was purely for compassionate reasons, but it gave me a chance to talk about recreational drug use as well. I am the only senator openly supporting recreational use.

And finally, there is my Freedom to Marry Bill which I foreshadowed at last year's Friedman conference. I've been busily telling all comers that gay people have a right to be miserable in marriage like the rest of us. The Bill is now on the senate notice paper but hasn't been debated yet because I am waiting for the right time to prod the Liberals into considering the conscience vote issue. I don't think it will get through parliament before the next election, but I do think we'll get the Libs to agree to a conscience vote. That will be progress.

In conjunction with my support for marijuana legalisation, that Bill has set me apart in the eyes of journalists. Not even the most left-wing publications dare to describe me as a right-wing extremist.

As a consequence, I can discuss things like lowering taxes, balancing the budget, free speech, reducing eligibility for pensions and other welfare, speed limits and of course shooters' rights, in left-wing media. The Guardian even likes to publish libertarian views as a counter to its left-wing norm.

In fact, quite a lot of the media are now starting to catch on to the idea that I don't fit the old left-right paradigm. They have discovered libertarianism, and some even try to tell me what it is and what I should believe in. I am regularly called by journalists who say, 'I think I know what your view will be but I just wanted to check.'

There are even rumours that certain journalists employed by a government owned media outlet did the quiz on our website and found they were actually libertarians themselves.

The term libertarian is being heard a lot more than it was 12 months ago.

Does this mean Australia is about to become Galt's Gulch, or Libertopia? No. The Abbott government is at its core authoritarian, big taxing and big spending. Its rhetoric is belied by its actions.

Labor is even more into taxing and spending, although I don't think it is quite so inherently authoritarian.

What I have been able to do is provide a contrary view – anti-big taxing and anti-big spending, and also anti-authoritarian and anti-corporate welfare.

Elements within the government like the fact I make it easier for them to look moderate when they try to achieve savings.

When the Minister for Small Business, Bruce Bilson, introduced the voluntary supermarket code, he defended it by saying that even I thought it was OK.

Elements within Labor like the fact that I am open to persuasion on matters that affect the civil rights of workers. I'm pro-liberty, not anti-worker or anti-union.

Even the Greens appreciate my consistent position on liberty, working to reduce the intrusion of the state in private matters.

My challenge, and indeed the challenge of everyone here, is to use this moment in history, this period in which I am living the dream, to ensure Australia is fundamentally changed as a result of my election.

Our joint aim must be to start a trend away from statism, towards individualism.

From high taxes to low taxes.

From nanny state to free state.

From group identification to individual choice.

From irresponsible to personally responsible.

And from entitled to self-motivated.

I have now spent ten months in my dream job, but the dream has only just begun.

Political party funding[98]

For some reason it is news when a minor party receives a million dollars in electoral funding, but not when the Liberals and Labor each receive over 20 million and the Greens over five million. What ought to have been news, but wasn't, is why any party received funding at all.

My party, the Liberal Democrats, opposes government funding of most things that private individuals or organisations are willing to pay for voluntarily. Since plenty of people are passionate enough about politics to stump up their own money, the question we ask is, why should everyone be forced to pay?

We would have returned the million dollars we received from the Australian Electoral Commission if it had led to the end of electoral funding. But giving it back without changing the system would be similar to a rich socialist giving his money to the government in the hope it would bring an end to capitalism. Like peeing in a wetsuit, you feel all warm but nobody notices.

As it stands, the major parties are totally hooked on public funding. It accounts for the bulk of their revenue and funds most of their election campaigns. Moreover, they rarely miss a chance to double dip with by-elections, even in safe seats. For every first preference vote they receive $2.48, indexed of course.

There is no opposition from the Greens either; they want to ban donations from for-profit organisations, cap them from individuals and not-for-profits, and limit election expenditure. All of which would increase reliance on public funding.

In NSW, the Liberal government has gone even further. Indeed, it is now so difficult for political parties in that state to raise funds that state-level public funding is inescapable. Only individuals on the electoral roll in NSW may donate, to a maximum of $5,000 per year; associations, unions, clubs and businesses may not. There is a ceiling on electoral expenditure (which only the major parties can hope to reach) and expenditure is reimbursed. It's an incumbent's dream.

The traditional argument is that public funding reduces the risk of donors buying favourable policies, based on the adage that he who pays the piper calls the tune. That is garbage. The vast majority of politicians are principled people whose opinions and votes cannot be bought. Those who are not can be bought in various ways and in any case tend to be more interested in personal rewards than donations to their party.

The rules in NSW were no barrier to Obeid or McDonald, for example. Nor do they prevent someone with plenty of money, like Clive Palmer, from using it to start a new political party and win the balance of power in the senate.

The underlying problem is that governments intrude too much into our lives. There would be less need to lobby a government that did less. As it stands, business success can often depend on favourable ministerial decisions and there is no shortage of people keen to enlist the government's support to impose their views on the rest of us.

A better option would be to leave political funding to those who care enough to put their hand in their pocket. Public funding forces taxpayers to contribute to parties they would never support voluntarily. It is ludicrous that their money pays for virtually every political poster, leaflet and television advertisement.

Even better would be to also leave voting to those who care enough to turn out voluntarily. Compulsory voting takes what purports to be a right to vote, something we regard as integral to democracy, and turns it into a legal obligation like paying taxes.

It is not a right when you can be prosecuted for not exercising it, and Australia is one of very few countries that thinks it is.

In short, it is high time Australia stopped treating democracy like an obligatory dose of castor oil and let people decide for themselves whether to donate their money and vote.

Political donations[99]

I thank the Greens Party for today's opportunity to talk about the need for urgent action on political donations.

You ought to be congratulated, just like Goodman Fielder – the producers of my favourite margarine, Meadow Lea.

I enjoyed my Meadow Lea on toast this morning, so allow me to also acknowledge George Weston Foods – good on you mum, Tip Top's the one.

The Liberal Democrats agree there needs to be urgent action on political donations – and this can be achieved by sending cheques made out to us directly to PO Box 636, Drummoyne NSW 1470 or joining the party through our web page at ldp.org.au.

While enjoying my Nescafé coffee this morning, (thank you Nestlé) I reflected upon the fact that at the last election, Australians were forced to hand over $58 million to the greedy major parties.

This paid for wasteful advertisements that drove us all crazy. Even the Greens produced enough junk mail to create a bare patch in the Amazon rainforest about the size of the ACT.

This is why long-suffering taxpayers should welcome anything to ease this burden – donations given willingly by individuals and corporations. So long as this process is transparent, it is something to be encouraged.

The Liberal Democrats certainly encourage it, which is why we regularly check on the contents of PO Box 636, at Drummoyne NSW, in the postcode 1470.

Speaking of transparency, the Liberal Democrats were proud to receive our first major corporate donation from Philip Morris International last year.

I don't recommend smoking, but I do support the right of people to choose to smoke. I would like to thank Philip Morris for their generosity to my party and remind other tobacco companies, chop chop merchants, and smokers that we are still waiting for a donation from them.

We also welcome all donations from developers, alcohol, gambling, and mining companies.

But as the Greens rightly point out, this is now a matter for urgent action.

It can be addressed by sending a cheque made out to the Liberal Democrats at PO Box 636, Drummoyne NSW 1470.

I must leave now Mr/Madam Acting/Deputy President to quench my hard-earned thirst, for which I thank Carlton and United Breweries, a subsidiary of the Fosters Group.

Gough Whitlam[100]

If it wasn't for Gough Whitlam I may well have been imprisoned or shot. Like so many of his legacies, people will argue about whether this was a good thing or not.

But by ending conscription he saved me, and thousands of others, from making a choice between going to jail or going into the army and being sent to Vietnam.

It is a common mistake where political debate resembles a Punch and Judy Show to characterise politicians as good or bad, evil or saintly, great or useless. But at the end of the day, what endures are good and bad policies. Gough Whitlam was responsible for plenty of both.

When Gough was sacked as Prime Minister, I was a young veterinarian and a member of the Labor Party. I remember exactly where I was, and was deeply shattered by the news. Australia would be a nastier place if not for Gough, and the policies he implemented that enhanced our personal freedoms were his most profound and enduring bequests.

He pulled our troops out of an unwinnable civil war in Vietnam, and lowered the voting age to 18 so that, in future, those who were old enough to die for our country could also have a say in how it was run.

He removed the death penalty from federal law which, while largely symbolic, was something for us to be grateful for. Governments are not terribly good at doing most things, and are best kept out of making decisions about whether people should live or die.

The introduction of no-fault divorces lifted a huge weight off the shoulders of many thousands of spouses and their children during a difficult time in their lives, avoiding the kinds of rancorous fault-finding we still see in some places overseas. And while there are still many legitimate complaints about its operation, the Family Court established by Gough was nonetheless an important departure from moralistic government passing judgement on our relationships.

He also cut the sales tax on the contraceptive pill and lifted the ban on it being advertised. He set in train the transfer of crown land, land owned by an impersonal and force-wielding state, to Aboriginal people in the Northern Territory. He removed the last elements of the White Australia Policy, and granted independence to Papua New Guinea.

With the establishment of the Industries Assistance Commission, now the Productivity Commission, he ushered in a more transparent approach to setting economic policy that focused on the national interest rather than sectoral interests. Opening up trade and diplomatic links with China was also far-sighted, as is now acknowledged by all sides of politics.

Those of us with economic perspectives drier than a toasted SAO might admire the fact he cut tariffs by 25%. Sadly, this initiative could not be sustained, with the automobile and other protected industries succeeding in having tariff rates restored to previous levels within a year.

When Gough committed to removing an overbearing government from people's lives, he did enormous good, accruing real benefits to many people. History tends to be kind to governments that give people greater freedom.

But when Gough decided something needed controlling, it often ended badly. Regulated wage rises brought inflation and unemployment, a cruel legacy that continued well beyond Gough's rein. 'Free' university education, with no obligation to repay costs later on, meant those with lower incomes over their lifetime paid more via their taxes to those who would come to be rich. 'Free' medical care, provided to all rather than just the least well-off, led to hurdles and restrictions on specialist care and ever increasing waiting lists.

The centralisation of power in Canberra also infantilised the states, which have acted like needy children ever since. Equally, welfare rises led to a major problem of welfare dependence and development of an entitlement mentality among those capable of providing for themselves. And the cost of the Whitlam Government's prolific spending policies brought dodgy loans, waste and deficits to be paid for by later generations.

And yet, such consequences were not a unique hallmark of the Whitlam Government; they are a hallmark of every government that fails to live within its means.

Perhaps none of us should look at Whitlam as either a great Prime Minister or a terrible one. The one man did some great and some lousy things. I am grateful for the great things.

AGRICULTURE

ESCAS: valuing animals more than people [101]

Animal welfare is important, but not something we should seek to impose on our customers while we show such little interest in human welfare.

When the former government allowed live exports to resume following the suspension in June 2011, it imposed a scheme on exporters known as ESCAS (Export Supply Chain Assurance Scheme).

Prior to the suspension, exporters of livestock were only required to track exported animals from the property of origin in Australia to the port of export and report on the outcome of the voyage.

Under ESCAS, permission to export requires the exporter to retain control over the animals through to slaughter in the destination country. That means either vertical integration or appropriate contractual agreements with the importer, feedlot operator, transporter and abattoir operator.

Evidence of traceability is also required so individual animals (cattle and buffalos) can be identified and located at any point. Exporters of sheep and goats must have a system based on counting and reconciliation at points along the supply chain. An end of processing report must be supplied for each consignment along with an independent performance audit report.

Exporting without a licence or intentionally contravening licence conditions carries a penalty of five years in prison.

What prompted the suspension was footage supplied to the ABC by Animals Australia showing cattle from Australia being inhumanely slaughtered in Indonesia. Since then Animals Australia has come up with further claims of cruelty to animals, mostly sheep, exported from Australia to Jordan, Kuwait, Israel and Lebanon, all of which the ABC has dutifully reported.

Animals Australia is an animal rights lobby group committed to forcing an end to all live exports. It takes no interest in other issues.

It has no policy on matters such as the oppression of women or persecution of Christians in destination countries, for example. It is all about the animals.

It does not insist that Australia stop exporting wheat to any of the 27 African countries, Yemen or Iraqi Kurdistan where female circumcision is practised. A 2013 UNICEF found that 125 million women and girls in those countries have been affected.

It has nothing to say about export destinations that do not allow women to vote or that treat women as chattels, or the growing number in which Christian churches are being burnt down and their congregations brutalised. Indeed, there is no equivalent to ESCAS for exporting anything other than livestock.

As a corollary of that, the ABC also has very little to say about those issues, especially in comparison to its coverage of the complaints raised by Animals Australia.

This prompts an interesting question. While a lobby group might be excused for focusing on one issue to the exclusion of all others, is it appropriate for the taxpayer-funded ABC to do the same?

Perhaps more importantly, what does it say about our priorities as a nation that we should seek to impose our standards of animal welfare on other countries under the ESCAS system while saying nothing about issues that scream out for attention, such as the oppression of women and persecution of Christians?

While there are international treaties that assert human rights are universal and should not be subject to cultural interpretation, that is not the case with animal welfare. Cultural differences are hugely important.

Both the halal and kosher methods for slaughtering sheep, for example, consist of using a well-sharpened knife to make a swift, deep incision that cuts the front of the throat, the carotid artery, windpipe, and jugular veins. There is no prior stunning. That, and images of animals being bled (consumption of blood is not permissible in either case) appals Animals Australia.

Similarly, Animals Australia considers images of sheep being dragged by their legs and stuffed into car boots as evidence of outrageous cruelty, despite it being not much different from what occurs in every shearing shed in Australia. Nobody seems to have explained to them that sheep are not good at walking on a lead.

There are undoubtedly instances of cruelty to animals in our export markets and we should obviously seek every opportunity to convince our export customers not to be cruel. A bit of information and education can often go a long way.

But the ability to use our influence is diminished by a holier-than-thou approach that assumes our animal welfare standards are universal when that is clearly not the case. Moreover, a disproportionate focus on animal welfare relative to concern for human welfare is just plain wrong.

Both the government and the ABC ought to stop allowing Animals Australia to set their priorities. Animal welfare is important, but not something we should seek to impose on our customers while we show such little interest in human welfare.

Agriculture is totally sustainable[102]

Modern agriculture is not only sustainable now, but more sustainable than it has ever been.

The most over-used and misused word in the English language currently is 'sustainable.' Although everybody uses it, there is no agreement as to what it means.

A manager might suggest that maintaining the current business course is not sustainable; a lawyer might argue a particular case is not sustainable; an athlete might declare a certain training program to be unsustainable; and increasingly, the impact of an activity on the environment might be described as unsustainable. The only thing you can be sure of is that being unsustainable is not good.

It has long been green dogma that modern agriculture is not sustainable. Terms such as monoculture, factory farming and industrial agriculture are used in a derogatory sense to reinforce that view. Plenty of people, either in a spirit of compromise or because they don't know any better, go along with the suggestion that agriculture should be 'more sustainable,' the assumption being that it isn't now.

My preferred definition of the word comes from former Norwegian Prime Minister Gro Harlem Brundtland, who said, 'Sustainable development is development that meets the needs of the present without compromising the ability of future generations to meet their own needs.'

Based on that definition, modern agriculture is not only sustainable now, but more sustainable than it has ever been.

Here in Australia we are often told that anything done by humans to change the environment is evidence in itself of unsustainability. The key assumption behind the term 'wilderness' is the absence of human impact, or at least of white Europeans.

That thinking is not so common outside the country. In Ireland recently, a farm owner told me there was evidence of human settlement in the area going back 5,000 years. He also said that his farm, which has been in the family for generations, could run 20 cows in the 1920s, 50 in the 1950s, 100 at the turn of the century and was now up to 120. He expects it to be running 150 within a decade.

Allowing for a bit of rounding, it is pretty obvious the farm has not only been capable of providing for its past and current owners, but will continue to do so for future generations (in this case the farmer's children) as well. In other words, it has long been sustainable and is sustainable now.

What's more, it is the use of modern technology, so despised by the green dogmatists, that makes this possible. Vaccines (some the product of genetic engineering) and chemicals help keep the cattle healthy. Pasture management using hybrid seeds and chemical fertiliser means there is enough food for the cattle. High tech nutritional supplements ensure they receive a balanced diet. Advanced artificial breeding technology means cows produce a calf each year and that the calves grow faster or produce more milk than ever before, and that there are more heifer than bull calves on dairy farms.

For agriculture to remain sustainable, it needs more of this. It will be modern technology, not a return to the last century or beyond, that ensures our soil and water are preserved. Genetically modified crops and pasture plants, for example, are not only fundamental to raising the nutritional value of pasture, but to combating desertification and drought.

What's needed in Australia is recognition that human impact on the environment is not only unavoidable but mostly highly positive. Moreover, the concept of virgin wilderness untouched by humans should be exposed for the lie that it is.

Large areas of the planet that today look like virgin forests were once farms. That includes much of the Amazon, which is actually forest regrowth growing in man-made 'dark earths,' which archaeologists believe were created by pre-Columbian farmers who added organic wastes and charcoal to improve nutrient supply and boost yields. It is a similar story in forests of West Africa and Borneo.

Nor is it just rainforests. The bison-grazed plains of North America were remade by Native Americans long before Europeans showed up. Many of the mist-shrouded treeless grasslands of the tropical Andes are the result of burning and grazing after locals cut down the natural forests centuries ago. Australia's 'old growth' temperate forests are all regrowth following repeated burning by aborigines over thousands of years.

Ecosystems have always been in a constant state of flux and humans have always left their mark. Nature is resilient and adaptable. In a thousand years the farms of today will be producing far more food and fibre they do now. That's sustainable.

Free range eggs[103]

To scramble the metaphors, various thin-shelled types are running around like headless chooks over free range eggs, proclaiming the sky will fall if the law doesn't tell us all what the term means. Facts and evidence are as scarce as hen's teeth, while market forces are disappearing faster than a randy rooster.

The cause is the fact that consumers are increasingly choosing free range eggs over cage eggs. There are no health, welfare, nutritional or environmental advantages to this. Cage and free range eggs are no different, although free range eggs are more likely to be contaminated by chook poo. The preference is mainly due to the fact that 'free range' sounds nicer than being in a cage.

Irrespective of their merits, consumers are entitled to make choices without being deceived. This question has come down to how many hens a farmer may keep in a particular area. Everyone purports to know what deceives consumers, and almost nobody has bothered to ask them.

The range of opinions is substantial. Choice wants no more than 1,500 hens per hectare while the Greens want 750. Coles and Woolworths accept 10,000, but the Australian Egg Corporation prefers 20,000.

The ACCC has quite strong views on the subject and launched legal action against an egg producer in Western Australia who labelled his eggs as free range when the ACCC did not think it legitimate. Its key concern was that the chickens did not want to go outside. At a Senate Estimates hearing in June, the Chairman of the ACCC, Rod Sims, insisted that, 'On most days we think most of the birds should [go outside]. Most people would think that 'free range' means the birds are outside of the barn.'

Like a lot of people with strong opinions on this subject, he doesn't know much about poultry. In fact, a sizeable proportion of hens in free range situations never venture outside, while many others do not go out on a daily basis. There are good reasons for this: barns are warm and provide food and water, and there are no predators such as foxes and hawks.

Indeed, it is not obvious that a rational chicken would prefer a free-range environment over a cage, if given a choice. The size and type of cages has a far more important influence on bird health than the ability to range freely. Plumage, fractures, body weight and general physiological state are all of better standard in properly caged birds than free range counterparts. Caged hens also live longer, due in part to less exposure to predation and natural hazards such as avian flu carried by wild ducks.

Hens are also hierarchical creatures with a definite pecking order that comes into play in free range situations. Those at the bottom of the pecking order are absolutely better off in a cage.

Whether or not hens are rational, human rationality is in short supply in the debate about what constitutes free range.

The Australian Egg Corporation's choice of 20,000 hens per hectare is at least based on something more than an arrogant assumption. The figure was arrived at with the help of consumer market research, in which participants were shown pictures of hens at various densities and invited to indicate which they considered to be compatible with the term free range.

The preference of the supermarkets for 10,000 reflects an attempt to strike a compromise between the AEC's position and the lobby groups, coupled with a desire to ensure the costs of production do not skyrocket and kill off what has become a very lucrative market.

Those pushing for much lower densities are motivated either by animal rights arguments (not the same as animal welfare) or visions of hens happily wandering in green pastures. There is a very strong anthropomorphic aspect to these. That is, they are based on the question, 'how would you like to live at that density?' What they overlook is that it only takes a visit to a sporting event to see that humans choose to congregate at high densities. And when they do, not everyone goes outside for some peace and quiet.

The idea that free range means happily pecking away in green pastures is also a myth, particularly in sunburnt Australia. Even if the pasture is green at first, as it might be during spring, that soon changes when the chickens start scratching (assuming foxes haven't eaten them).

Concern for consumers is far from the main concern of those pushing for low hen densities. If densities were lowered to 1,500 or less, for example, the price of free range eggs would increase to more than $12 a dozen. Many people who currently buy free range eggs would stop, and some would undoubtedly reduce their consumption of eggs.

Prompted in large part by the ACCC's obsession, the states and territories are negotiating to adopt a common standard for free range, backed by legislation. In other words, politicians and bureaucrats are proposing to agree on what free range means so that consumers don't need to decide for themselves. This is paternalist and offensive.

Without the interfering ACCC, politicians, and bureaucrats, consumers could continue to decide for themselves if they are being deceived. Producers who want to prove they are not deceptive could print their hen densities on egg cartons, allowing consumers to decide whether $12 per dozen is a reasonable price for something that sounds nice.

For those who suspect 'free range' might have lost its original meaning, there are plenty of other nice sounding terms that might be employed. Semi-free range, for example, may suit those who want a bet each way. And what about ultra-free range, unconfined, spacious or liberated? I suggest they sound equally nice as free range.

But I bet if an egg producer sought to use such terms in today's environment, it wouldn't be long before some interfering bureaucrat or politician – convinced he or she is smarter than the average consumer – would want to impose a meaning on everyone else. They just can't help themselves.

The PETA campaign against the wool industry[104]

The PETA campaign against the wool industry, using a fake sheep that appears to have major shearing cuts, signals a new episode in the organisation's long-standing crusade to demonise the industry.

And just as when it engaged in the campaign against mulesing, its goal is not to encourage improved animal welfare. Rather, the ultimate aim is to close down any livestock industry on the grounds that humans should not utilise animals for food, clothing or recreation.

The campaign is based on lies and misrepresentation. Serious shearing cuts are rare, good animal welfare is good for business, and farmers take care of their sheep. But PETA is not really arguing about these. They are the jihadists of the animal rights world, with a messianic ideology that they seek to impose on everyone else. And like jihadists elsewhere, their record shows they are willing to use violence to pursue their aims.

Predictably, most responses from the wool industry have been civil and soothing. The facts are on our side, they say. We are really serious about improving animal welfare. Maybe if we agreed to a little bit more regulation they'd be happy. And of course, why don't we just sit down and work things out like nice people?

Here's what I think – PETA are not nice people. If they talk to the industry, it is merely to gather information to use against it. They will compromise today, but only to give themselves time to commence a fresh attack tomorrow. Hysterical claims are what prompt donations from the gullible public. And the only reason they might leave the sheep industry alone for a time is because they are focusing on another sector, like chickens or pigs.

Quite simply, PETA is the enemy of the livestock industries. PETA must not only be defeated, it should be destroyed by any legal means available.

When PETA launched its campaign against mulesing a decade ago, Australian Wool Innovation adopted a strategy of appeasement. Millions of dollars were spent promoting alternative means of flystrike control and finding non-surgical alternatives to mulesing. As a consultant at the time, I had a small role in seeking commercial partners for some of these alternatives.

In the end it became obvious that AWI had misjudged its members. Mulesing is cheap, effective and, especially compared to flystrike, totally defensible. As I predicted to AWI at the time, wool producers simply refused to give it up. Moreover, the market for wool from unmulesed sheep, supposedly driven by garment manufacturers and retailers intimidated by PETA, never developed. In the end it is consumers, not retailers, who make markets. The PETA roar was exposed as the squeak of an impotent mouse.

The wool industry should not forget that lesson. PETA is not invincible; it can be challenged and beaten.

There are many ways in which the fight can occur, and it is likely it won't be limited to one. In the court of public opinion there are social media and mainstream media, where opinions can be influenced. In the courts of justice there are criminal and civil remedies against such things as trespass, incitement, malicious damage, defamation and nuisance. And of course there is the court of political opinion, where politicians with little knowledge of and no interest in the sheep industry might find themselves being asked to do something.

But wherever the fight takes place, there should be no appeasement. Any step backwards, even of a minor nature, will never be regained. The wool industry must stand its ground, fight back, and not give an inch.

Dealing with low profitability[105]

As most people are aware, the profitability of primary production is a function of the difference between prices received and costs of production. Profitability suffers whenever prices are too low or costs too high.

For many people, the solution to low farm profitability is higher prices. Indeed, quite a few believe prices are kept low deliberately, with the assumption that everyone is making money at the expense of primary producers.

A recent investigation by another media organisation found farmers receive a relatively small proportion of the retail price of the food they produce. The average, according to the report, was 28%, with a range between 2 and 49%.

Such a low percentage, some suggest, is proof that others are making money at the expense of farmers. Top of the list of 'usual suspects' is supermarkets, with Coles and Woolworths the main culprits.

One way of examining this argument is to take a counter-factual position. In other words, what would be the situation if everything supposedly wrong with the supermarkets were fixed? What if they did not exist? Or, perhaps more realistically, what if the retail market were much more diverse, with Coles and Woolworths each having less than 10% of the market? Would there still be complaints about low prices?

That question is, or ought to be, occupying the minds of the ACCC in their quest to find something illegal about the way supermarkets do business or, if that's not possible, to change the law so they can (find something illegal). Like those who blame supermarkets for low commodity prices, the ACCC's starting assumption is that supermarkets are up to no good.

A substantially more diverse retail market would have considerably higher costs than at present. Coles and Woolworths each have very efficient logistics networks for moving produce from where it is grown to where it is purchased. If there were 100 different supermarket networks, for example, there would be 100 freight and warehouse networks to supply them, with everything on a much smaller scale. Goods now transported on B-doubles would be carried on tray trucks. The fixed costs of supermarkets would have to be recovered from lower turnovers.

The result of this would be higher consumer prices, but would it mean higher producer prices? Probably not. In the end, the same number of consumers are buying food. Whether they are buying it from Coles or Woolworths, or from one of a hundred alternatives, they would buy the same amount.

However, they would not necessarily buy the same things. Although food is largely non-discretionary and demand is insensitive to price within a certain range, price has a big effect on substitution. When prices rise, consumers may not buy less food, but they will choose cheaper options.

It's not uncommon to hear it said that Coles and Woolworths work in concert to keep prices down. Leaving aside the fact that this is illegal and would give the ACCC the opportunity it has been looking for, it makes no rational sense. Producers of tomatoes, potatoes, chicken, beef or any of the other food commodities that supply Coles and Woolworths are neither operating at a loss nor acting involuntarily. Indeed, most producers would love to have a contract to supply them. And if the prices they received were less, they would stop.

Some of the loudest complaints about low prices, and accusations levelled at supermarkets, come from beef and wheat producers. Yet in both cases, prices are determined more by international markets than domestic factors. Whether Russia allows its wheat growers to export their wheat, and by how much the US subsidises the conversion of corn into ethanol, have far more impact on prices than what Coles or Woolworths do in the process of retailing bread in their stores. Similarly, Korea's quota for importing beef has much more impact on beef prices.

None of this is to suggest that profitability cannot be increased. It can be. But blaming others for low profitability is not only fruitless, it is wrong. The solution is within the grasp of each industry and producer.

Reducing the cost of production is obviously a good place to start. It is rare to find a farm where inputs cannot be used more sparingly to reduce costs or more effectively to boost output. That includes capital. And of course, increasing the scale of production will drive down unit costs. Buying out the neighbours is often a good way to achieve higher profitability.

Another obvious option is to increase demand, whether domestic or international. So long as supply does not increase in response, prices will rise. Thus access to export markets and discovering new uses for products can be very helpful.

Equally obvious is to reduce supply, by some producers switching to something else or selling the farm and letting someone else have a go. Demand will rarely decline if supply is reduced, meaning higher prices must eventuate.

And for those who sell do out, it would be entirely rational to use the proceeds to buy shares in Wesfarmers, the owners of Coles, or Woolworths. The dividends will almost certainly offer a higher rate of return on capital than they achieved from farming. And calls for these companies to reduce their profits might not be viewed in the same way, either.

Drought assistance[106]

We all know that those who fail to learn from history are bound to repeat it, and with drought spreading in Queensland and beyond, I wish I could be more confident that people were listening to their history teachers.

Lesson one is that droughts will happen. The reality of drought always seems to come as a huge shock to city people, who find images of dried up creeks and bones of livestock in the paddock particularly confronting.

But as Dorothea Mackellar told us, you shouldn't need a degree in meteorology to understand that drought is not a disaster in this country so much as a part of life.

Indeed, any farmer or grazier older than 12 will have experienced drought, and knows that managing it is as much a part of their job description as dealing with stormy weather is part of the job of the captain of a ship.

The other part of history that I wish we had learnt from is that drought assistance programs quickly become a bottomless pit. The Exceptional Circumstance Schemes of recent times gave aid to whole regions for long periods regardless of individual circumstances, gobbling up $2.6 billion on interest rate subsidies alone from 2001 to 2011.

Several reviews subsequently recommended abolishing EC interest rate subsidies, not least because they can have the effect of rewarding farmers who managed their farms badly, and encouraged them to take on debt at the beginning of a drought.

Farmers are no different to anyone else when it comes to a liking for other people's money, which might explain why the schemes quickly blew out. Many farmers can tell you stories of neighbours who they suspect of rorting the system or who benefited from it despite living on extremely valuable holdings.

The Productivity Commission found that none of these drought assistance programs helped farmers improve their self-reliance, preparedness and climate management. It found that interest rate subsidies and state-based transaction subsidies were ineffective, and can perversely encourage poor management practices. What's more, it found that household relief payments were inequitable because they were limited to those in drought-declared areas.

Not surprisingly, given these findings, Exceptional Circumstances schemes were abolished. However, because of our apparent collective amnesia, and the persistence of lifelong whingers, they have only been replaced by new handouts that have little more going for them.

Using federal money – money that might otherwise be used to lower taxes – state governments are now being allowed to hand out concessional loans that pay little heed to old fashioned market concepts like viability. Where once it was up to financial organisations to decide who received loans, now it is up to state government agencies. It's a scary thought.

Speaking of failing to learn from history, it will also now be up to state governments to make the inevitable, painful foreclosures. State loans to farmers were discontinued in the 1990s because of the political fallout that inevitably followed.

Right now, these loans not only put farmers deeper in debt, they put all the rest of us further in debt too because they worsen Australia's budget position. As the drought expands, we will not be able to afford this kind of largesse, however we give it out, and whatever name we deem to give it.

Providing income support to see people through really bad periods is a given, but safety nets are already available for this, as they should be.

Drought assistance schemes should not be considered unless they can be shown to succeed when others have failed. Farmers who cannot survive drought without help from their fellow Australians should not be propped up or encouraged to sit on their hands until it rains. The only incentive they need is the one that motivates any business, which is to remain profitable and sustainable. If they cannot do that, they should sell their property to someone who can.

Socialism was an experiment that failed repeatedly in the twentieth century when the money eventually ran out. Dabbling in agrarian socialism will inevitably have the same outcome.

It's not 'ag-gag.' It's private property[107]

The eighteenth century Scottish philosopher, David Hume, wrote that once laws for protecting private property were established, 'there remains little or nothing to be done towards settling a perfect harmony and concord.'

When it comes to businesses that involve the production of livestock products for food, animal rights activists and their cheerleaders in the Greens do not respect private property. They insist they have a right to enter the property, take photos and videos, misrepresent what they see, and pass it on to sympathetic and gullible members of the media. Their argument is that animal rights outweigh all other rights and that companies have no right to privacy.

State and federal governments are now contemplating measures to clamp down on this activity. The NSW Agriculture Minister recently described such people as 'terrorists.'

There are laws in several US states that outlaw such covert filming. An article in the *New York Times* described the laws as making it illegal for employees to covertly videotape livestock farms, or apply for jobs at related businesses, without disclosing ties to animal rights groups. Any videos which are claimed to disclose ill treatment of animals must also be handed to authorities almost immediately.

One law, 'The Animal and Ecological Terrorism Act,' prohibits the filming or taking of pictures on livestock farms to 'defame the facility or its owner' with any violators placed on a 'terrorist registry.'

The laws are said to have helped curtail such activism in those states, and more states are contemplating introducing laws of their own.

There are objective reasons why farm intrusions are undesirable, including animal welfare. Some animals, particularly broiler chickens, are easily panicked by strangers and prone to pile up in corners where they crush each other to death. Pigs can also behave undesirably when frightened, while dairy cows stop releasing their milk and tend to release an almost endless supply of manure.

There is also the question of biosecurity. Most farms, especially pig and poultry farms, maintain strict quarantine to keep out unwanted diseases. It's a very important part of keeping the animals healthy so they don't require antibiotics or other medications. Unwelcome visitors to the farm can carry all kinds of bugs.

And of course there is a commercial penalty incurred when the public believes the propaganda issued by the activists and avoids buying the food involved. There is rarely any opportunity to correct the public record once the emotive images are broadcast.

The activists argue from the perspective that the end justifies the means, labelling poultry, pig and dairy farms as factory farms and insisting they are inherently cruel. Capturing and exposing this 'cruelty' on video, they claim, is the only way of ensuring it ceases.

They maintain there are civil rights at stake and claim the public has a right to know 'what happens behind closed doors,' and 'consumers have a right to know the conditions under which animals are raised and slaughtered.' They insist the US type laws are an attack on free speech, referring to them as 'ag-gag' laws.

What they do not disclose is that, like those who attack live exports (who are mostly the same people), their objective is to stop people from eating meat. Or that in their authoritarian world, coercion and violation of property rights are legitimate tools in the pursuit of their goals.

Their rights-based claim is ridiculous. The public has no more right to know what goes on in a piggery than in a family home. Indeed, the activists would be the first to complain if their own homes were broken into and the management of their children filmed. And yet it could easily be argued that the public has a greater right to know about the rights of children than animal rights.

And while we place a high value on animal welfare and expect genuine cruelty to be disclosed and those responsible held to account, cruelty is primarily an individual failing rather than an organisational deficiency. Yet it is 'corporations' that are targeted by the activists, exposing their anti-capitalist attitudes.

There is a case for doing something to stop these people. With their fanaticism they are impervious to social disapproval.

The question is whether our governments should adopt a similar legislative approach to that taken in America. While it is obvious the activists have no respect for the rights of those they are targeting, we should not invite laws that undermine our rights.

In particular, the claim by the activists that such laws threaten their free speech should not become reality. Free speech means nothing unless it includes those we don't want to listen to. We also do not want to suppress the reporting of cruelty.

A general obligation to report cruelty as soon as it is identified might be an option, accompanied by a condition that those lodging reports later found to be false and malicious could be held liable for any damage they cause. That would leave genuine whistle blowers with nothing to fear, but mischief makers would find it expensive.

But for promoting 'harmony and concord' it may be best to focus on upholding private property rights. In earlier years the law would have permitted property owners to wield a shotgun to deal with malicious trespassers. Governments now claim the sole right to deal with such criminals, which leads to the thought that perhaps it is time to create a specific, serious offence of entering a piggery, poultry farm, dairy farm or abattoir without permission. And for employees of these premises, a legal obligation not to harm the property of their employers may be an option.

There are sure to be ways in which property rights can be protected without infringing other rights.

GMOs[108]

Many people will have heard of the Luddites – nineteenth century workers in the wool and cotton mills of West Yorkshire and Lancashire who were so fearful of industrialisation that they wrecked machinery and burnt down mechanised mills.

Some of them were punished with transportation to Australia, a nation that benefited profoundly when those mills were able to process our wool in ever larger amounts.

History showed the original Luddites were wrong to be afraid of the future. We now know the industrial revolution lifted millions of people out of poverty in a way that revolutions seldom do. People in countries that embrace new technologies, including Australia, have become healthier and wealthier than ever before.

But every generation spawns a new pack of Luddites. Luddites claimed that metal ploughs would contaminate the soil; that train passengers would not survive travelling at high speed through tunnels; that gramophones would make musicians redundant; that microwave ovens would make food carcinogenic; and that vaccines were responsible for autism.

The philosopher Bertrand Russell once noted that every great advance in civilisation has been denounced as unnatural. This might explain why the Luddites of today call themselves environmentalists.

Unfortunately, while Luddites were once just ill-informed vandals destroying workplaces in their own communities, now their ideas are sometimes lethal on a global scale.

Consider, for example, the case of genetically modified food. In the twenty-odd years in which GM crops have been grown, there have been no documented negative human health effects. There are many documented benefits, including better nutrition, more efficient production, and reduced use of pesticides.

But unfortunately, this hasn't stopped South Australia and Tasmania, our two worst performing economies, from banning GM crops.

At a global level, one GM crop, golden rice, has the potential to save millions of children who suffer from vitamin A deficiency. Its yellow appearance is due to genetic modification to contain beta-carotene, a source of vitamin A. A single bowl of golden rice can supply 60% of a child's daily vitamin A requirement.

Regular white rice does not provide this vital nutrient and with three billion people worldwide reliant on rice, there are many cases of deficiency. The British medical journal *The Lancet* reported that, in total, vitamin A deficiency kills 668,000 children under the age of five each year. Those children who do not die often go blind.

But Luddites such as Greenpeace have been openly denying the benefits of golden rice for at least 15 years, with complete disregard for the science and in full knowledge of the impact of vitamin A deficiency. The consequences have been catastrophic.

While golden rice is now finally being grown overseas, some eight million children died while Greenpeace was successfully campaigning against it.

Greenpeace has also played a part in preventing famine-hit people in Africa from accepting food aid – because it was genetically modified.

These modern-day Luddites are willing to let other people pay the ultimate price for their attitudes.

The government of India indicated recently that it would suspend Greenpeace India's foreign funding licence on the entirely sensible grounds that the organisation works against the country's economic interests.

This follows the stripping of Greenpeace Canada's charitable status in 1989.

Australia should follow suit. Greenpeace Australia demonstrated that they are philistines when they destroyed wheat crops being trialled by scientists from CSIRO here in Canberra.

In a world where millions still lack adequate nutrition, improving food quality and productivity must be one of the most noble of scientific pursuits. Yet Greenpeace Australia sought to ensure that research isn't carried out. They should be stripped of their charitable status. They should reap what they sow.

Endnotes

1   Delivered 9 July 2014, the day after I was sworn in.

2   Delivered 12 February 2015.

3   Published in the *Australian Financial Review* on 20 June 2014.

4   Published in the *Australian Financial Review* on 26 April 2016.

5   Delivered 16 March 2016.

6   Published in the *Australian Financial Review* on 3 December 2014.

7   Published in *The Australian* on 5 December 2014.

8   Second reading speech delivered 16 June 2016.

9   Second reading speech delivered 24 Nov 2015 by singing.

10   Second reading speech delivered 22 Feb 2016.

11   Adjournment speech delivered 2 Feb 2016.

12   Second reading speech delivered 9 Nov 2015.

13   Second reading speech delivered 24 June 2015.

14   Published in the *Australian Financial Review* on 17 December 2015

15   Published in the *Australian Financial Review* on 18 June 2015.

16   Published in *The Australian* on 19 February 2016.

17   Second reading speech delivered 21 June 2015.

18   Published in the *Australian Financial Review* on 4 February 2014.

19   Published in *The Australian* on 6 February 2015.

20   Published in the *Australian Financial Review* on 23 June 2016.

21   Published in the *Australian Financial Review* on 12 February 2015.

22   Second reading speech delivered 23 Nov 2015.

23   Published in the *Australian Financial Review* on 21 March 2014

24   Published in the *Australian Financial Review* on 7 March 2014.

25 Published in the *Australian Financial Review* on
    10 September 2015.
26 Senator statements delivered 30 November 2016.
27 Delivered 17 September 2015.
28 Second reading speech delivered 17 June 2015.
29 Published in the *Australian Financial Review* on
    11 December 2013.
30 Delivered 1 September 2016.
31 Delivered 14 September 2015.
32 Published in the *Australian Financial Review* on 4 June 2015.
33 Published in the *Australian Financial Review* on
    8 January 2015.
34 Published in the *Australian Financial Review* on
    27 October 2016.
35 Second reading speech delivered 11 November 2015.
36 Published in *The Spectator* on 4 June 2016.
37 Published in the *Australian Financial Review* on
    14 February 2014.
38 Published in the *Australian Financial Review* on 3 July 2015.
39 Published in the *Australian Financial Review* on
    23 August 2014.
40 Published in the *Australian Financial Review* on
    19 September 2014.
41 Published in the *Australian Financial Review* on 16 July 2015.
42 Published in the *Australian Financial Review* on 22 July 2016.
43 Published in the *Australian Financial Review* on
    12 December 2014.
44 Published in the *Australian Financial Review* on
    23 October 2015.
45 Delivered 26 November 2014.
46 Published in the *Australian Financial Review* on 5 May 2017
47 Delivered 10 November 2016.

48 Published in the *Australian Financial Review* on 30 May 2014.

49 Delivered 7 September 2015.

50 Published in the *Australian Financial Review* on 7 May 2015.

51 Delivered 16 September 2015.

52 Published in the *Australian Financial Review* on 6 November 2015.

53 Published in the *Huffington Post* on 21 September 2015.

54 Delivered 10 November 2016.

55 Published in the *Daily Telegraph* on 11 August 2015.

56 Delivered 4 March 2015.

57 Second reading speech 3 March 2016.

58 Delivered 1 October 2014.

59 Published in the *Australian Financial Review* on 2 May 2014.

60 Published in the *Daily Telegraph* on 1 July 2015.

61 Published in the *Australian Financial Review* on 25 July 2014.

62 Delivered 24 February 2016.

63 Published in the *Australian Financial Review* on 4 April 2014.

64 Delivered 25 November 2014.

65 Published in the *Star Observer* in June 2016.

66 Delivered 1 December 2015.

67 Published in the *Daily Telegraph* on 20 August 2014.

68 Published in *The Guardian* on 5 November 2014.

69 Delivered 28 October 2014.

70 Published in *The Drum* on 27 October 2014.

71 Published in *The Guardian* on 17 October 2014.

72 Published in *The Guardian* on 19 September 2014.

73 Published in *The Guardian* on 22 January 2015.

74 Published in the *Australian Financial Review* on 20 February 2014.

75 Published in the *Australian Financial Review* on 23 January 2015.

76 Delivered 30 August 2016.

77 Delivered 24 November 2016.

78 Published in the *Sydney Morning Herald* on
18 December 2014.

79 Published in the *Daily Telegraph* on 27 April 2016.

80 Published in Fairfax Rural Media on 15 December 2016.

81 Delivered 15 October 2014.

82 Published in the *Australian Financial Review* on
28 October 2016.

83 Published in the *Australian Financial Review* on
10 January 2014.

84 Delivered 15 September 2015.

85 Delivered 13 October 2016.

86 Published in *The Australian* on 11 May 2015.

87 Delivered 22 February 2016.

88 Published in the *Huffington Post* on 28 August 2015.

89 Delivered 25 March 2015.

90 Senators' Statements 18 March 2015.

91 Published in *The Australian* on 10 June 2015.

92 Published in *The Australian* on 23 December 2016.

93 Published in *The Australian* on 24 March 2016.

94 Published in *The Australian* on 18 December 2014.

95 Published in *Australian Financial Review* on 20 June 2014.

96 Published in the *Australian Financial Review* on
24 March 2016.

97 Third ALS Friedman Conference May 2–3 2015.

98 Published in the *Australian Financial Review* on
31 October 2013.

99 Delivered 24 February 2016.

100 Published in the *Sydney Morning Herald* on 23 October 2014.

101 Published in *Farm Weekly* on 4 November 2013.

102 Published in *Farm Weekly* on 24 June 2016.

[103]   Published in the *Daily Reckoning* on 16 July 2015.

[104]   Published in *Farm Online* on 22 April 2015.

[105]   Published in *Farm Weekly* on 5 May 2014.

[106]   Published in *Farm Weekly* on 26 November 2014.

[107]   Published in the Rural Press in June 2014.

[108]   Delivered 18 August 2015.

ABOUT THE AUTHOR

David Leyonhjelm is an Australian Senator for the Liberal Democratic Party. He was elected in 2013 and re-elected in 2016. As the first politician to be elected to an Australian parliament representing a genuinely libertarian party, David bears a major responsibility. While the libertarian concept is relatively well known in the United States, and classical liberalism is somewhat understood in Britain and Europe generally, neither is part of the usual political dialogue in Australia.

David has held an interest in politics since the early 1970s when, as a member of Young Labor, he worked on the *It's Time* campaign to help end military conscription. He later joined the Liberal Party but resigned in 1996 due to John Howard's extremist gun laws.

He is a former veterinarian and has degrees in business and law.